C0-BPT-789

MORAVIAN AND METHODIST

MORAVIAN AND METHODIST

Relationships and Influences in the Eighteenth Century

BY

CLIFFORD W. TOWLSON

M.A.(Oxon.), B.A., B.D., Ph.D.(Lond.)

LONDON : THE EPWORTH PRESS

THE EPWORTH PRESS
(FRANK H. CUMBERS)
25-35 City Road, London, E.C.1

MELBOURNE CAPE TOWN
NEW YORK TORONTO

Made in Great Britain
Published in 1957

SET IN MONOTYPE BASKERVILLE AND PRINTED IN
GREAT BRITAIN BY THE CAMELOT PRESS LTD
LONDON AND SOUTHAMPTON

To

MY WIFE

PREFACE

THIS BOOK is a thesis which was presented to London University for the Degree of Doctor of Philosophy. In order to facilitate publication in these days of high costs, it has been shortened—by the omission of three Appendices, consisting of 'The Orders of the Poplar Religious Society', 'The Orders of the Fetter Lane Society', and 'The Nature, Design, and General Rules of the United Societies', by some excisions from the text, and by the reduction of the bibliography of nearly three hundred items to a brief summary.

The influence of the Moravians upon the Wesleys in the early days of their ministry has often been discussed, with conspicuous ability by Dr J. Ernest Rattenbury in *The Conversion of the Wesleys*; but there seems to have been little attempt to trace the relationships of the two Communions throughout the century. This book is an attempt to remedy the omission. After reviewing and examining the causes of the disruption of 1740, it discusses John Wesley's share in 'The Battle of the Books', and records the increasing good will of the later years, culminating in the negotiations for union in 1785-6.

It then assesses the influences, temporary and lasting, of Moravian teaching and example upon Methodist organization and practice, in the 'band-system', hymn-singing, the Love-feast, the Watch-night, education, and, to a smaller degree, lay-preachers and field-preaching; and concludes with a chapter on the Methodist contribution to Moravianism, in its contemporary restraints on its doctrine and practice, its hymnody, its example of evangelism, and especially the personal influence of the Wesleys on its English leaders.

In the making of this book, I am indebted to many people: to the Right Revs. G. W. McLeavy and C. H. Shawe and the Revs. J. H. Foy, H. Hassall, and A. J. Lewis, of the Moravian Church, for granting me access to Moravian books and documents; to Dr Frank Baker and Mr Leslie T. Daw, of the Wesley Historical Society, for advice and the loan of books; to Mr W. H. Leadley, of Kirbymoorside, for a gift of books which saved me much time and trouble; to the Revs. Frederick Hunter and Walter Goss, for valuable suggestions contained in their Eayrs Essays; and to Mr H. P. La Trobe, a worthy son of a distinguished family, for his commendation of Moravianism by his life and example. I am glad, too, to acknowledge the kindness of Dr W. G. Addison and the S.P.C.K. in allowing me to quote from Dr Addison's translation of the Loretz–La Trobe correspondence in his book, *The Renewed Church of the United Brethren 1722-1930*, published by the S.P.C.K. for the Church Historical Society; and also to express my gratitude to the Revs. W. N. Schwarze and S. H. Gapp, of the Moravian Church, Bethlehem, Pennsylvania, U.S.A., and the publishers of *World Parish* (November 1949), for permission to use the translation of Peter Böhler's letters to Zinzendorf in the spring of 1738. If I have omitted the name of any other helper, I trust I shall be forgiven.

Most of all, I am indebted to my wife for her constant encouragement and her valuable help in preparing this book for publication.

CLIFFORD W. TOWLSON

CONTENTS

CHAPTER ONE

PREPARATION

THE SOMEWHAT dissembled love of Robert Southey for the Methodists revealed in his *Life of Wesley* (1820) received a dignified reply from an unexpected source. In *A Letter to Robert Southey, Esq., Poet Laureate, etc., on his Life of the late Mr John Wesley, and especially that part in which he treats of the Moravians*, Dr William Okely, a Bristol physician, made a spirited defence of the Moravians against Southey's animadversions. That was to be expected, for the charges against the Moravians, in so far as they were true, had by 1820 long been outgrown. It is somewhat surprising, however, to find in Dr Okely a sturdy champion of the Methodists, once so closely linked to the Moravians but by this time far removed. 'I do not mean to assert', he wrote, 'that enthusiasm and fanaticism did never mingle with the proceedings of Methodism—neither do I mean to say that in many instances the spiritual agency of Methodism did not exhibit specimens of what are called nervous disorders. The many blemishes which I discern in them have not made me blind to the extent of the undeniable good of which they have been the instruments.'

These two sentences not only reveal one of the factors which separated two Christian groups which had at one time promised to work in intimate and perhaps organic association, but they also give a hint of how close that association might have become but for differences of opinion and practice which were largely superficial and transitory.

An estimate of the extent of the mutual influence exercised by these Communions, and especially of that of the Moravians upon the Methodists, must depend in large part upon the importance assigned to the 'conversion' of John Wesley on 24th May 1738. Throughout the Methodist world this day is regarded as crucial, as the birthday of the Methodist Church, and in this country commemorative services are held in every District and in a great many Circuits, services in which Charles Wesley's hymns are sung, extracts from the *Journals* of the two brothers are read, and prayers of thankfulness for their life and work are offered. There are some writers, however, who take a different view, and who either question the importance of the Aldersgate Street experience or doubt its permanence. Dr Maximin Piette, for example, in his sympathetic study, *John Wesley in the Evolution of Protestantism*,[1] regards the events of Whitsuntide 1738 as merely incidents, and as ordinary experiences which would lose their effect with the process of time. He holds that the word 'conversion' should be applied, if at all, to the events of 1725, the year in which John Wesley entered upon Holy Orders. Canon J. H. Overton[2] realizes the importance of the day, but regards it as a result of Moravian influence of an impermanent character, though he admits that the indirect effect of their teaching pervaded all the remainder of Wesley's life. Professor Umphrey Lee, in *John Wesley and Modern Religion*,[3] like Piette, minimizes the Whitsuntide experience. He points to John Wesley's later doubts, to the meagre subsequent references to the event, to Wesley's avowed lack of faith (in a particularly gloomy letter[4] to his brother in June 1766), and to the modifications in his description of his pre-Aldersgate religious experience—objections which are very different from one another, and which are not difficult to answer. In that letter Wesley wrote:

I do not love God. I never did. Therefore I never believed in the Christian sense of the word. . . . I never had any other evidence of the eternal or invisible world than I have now: and that is none at all, unless such as fairly shines from reason's glimmering ray. I have no direct witness, I do not say that I am a child of God, but of anything invisible or eternal.

But in the same letter he wrote:

I dare not preach otherwise than I do, either concerning faith, or love, or justification, or perfection. . . . I find rather an increase than a decrease of zeal for the whole work of God and every part of it.

I am borne along, I know not how, that I can't stand still.

And then he urged his brother to insist on *full* redemption, receivable by faith alone. It is not surprising that Wesley had his times of depression and questioning. Faith is faith in defiance of doubt.

Dr Piette's contention that Wesley's 'new life' began in 1725

[1] Sheed and Ward (1937), p. 306. [2] *John Wesley* (1891), pp. 67-8.
[3] Cokesbury Press, Nashville, U.S.A., Chap. 5. [4] *Letters*, V.16.

requires similar qualification. It was on 19th September of that year that he was ordained deacon, and on 1st December his *Diary* records the following:

Breach of vows: hence careless of fixing days of mortification, etc.

Pride of my parts or holiness: greedy of praise: peevishness: idleness.

Intemperance in sleep: sins of thought: hence useless or sinful anger.

Breach of promise: dissimulation: lying: rash censures: contemning others: disrespect of governors: desire to seem better than I am. Lord, have mercy.[5]

The slender reference to the Moravian influence must be read in the light of Wesley's subsequent relations with them, and must be compared with his high tributes at other times. His friendship with Böhler persisted, as will be seen, but his differences with Zinzendorf had been acute, and there was a long suspension of his fellowship with Spangenberg, Gambold, and Hutton.

In any case, John Wesley, whatever his mood, did not allow depression to interfere with his work. This is what he wrote on his eighty-fifth birthday:

What cause have I to praise God, as for a thousand spiritual blessings, so for bodily blessings also! How little have I suffered yet by 'the rush of numerous years'! . . . To what cause can I impute this, that I am as I am? First, doubtless, to the power of God, fitting me for the work to which I am called, as long as He pleases to continue me therein. . . . May we not impute it, as inferior means . . . to my having constantly, for above sixty years, risen at four in the morning? to my constant preaching at five in the morning for above fifty years?[6]

It would have required more than a vague ethical altruism to sustain him for that; and if the impulse which fortified and inspired him did not come in 1738, when *did* it come?

Contemporary Methodist biographers, Clarke, Moore, Whitehead, and Hampson, living comparatively close to the event, agree about its vital importance; Lecky,[7] not unduly sympathetic, regards the day as 'the true source of Methodism', and declares that the humble meeting in Aldersgate Street formed 'an epoch in English history'; and later Methodist historians, from Tyerman[8]

[5] *Journal*, I.51.

[6] *Journal*, VII.408.

[7] *History of England in the Eighteenth Century* (1879), II.558.

[8] *The Life and Times of the Rev. John Wesley* (1871), pp. 175ff.

to Bett,[9] look upon the Aldersgate Street experience as of supreme significance in the history of Methodism and the life of its founder. The case has been fully examined and adequately argued by Dr J. Ernest Rattenbury in *The Conversion of the Wesleys*,[10] and Dr A. S. Yates, in a more recent study,[11] while admitting that the experience was not a catastrophic change from sin to piety, or a sudden dawning of compassion for men and women, or even primarily an intellectual change, claims that 24th May 1738 was the first occasion on which John Wesley was *assured* of salvation in Christ, and that the Aldersgate Street experience was the foundation on which his doctrine of Assurance, or the Witness of the Spirit, was based.

Wesley's own testimony on this point is convincing. In the historic account of the events of 24th May he wrote:

> I felt I did trust in Christ, Christ alone for salvation; and an assurance was given me that He had taken away *my* sins, even *mine*, and saved *me* from the law of sin and death.[12]

On the other hand, he seems to have had some appreciation of this doctrine as early as 1725, for in a letter to his mother he quoted a sentence from Jeremy Taylor's *Holy Living* and *Holy Dying*, 'Whether God has forgiven us or no we know not', and commented:

> If his opinion be true, I must own I have always been in a great error; for I imagined that when I communicated worthily, i.e. with faith, humility, and thankfulness, my preceding sins were *ipso facto* forgiven me. . . . But if we can never have any certainty of our being in a state of salvation, good reason it is that every moment should be spent not in joy but fear and trembling; and then undoubtedly in this life WE ARE of all men most miserable.[13]

The difference between the 'assurance' of 1725 and that of thirteen years later lay in their origins, 'ordinance' or 'faith'—a crucial distinction.

The consensus of opinion is that, whatever were the influences leading up to the experience, and whatever name is given to it—conversion, decision, or re-dedication—it was the experience itself which changed the direction and impact of John Wesley's life, and which may therefore be said to have given birth to the

[9] *The Spirit of Methodism* (1937), pp. 23-7. [10] 1938.
[11] *The Doctrine of Assurance* (1952). [12] *Journal*, I.476. [13] *Letters*, I.20.

Methodist revival. A letter sent by him to his brother Samuel is some evidence, though it must be borne in mind that it was written within a few months of Whitsuntide, 1738:

By a Christian, I mean one who so believes in Christ as that sin hath no more dominion over him; and in this obvious sense of the word I was not a Christian till May the 24th last past.[14]

More conclusive still is the frequency with which Wesley at much later dates takes the year 1738 as a *terminus a quo*, a climactic date in his spiritual pilgrimage. On 22nd June 1740, for instance, he wrote:

About two years ago it pleased God to show us the *old way* of salvation by *faith only*.[15]

On 14th May 1765, in a letter to John Newton, he said:

I think on Justification just as I have done any time these seven and twenty years;[16]

and as late as 1st September 1778, he said:

Forty years ago I knew and preached every Christian doctrine which I preach now.[17]

The influences which shaped the religious life of John Wesley and prepared the way for his heart-warming experience were many and varied. They were not of uniform strength, nor did they all follow the same direction. They were like strands of different colour, texture, and thickness, in a cord which at first gave little promise of coherence and beauty, but which in the event was strong enough to endure to the end. The range of experiences and emotions through which Wesley passed in his early years was so wide that the description of him by the Marienborn congregation as *homo perturbatus* is not surprising; nor is it difficult to appreciate why fifty years later another Moravian, Benjamin La Trobe, could say: 'It is very doubtful whether John ever knew himself as a sinner, or our Lord as his Saviour.'[18] The marvel is that in spite of his composite spiritual ancestry and of the extraordinary difficulties which beset his evangelical journey he could keep a stable faith, and it is no wonder if doubts assailed him in his moments of depression.

[14] *Letters*, I.262. [15] *Journal*, II.354. [16] *Letters*, IV.298.
[17] *Journal*, VI.209. [18] Letter to Loretz (Herrnhut MSS); see p. 157, *infra*.

A—EPWORTH RECTORY

It is a truism to say that the religious outlook of children depends in the main upon the atmosphere and training of the home. John Wesley and his many brothers and sisters knew it to be more than a truism, and were always gratefully conscious of the wise guidance of their saintly mother and their devout if somewhat unpractical father. The possession of a living in the seventeenth and eighteenth centuries did not necessarily carry with it a deep religious experience or even posit a high moral character, but John Wesley's parents and grandparents could have satisfied the most critical on both scores. His grandfather and one great-grandfather had been ejected from their livings in the great 'purge' of 1662, and this independent strain, if not transmissible, was at least an example which might be followed. John's father and mother did not follow it, and his elder brother Samuel was eminently conservative, but the atmosphere of the Epworth home favoured sincere belief and conscientious worship. John took his first Holy Communion at the early age of eight.

In particular, he owed more than he could ever repay to his mother, Susanna Wesley. There can be little doubt that at her hands he and his brother Charles learned the methodical habits which were to earn for the Holy Club the nickname which was to become the prized title of their followers; and that from both parents they inherited their religious emphasis and their unshakable belief in an overruling Providence. But the influence of Epworth Rectory was more general than specific, and it is by no means certain that it was closely linked with the Whitsuntide experience. On the contrary, it may even, by its somewhat academic discussions of abstract virtues like hope and faith, its insistence upon moral conduct, and its stress on the Sacraments, have deferred it. All these matters are freely discussed in the letters exchanged between John Wesley and the other members of the family, especially after his ordination in 1725, but there is nowhere any recognition of Christ as a personal Saviour.

Tyerman, always inclined to overstate, speaks disparagingly[19] of the evils of public-school education, and assumes that the effect of Charterhouse upon Wesley was altogether evil. There is no reason to suppose that the young scholar was unduly pious

[19] op. cit., p. 22.

at home or abnormally wicked at school. Though he himself (writing in 1738) speaks of 'outward sins',[20] he admits that he regularly read the Scriptures and said his prayers, habits he had learned at home. There can be no doubt that his rescue at the age of six from the fire which destroyed the parsonage made a deep impression upon his mind. Nearly fifty years later, when seriously ill, he drafted his own epitaph, which contained the words, 'Here lieth the body of John Wesley, a brand plucked out of the burning',[21] a phrase which his brother Charles acutely altered to 'a brand, not once only, plucked out of the fire'. It was this conviction that God had saved him for a specific purpose which guided him through all his long and toilsome life. It is probable too that the special care devoted by Susanna Wesley to this one of her brood of children arose from a similar conviction. 'I do intend', she wrote, 'to be more particularly careful of the soul of this child, that Thou hast mercifully provided for, than ever I have been, that I may do my endeavour to instil into his mind the principles of Thy true religion and virtue.'

B—OXFORD

If schooldays presented the young student with grave temptations, those which faced him at Oxford were much more threatening. Ostensibly and historically the custodian of High Church principles, the ancient University displayed little scholarship and less religion, and little improvement took place during the century. John Wesley, however, in spite of his own confession of having 'gone on contentedly in some or other known sin', does not appear to have sown any unusual amount of wild oats. His willingness to confess was probably more an indication of spiritual sensitiveness than a revelation of culpability. Indeed, it is probable that the prevailing atmosphere, which might have corrupted a weaker man, acted as a challenge to Wesley and prepared him for his decision to take Holy Orders. It is true that this decision was made at the instance of his father and in accordance with the fervent hope of his mother; but the necessity for it forced him to take stock of his own spiritual condition. As will be seen, he had been much influenced in this direction by the books he had read.

There is no doubt that a profound change in his attitude to religion took place in 1725. Whether this 'conversion' was

[20] *Journal*, I.466. [21] *Journal*, IV.90.

comparable with that of 1738, or whether, as Piette maintains,[22] it was of even greater importance, is a matter of debate, and depends to some extent on the connotation given to the word 'conversion'. Augustin Léger, in *La Jeunesse de Wesley*,[23] calls the 1725 experience '*la première conversion*' and that of 1738 '*le coup de grâce*', and, making it clear that he is referring to the moment when the soul begins to turn to God, adds: '*En ce sens, la conversion de Wesley date de 1725, non du 24 mai 1738.*' This contention is at least tenable, if conversion is the decision to follow God and to adopt the Christian way of life. But to Methodists, as to other evangelicals, it is much more than that—it is the establishment of a relationship with God through His Son, accompanied by a new sense of power, and indeed by a new power itself.

It was at first a lonely business. It was not until 1729 that Charles Wesley gathered together two or three Oxford friends for study, and a few weeks later John joined the little group, of which he soon became the acknowledged leader. It was at this time that the name 'Methodist' was applied to the tiny band of students, a term by no means new, but in this instance given in jocular reference to their 'strict conformity to the method of study prescribed by the statutes of the University'—not the first nor the last occasion on which a name given in derision has become a title of honour. Strict they were, not only in the self-imposed discipline with which they read, discussed, worshipped, prayed, partook of the Holy Communion, and performed acts of charity—they paid regular visits to the prison and the workhouse—but in the austerity of their life, though it is probable that in some instances this was imposed upon them by their penury. It is clear that this fellowship must have been a safeguard and an inspiration to John Wesley and his companions, several of whom were to be associated with him in after years—George Whitefield, James Hervey, John Gambold, Benjamin Ingham, and Charles Kinchin; and it is no coincidence that several of them afterwards joined the Moravian Brethren, and that one of them, Gambold, became their first English Bishop.

C—BOOKS

Much of the time of the Holy Club was spent in reading, and John Wesley has himself testified to the effect of some of the books

[22] op. cit., p. 244. [23] 1910, p. 77.

on his spiritual growth, books which indeed impelled him to join that sodality. When he laid the foundation stone of 'the new chapel, near the City Road, London', in 1777, he spoke of the influence of two of them—Thomas à Kempis's *Christian Pattern* and Jeremy Taylor's *Holy Living* and *Holy Dying*—and he began his *Plain Account of Christian Perfection* by saying that the reading of these books and of William Law's *Christian Perfection* made him see that true Christianity involved a complete dedication to God. It will be noticed that in all these books, as well as in Law's *A Serious Call to a Devout and Holy Life*, the emphasis is on *conduct*, an emphasis which, though it may for a time have hindered the complete surrender which Aldersgate Street supplied, was to modify profoundly his later views.

Thomas à Kempis's *Christian Pattern* or *Imitation of Christ* was, after the Bible, the first book to move Wesley toward a new life. He says:

> When I was about twenty-two my father pressed me to enter into holy orders. At the same time, the providence of God directing me to Kempis's *Christian Pattern*, I began to see, that true religion was seated in the heart, and that God's law extended to all our thoughts as well as words and actions. I was, however, very angry at Kempis for being too strict. . . . Yet I had frequently much sensible comfort in reading him, such as I was an utter stranger to before. . . . I began to alter the whole form of my conversation, and to set in earnest upon a new life. I set apart an hour or two a day for religious retirement. I communicated every week. I watched against all sin, whether in word or deed. I began to aim at, and to pray for, inward holiness. So that now, 'doing so much, and living so good a life', I doubted not but I was a good Christian.[24]

The implication is that by the time this was written (May 1738) serious doubts had arisen.

Elsewhere he writes:

> In the year 1726 [*sic*], I met with Kempis's *Christian Pattern*. The nature and extent of inward religion, the religion of the heart, now appeared to me in a stronger light than ever it had done before. I saw, that giving even all my life to God (supposing it possible to do this, and go on farther) would profit me nothing, unless I gave my heart, yea, all my heart, to Him.[25]
>
> I sought after this [Christian Perfection] from that hour.[26]

[24] *Journal*, I.466-7. [25] *Works*, XI.366-7. [26] ibid., III.213.

Wesley wrote to his mother about some of the difficulties he found in à Kempis. Here is part of a letter sent to her in May 1725:

I think he must have been a person of great piety and devotion, but it is my misfortune to differ from him in some of his main points. I can't think that when God sent us into the world He had irreversibly decreed that we should be perpetually miserable in it.[27]

John found similar doubts in Jeremy Taylor's *Holy Living* and *Holy Dying*, though these books seem to have made a more lasting impression upon him. He begins the preface to the first edition of his *Journal* thus:

It was in Pursuance of an Advice given by Bp. Taylor, in his *Rules for Holy Living and Dying*, that about fifteen years ago, I began to take a more exact Account than I had done before, of the manner wherein I spent my Time, writing down how I had employed every Hour.[28]

Jeremy Taylor's *Rules* therefore supplemented and strengthened the habits of discipline and method which Wesley had learned at Epworth Rectory and which formed so large a part of his life in Georgia. As late as 1765 he writes, in a letter opposing the doctrine of Predestination:

How came this opinion into my mind? I will tell you with all simplicity. In 1725 I met with Bishop Taylor's *Rules of Holy Living and Dying*. I was struck particularly with the chapter upon Intention, and felt a fixed intention *to give myself up to God*. In this I was much confirmed soon after by the *Christian Pattern*, and longed to *give God all my heart*.[29]

Again he wrote to his mother, pointing out some apparent contradictions in Taylor's book, and indicating that his belief in Assurance was already taking shape:

Surely these graces [viz. those necessary for an immortal life] are not of so little force, as that we can't perceive whether we have them or no; and if we dwell in Christ, and Christ in us, which He will not do till we are regenerate, certainly we must be sensible of it.[30]

In a later letter to her, written in 1730, though he dislikes Taylor's account of Hope, he writes with warm appreciation of his account of the pardon of sins, which, he says, 'is the clearest I ever met with'.[31] And again:

[27] *Letters*, I.16. [28] *Journal*, I.83. [29] *Letters*, IV.298-9.
[30] *Letters*, I.20. [31] ibid., I.47.

In reading several parts of this book, I was exceedingly affected; that part in particular which relates to purity of intention. Instantly I resolved to dedicate all my life to God, all my thoughts, and words, and actions; being thoroughly convinced, there was no medium; but that every part of my life (not some only) must either be a sacrifice to God, or myself, that is, in effect, the devil.[32]

There were other books on which he fed at this time—Scougal's *Life of God in the Soul of Man* (an edition of which he afterwards published), the books of Beveridge and Nelson, which, he claims, relieved him a little from certain 'well-meaning, wrong-headed' Lutherans and Calvinists; and, according to his diaries, the writings of Hickes, Herbert, Heylin, Ephrem Syrus, and Bishop Patrick. But it was probably William Law who had the greatest *immediate* influence upon him, just as it was he from whom, on some matters, he differed most widely in later years. Law is hardly in the same category as à Kempis and Taylor, for Wesley had the advantage of knowing him and meeting him. Perhaps their relations would have been more friendly if they had met less often, for they did not mix well. Law was an able debater, and little inclined to compromise, and the differences of opinion between two men of deep convictions and firmly held views led to an open quarrel. There is no doubt, however, that in these formative years Wesley was deeply impressed by Law's *Serious Call to a Holy Life* and *Christian Perfection*, and that the later differences about mysticism did not eradicate the impression. Certainly, some of Wesley's critics associated Law with the beginnings of Methodism. The Rev. Joseph Tucker, for instance, in 1742 asserted that Law's system was 'the creed of the Methodists';[33] and Dr Joseph Trapp said: 'When I saw these two books, *The Treatise on Christian Perfection* and *The Serious Call to a Holy Life*, I thought, These books will certainly do mischief. And so it proved; for presently after up sprung the Methodists. So he (Mr Law) was their parent.'[34] Another of Law's opponents, Bishop Warburton, declared that the Methodists were the offspring of Law and Zinzendorf. In some ways, Law's influence did not last; but it is clear that, in the early years of their ministry, both John and Charles Wesley were profoundly impressed by him; and that the elder brother's continued emphasis, all through his

[32] *Works*, XI.366. [33] *A Brief History of the Principles of Methodism* (1742).
[34] *Works*, VII.203.

life, on 'doing all the good you can', was largely due to him. Late in the eighteenth century, Coke and Moore, Wesley's contemporaries, referred to Law as 'the great fore-runner of the Revival which followed, who did more to provoke it than any other individual whatsoever'.[35]

Both Wesleys pay their own tributes. In his autobiographical review in the *Journal*, under the date 24th May 1738, John says:

> But meeting now with Mr Law's *Christian Perfection* and *Serious Call*, although I was much offended at many parts of both, yet they convinced me more than ever of the exceeding height and breadth and depth of the law of God. The light flowed in so mightily upon my soul, that everything appeared in a new view. I cried to God for help, and resolved not to prolong the time of obeying Him as I had never done before. And by my continued endeavour to keep His whole law, inward and outward, to the utmost of my power, I was persuaded that I should be accepted of Him, and that I was even then in a state of salvation.[36]

Again there is the implication, in the 'even then', that his belief was unjustified. In 1765, writing to John Newton, he makes no reference to this conviction, but testifies to his renewed determination to give himself to God.[37] Even after his petulant letter of May 1738,[38] in which he reproaches Law for not revealing the source of power, he could say (in August 1744): 'I love Calvin a little, Luther more; the Moravians, Mr Law, and Mr Whitefield far more than either'—though he is careful to add: 'But I love truth more than all.'[39]

These tributes are difficult to reconcile with Wesley's statement, in his reply to Joseph Tucker, that he had been eight years at Oxford before he had read any of Law's writings, and that, when he did, he was so far from making them his creed that he had objected to almost every page.[40] It is perhaps kind to assume that, in the heat of controversy, Wesley's memory sometimes failed him.

His brother Charles was also deeply impressed by Law at first—even in old age he referred to him as having been 'our John the Baptist'[41]—but there are evidences in his *Journal* of increasing dissatisfaction. But this concern, as with John, arose primarily

[35] *Life of the Reverend John Wesley* (1792). [36] I.467.
[37] *Letters*, IV.299. [38] ibid., I.239. [39] ibid., II.25.
[40] *The Principles of a Methodist* (1742), *Works*, VIII.366.
[41] H. Moore, *Life of Wesley* (1825), I.107.

from Law's mysticism and not from his insistence on personal holiness.

What then did the Wesleys owe to Thomas à Kempis, Jeremy Taylor, and William Law? John Wesley paid them a general tribute when he said:

> They convinced me more than ever of the absolute impossibility of being half a Christian; and I determined to be all-devoted to God, to give him my soul, my body, and my substance.[42]

From à Kempis they learned the paramount importance of uprightness of heart, from Taylor the need for an ordered, methodical, pious life, and from Law an ethical impulse as a corrective to mere pietism. It has been maintained[43] that without the moral awakening which John Wesley owed to Law the conversion of 1738 would not have happened. That is not self-evident. Moral awakening does not always, or necessarily, *precede* conversion—it often follows it, for it is possible to realize the grace of God without being immediately conscious of its implications in conduct.

Indeed, it may be contended that the teaching of Law, and to a lesser degree that of à Kempis and Taylor, may have *postponed* Wesley's conversion, and may help to explain the 'long and painful period of impotence, amounting almost to despair' which intervened between the decision of 1725 and the experience of 1738. Wesley had to learn, through years of frustration and disappointment, that a life of piety and altruistic endeavour is neither adequate nor indeed possible without the inward power given by faith in God, and that his efforts to achieve sanctification were doomed to failure simply because they *were* his efforts, for only God through His Holy Spirit could avail for salvation.

In one way, however, in spite of the serious differences which separated John Wesley and William Law in after years, differences which showed themselves painfully in the famous open letter of 1756, Law's influence persisted. His emphasis on personal conduct and his teaching on Christian Perfection may help to explain the breach which was subsequently created between Wesley and the Moravians. If so, the wheel had turned full circle, for it was undoubtedly the influence of the Moravians, and especially of

[42] *Works*, XI.367.

[43] e.g. by E. W. Baker, in *A Herald of the Evangelical Revival* (1948), pp. 65-6, 183.

Peter Böhler, which was to make Wesley dissatisfied with the 'eudaemonistic ethicism' of Law. More permanently, the effect of Law's teaching is to be seen in the ethical emphasis which has always characterized Methodism.

D—THE RELIGIOUS SOCIETIES

It would seem therefore that sufficient impulse already existed—in Epworth Rectory, in the Holy Club, and in devotional books—to prepare the way for the culminating experience of Aldersgate Street. There were, however, other important factors which ought not to be ignored. It was in a Religious Society, for example, that John Wesley 'felt his heart strangely warmed';[44] the Holy Club at Oxford was probably suggested by, and certainly had many similarities to, the early Societies; and though the class-meetings of Methodism had a more intimate and direct origin, some of their characteristics, as will be seen in a later chapter, reproduced the rules and structure of the first Societies. It is probable that John Wesley intended his early Societies to be modelled on the Society at Epworth, though other influences, from without and within, caused him to alter his plans.

In 1760, in a letter to the *London Magazine*, Wesley ascribed the foundation of the Holy Club to a book entitled *The Country Parson's Advice to his Parishioners*. 'There', he says,

> I read these words: 'If good men of the Church will unite together in the several parts of the kingdom, disposing themselves into friendly societies, and engaging each other in their respective combinations to be helpful to each other in all good, Christian ways, it will be the most effectual means for restoring our decaying Christianity to its primitive life and vigour and the supporting of our tottering and sinking Church.' A few young gentlemen then at Oxford approved of and followed the advice. They were all zealous Churchmen, and both orthodox and regular to the highest degree. For their exact regularity they were soon nicknamed Methodists; but they were not then, or for some years after, charged with any other crime, real or pretended, than that of being righteous over-much. Nine or ten years after, many others 'united together in the several parts of the kingdom, engaging in like manner to be helpful to each other in all good, Christian ways.' At first all these were of the Church; but several pious Dissenters soon desired to unite with them. Their one design was to forward each other in true, scriptural Christianity.[45]

[44] *Journal*, I.476.

[45] *Letters*, IV.119-20.

The book to which Wesley referred had been published as early as 1680, and had already been preceded by the formation of at least one such Society. About 1678, through the influence of Dr Anthony Horneck and Mr Smithies, a number of young Churchmen in London began to meet once a week in order 'to apply themselves to good discourse and to things wherein they might edify one another'. By the beginning of the eighteenth century there were many such Societies, and Dr Josiah Woodward's *Account of the Rise and Progress of the Religious Societies in the City of London*[46] gives an interesting description of their constitution and methods. Both Woodward's *Rules* and those of Horneck show that these Societies were confined to members of the Church of England (though the former enjoined 'due Christian charity, candour, and moderation toward all such Dissenters as are of good conversation'—a proviso which John Wesley at first would not have welcomed), that the Liturgy of the Church of England was to be used, that charity should be dispensed, and that the members should not only make regular use of the means of grace in prayer and sacrament but should cultivate the highest probity in their parochial lives. This programme is too close to that of the Holy Club to be accidental, and the Religious Societies must therefore be regarded as one more strand, if only a slender one, in the composite cord of John Wesley's spiritual development.

The existence and spread of these Societies should modify the commonly held and commonly stated view that the clergy were, as a whole, time-servers, negligent, or corrupt. All over the country were rectories where the Bible, the Prayer Book and *The Whole Duty of Man* were read and followed. John Wesley's own *Journal* tells of many incumbents who welcomed him to their pulpits, a magnanimous gesture in view of the many criticisms of the Methodists in Anglican circles. The friendliness of William Grimshaw of Haworth is well known—it was due to a loan from him that the first preaching-place in Halifax was built; Dr Legh, Vicar of Halifax, was described by Wesley as 'a candid inquirer after truth' and opened the Parish Church to him;[47] Henry Venn, Vicar of Huddersfield, invited him to his church,[48] and was so evangelical in his methods that the Methodists made no attempt to establish their work in his neighbourhood as long as he lived; while, as late as 1786, Wesley preached twice in one day at Holy

[46] 1701. [47] *Journal*, III.16. [48] ibid., V.82, etc.

Trinity Church, Hull.[49] But the age was a loose and vicious one, and great masses of the population were hungry with a hunger which little groups of students, however devout, could not satisfy. It is probable that John Wesley felt this himself long before 1738. In his early days at Oxford, at any rate after 1725, he had seemed almost exclusively concerned with his own spiritual condition. When, for example, it was suggested that he should follow his father as Rector of Epworth, he wrote thus in reply:

> The question is not whether I could do more good to others there or here; but whether I could do more good to myself: seeing wherever I can be most holy myself, there I can most promote holiness in others. But I can improve myself more at Oxford than at any other place.[50]

When his father wisely pointed out that our main consideration in choosing a course of life 'is not dear self, but the glory of God and the different degrees of promoting it', he replied in a long letter,[51] full of debating points (a device to which he became more and more prone), in which he argued that he could best promote the glory of God by achieving holiness in himself and in others. The letter, however, has very little to do with 'the others', except for visiting the prisons and helping the poor, and a great deal to do with his own spiritual life. It is a far cry from the evangelistic zeal of the John Wesley who took 'the world as his parish', and suggests that, in spite of the wholesome influences which were already at work, he still had a long way to go.

On the whole then it appears that, though the history of Methodism, especially in its later organization, may have been affected by John Wesley's connexion with the Religious Societies,[52] the direct connexion with his growing religious experience and especially with his Aldersgate Street crisis was slight.

E—THE PIETISTS

It is remarkable that in the list of books to which Wesley pays a tribute the name of Martin Luther does not appear. Indeed, the first reference to Luther in the *Journal* is under the date 24th May, 1738, when, as he tells us, 'one was reading Luther's preface to the *Epistle to the Romans*.[53] Charles Wesley antedates this by

[49] *Journal*, VII.170-1.
[50] Priestley's *Original Letters*.
[51] *Letters*, I.166ff.
[52] See p. 191, *infra*.
[53] *Journal*, I.475-6.

a week: it was on 17th May that he was introduced by William Holland to Luther's *Commentary on the Epistle to the Galatians.*[54] In view of the crucial importance of these two dates, and of the consistent emphasis laid by the Wesleys and the Moravians on the doctrine of Justification by Faith, this omission is striking. No doubt, Luther's writings were not widely known in England at that time, and Holland refers to Luther's *Galatians* as 'a very precious treasure that I had found'. It would be wrong, however, to assume from this that Luther's influence before 1738 was negligible. But it was an indirect influence, and made its presence felt through the Pietists, and to a lesser extent through the Religious Societies. It is interesting to observe that Dr Anthony Horneck, the principal promoter of these Societies, was the Lutheran minister at the Savoy Church, and it is probable therefore that they were, at any rate in part, suggested by the *collegia pietatis* which characterized the Pietist movement in Germany.

Pietism had many points of similarity to Methodism, both in its spirit and in its effects. It brought a personal emphasis and a social consciousness to religion in Germany in much the same way as the Evangelical Revival was to do in England. It arose out of a recognition of the low spiritual condition of the Lutheran Church in Germany in the second half of the seventeenth century, not unlike that of the Church of England in the first half of the eighteenth, and owed its origin to Philipp Jakob Spener, pastor at Frankfurt. Spener had himself been influenced in early life by some Puritan writings, especially those of Richard Baxter, whose *Reformed Pastor* probably helped to shape Spener's thought and methods. These methods included not only more evangelical preaching, but what would now be called 'group discussions', with catechetical instruction and book-study. At first these groups were informally arranged, in private houses, but later on Spener held his *collegia pietatis* in the church.

His successor was August Hermann Francke, who, after some little time at Leipzig and Erfurt, became Professor of Theology at the new University of Halle. His teaching took a more practical turn, in the provision of an orphan home, a charity school, a dispensary, and a publishing house. Wesley was familiar with the description of this work in Francke's book *Pietas Hallensis*, and

[54] *Journal*, I.476, n.

in August 1739 visited Francke's charitable institutions. 'I waited', he says, 'on Professor Francke, who behaved with the utmost humanity.'[55] It has been suggested[56] that Wesley intended the Orphan House at Newcastle to be modelled on the lines of Francke's Waisenhaus at Halle, but it is probable that he received his first stimulus from another quarter.[57] Other Pietists to whom Wesley was indebted were Francke's son-in-law and successor, Johann Anastasius Freylinghausen, the compiler of the famous *Gesangbuch*, from which he was to translate several hymns by Pietists to which the Moravians introduced him, and the great expositor Bengel, on whose *Gnomon of the New Testament* Wesley based his own *Notes on the New Testament*.

It cannot, however, be claimed that the Pietists had any considerable influence on Wesley's spiritual pilgrimage. *Notes on the New Testament* was not published until 1755; Wesley owed his knowledge of the hymns of the Pietists to his Moravian friends; and it was left for Peter Böhler and August Spangenberg to introduce Luther to him, even though the Luther they knew may not have been the true Luther.[58] Even the indirect influence of Pietism, through the Moravians, must not be exaggerated. Count Zinzendorf, it is true, owed much to his Pietistic upbringing. As a child, he had been under the guidance of Spener himself, he had come as a boy into contact with Francke's institutions at Halle, and in late adolescence he came to cherish Spener's (and Luther's) conception of '*ecclesiolae in ecclesia*' as the way to renewal and revival. But divergence and even hostility arose between Zinzendorf and his Pietist mentors. Pietism had begun as a revolt against a cold dogma devoid of religious feeling and practical piety, but by the time of Wesley's contacts with it was itself becoming hidebound in a narrow legalism and a prescribed devotional experience. It was on this latter interpretation that Zinzendorf was most at variance with it. To the Pietist, the one thing needful for reconciliation with a just and provoked God was a long and painful struggle for repentance; to Zinzendorf, as later to the Methodists, the essential mark of salvation was an immediate and joyous acceptance of forgiveness:

[55] *Journal*, II.58.

[56] By Henry Bett, in *The Spirit of Methodism* (1937), pp. 30-3.

[57] See p. 242, *infra*.

[58] Franz Hildebrandt, *From Luther to Wesley* (1951).

My God, I am Thine;
What a comfort divine,
What a blessing to know that my Jesus is mine!
In the heavenly Lamb
Thrice happy I am,
And my heart it doth dance at the sound of His name.[59]

In his early years, John Wesley had more in common with the Pietists than with Zinzendorf, though both Pietism and Moravianism preserved more belief in mysticism than he was ever able to accept. Much as he later owed to Francke, to Bengel and to Freylinghausen, the Pietistic contribution to his journey toward Whitsuntide 1738 was small.

SUMMARY

From the foregoing considerations, the following conclusions seem to be established:

(1) Though John Wesley's ordination in 1725 was a decisive step in his spiritual career, it differed not only in degree but in kind from the experience of Whitsuntide 1738. It was the logical and almost conventional outcome of his life hitherto, which had been founded on his Epworth home and encouraged by all the traditions of his family and associations. The events of 1738, on the contrary, were catastrophic. They were less an intellectual assent than the response to an emotional impulse. Wesley's ordination in 1725 was in the main the recognition of a fact, and by itself could not have sufficed to carry him through a life of amazing toil and unabated enthusiasm. Such a response demanded a change of heart. In Wesley's own records, there is a new note after May 1738—a new direction and a new emphasis—well-expressed in his brother's hymn which they sang together in Little Britain on that historic Wednesday:

Outcasts of men, to you I call,
Harlots, and publicans, and thieves!
He spreads His arms to embrace you all;
Sinners alone His grace receives:
No need of Him the righteous have;
He came the lost to seek and save.[60]

[59] Charles Wesley, *Methodist Hymn-book* (1933), No. 406.

[60] ibid., 361. It has been maintained that the hymn sung was No. 371—'And can it be'.

There is no such note in 1725.

(2) The contribution made therefore by the various factors enumerated above to the events of Whitsuntide 1738 must be assessed in the main on the basis of their *emotional* effect.

(*a*) The encouragement given by the training in the Epworth home cannot of course be ignored, but it was in the nature of a foundation rather than of a dynamic impulse, and may be said to have reached its fulfilment in 1725.

(*b*) Wesley's life at Oxford, with its historic surroundings and traditional association with the Church of England tended to fix Wesley in his love for that Church and his respect for its ordinances, and to postpone any departure from established beliefs and practices.

(*c*) The books he read were by no means revolutionary: they enunciated no new doctrine, but only interpreted accepted beliefs and compelled him to apply them to his own life.

(*d*) So too the influence of the Religious Societies was largely conservative. The fact that they were confined to members of the Church of England and that their proceedings were in the main liturgical shows that there was little that was revolutionary about them in conception or practice; and there was certainly no anticipation in them of Wesley's later evangelical zeal. They expressed themselves in study and discussion, in the deepening of the spiritual life of their members, and in the extension of their theological knowledge. Like the Epworth home, they established a foundation, they did not suggest a design or direct an impulse.

(*e*) The effect of the Pietists, though not negligible, was of a longer term, and was not to be realized until after the events of 1738.

(3) It seems clear therefore that some other factor beyond these was needed to give the Wesleys the impulse and vision which changed the whole direction of their work, and gave their life a new meaning. Where that influence was to be found the following chapters will indicate.

CHAPTER TWO

THE MORAVIANS

A—THE ANCIENT CHURCH OF THE BRETHREN

ANY MENTION of the Moravians is bound to call to mind the great Bohemian reformer, John Huss. The history of the Bohemian Church is, however, very obscure, and Huss, notable figure though he is, is only one of a long line of distinguished preachers whom that tiny country has produced. The beginnings of Christianity in Bohemia lie much farther back: it is probable that the conversion of the Goths in Moesia and Dacia in the third century took the Gospel to the Teutonic tribes much farther north than the Macedonia to which Paul was invited.[1] Later German infiltrations caused much the same difficulties, political and religious, as have persisted in Ireland. In the ninth century a great impression was made by Cyril and Methodius, Greek monks from Thessalonica. They adapted themselves to local conditions, preached in the Bohemian language, and became as popular as if they were Bohemian born. The attempt of the German Archbishop of Salzburg to introduce German priests led to bitter controversy and to a serious deterioration in the moral character of the clergy, whether native or German. The Bohemian Church was not fully Romanized until after the Reformation, though the creation of a University in Prague did much to ensure the acceptance of the Latin rites.

Many attempts had been made, by both Germans and Bohemians, to purify the Church and nation, notably by Matthew of Janow (1381-93), during the Papal Schism, when there were two or three rival claimants for the Papacy, and when Popes were politicians rather than preachers. The time was ripe for the influence of Wyclif, and his attacks, not only on the corruption of Pope and hierarchy but on what he believed to be false doctrine, supplied the spark which, in the person of John Huss, was to set on fire a people already glowing with patriotic enthusiasm and earnestly desirous of a return to Primitive Christianity. The Moravian influence on evangelical religion in the British Isles in

[1] K. S. Latourette, *A History of the Expansion of Christianity*, Vol. I.

the eighteenth century was therefore a kind of repayment for the work of Wyclif.

The prevailing discontent found a spokesman in John Huss, whose judicial murder in 1415 caused intense excitement and almost rebellion. Unfortunately, his death removed the link which had kept together discordant groups—the Utraquists or Calixtines, who contended that laymen should be allowed to take the wine at the Communion service, the Taborites, rebels against authority, political in aim and negative in doctrine, the Chiliasts or Millenarians, who believed that the end of the world was at hand, and the Waldenses, immigrants from Northern Italy and Southern France, who were religious radicals and at that time strongly anti-sacerdotal. The Hussite Wars tell a tragic story of bloodshed and confusion, distinguished by the military genius of Ziska, the blind Bohemian general, who for years kept at bay the Catholic armies which had been summoned by the Pope to a new Crusade, but his death of fever hastened the defeat of the patriotic forces, and the concordat between the Council of Basle and the Utraquists patched up an uneasy peace. From this welter of blood and fire the Moravian Church arose.

In this achievement, the leader and prophet was Peter of Chelcic, a man of humble origin but of great power as a writer. He was a pacifist, and regarded the Hussite Wars as a disgrace to both sides. He preached a gospel of primitive simplicity, opposed a State Church, and indeed discountenanced the participation by Christians in local or national affairs, decried the 'profit motive', and vigorously attacked the priesthood. In many parts of the country, men took him as a guide and wore a distinctive dress. His work was carried on by John Rockycana, Archbishop-elect of Prague, a great preacher but no leader; and his weakness caused his followers to support the leadership of his nephew Gregory, who formed a little community in the village of Kunwald, on the north-east border of Bohemia, within the King's estates. Hither came men and women of diverse ranks and views, and here was formed the first settlement of the Church of the Brethren, the fore-runner of Herrnhut, Marienborn, Fulneck, and Fairfield. The first Synod of the Brethren, the *Unitas Fratrum*, was held in 1467; it decided to break away from the Papacy; pastors were chosen by lot and ordained by Stephen, a Bishop of the Waldenses. By him Michael Bradacius was consecrated a Bishop, and thus arose those episcopal orders which have been maintained in the Church of the Brethren to the present day.

The Brethren were subjected to much persecution during the fifteenth century, and shared with other Protestants the difficulties of the sixteenth. In 1609 the Bohemians were so strong that they were able to compel Rudolph to grant, by the Letter of Majesty, religious toleration to all. All adherents of the Confession (i.e. the Bohemian National Protestant Confession) could worship as they pleased, and all classes except the peasantry could build schools and churches on Royal estates. 'No decree of any kind', ran one sweeping clause, 'shall be issued either by us or by our heirs and succeeding kings against the above established religious peace.'

The delight of the Brethren was short-lived. The hostility of the Jesuits, whose power was increasing, difficulties in interpreting the Letter of Majesty, especially with reference to royal tenants who were Catholics, and the weakness of King Matthias produced a dangerous situation, which was made critical by the election as his successor of Ferdinand, a determined supporter of Catholicism. The first blow of the Thirty Years War was struck in 1618, when the Protestant Defenders broke their way into the royal castle, and in the famous 'defenestration of Prague' threw the King's Councillors, Martinitz and Slawata, into the courtyard. The battle of the White Hill two years later, in which the Protestant army was routed, ended, however, the hope of a peaceful settlement, and twenty-seven leaders, including a dozen of the Brethren, were executed. The Brethren were expelled from Bohemia. Thirty-six thousand families left Bohemia and Moravia; their property was confiscated; the University of Prague was handed over to the Jesuits; and the Ancient Church of the Brethren ceased to exist.

But not for ever! John Amos Comenius, of whom more will be said in a later chapter,[2] kept the 'hidden seed' of the Church in his exile in Poland; other Brethren went to Hungary, Saxony, and Holland; some, including the Kennicks or Cennicks, found a home in England; and a few remained in Bohemia and Moravia, worshipping in secret and longing for the renewal of their ancient Church.

It is opportune here to ask in what ways the Brethren differed from other Protestant Communions. The differences were in attitude and practice rather than in doctrine. Indeed, it may be

[2] See p. 238, *infra*.

claimed that their doctrine was on the whole negative, not only in the early days of their Church, in the fifteenth and sixteenth centuries, but even in the eighteenth. They preferred to resist what they deemed to be error rather than to propagate theological propositions. They sought as far as possible to recapture the spirit and practice of Apostolic times. Indeed, it is probable that the similarity between Moravianism and the Apostolic Church was the primary cause of Wesley's association with the Brethren. In pursuance of this ideal preservation of the practice of the early Christians, without the accretions which had been gathered during the ages by other Communions and especially by the Roman Catholics, the Brethren endeavoured to keep their lives simple and their institutions unadorned. 'Above all things', they declared at a Synod held in 1464, 'we are one in this purpose. We hold fast the faith of the Lord Christ. We will abide in the righteousness and love of God. We will trust in the living God. We will do good works. We will serve each other in the spirit of love.'[3]

The emphasis on 'good works' is in interesting contrast to the suspicion entertained of them by their descendants in the eighteenth century; and the recognition of the value of moral conduct as evidence of faith shows that Molther's doctrine of 'stillness'[4] was not in accordance with Moravian tradition. But two things must be remembered. Luther had yet to formulate and enunciate his doctrine of Justification by Faith, the rock upon which the Reformation was to be built and, because of differing interpretations, the fellowship of Methodists and Moravians to be shattered. Moreover, in this declaration of 1464, though good works were included as an essential part of the Brethren's practice, they seem to have been limited to their own fellowship: 'We will serve *each other* in the spirit of love. . . . We will show obedience *to one another*.' John Wesley drew attention to this limitation in a letter to his brother Charles on 21st April 1741: 'They are by no means zealous of good works, or, at least, only to their own people.'[5] On the other hand, Benjamin Ingham took a very different view, for, writing on 1st May 1736, he said: 'They are more ready to serve their neighbours than themselves.'[6] Perhaps Wesley could have expressed equal admiration in 1736!

[3] J. E. Hutton, *History of the Moravian Church*, pp. 71-2.
[4] See p. 84, *infra*.
[5] *Letters*, I.353; and see p. 140, *infra*.
[6] Tyerman, *The Oxford Methodists* (1873), p. 68.

The emphasis evident in this declaration of 1464 governed every aspect of their lives. In their ministry they were less insistent on theological learning than on personal character. As a consequence, they were tempted to decry learning, especially classical learning, though the literacy of the rank and file was remarkably widespread. The ministers, who were unpaid, were subject to a severe discipline in their manner of living, and could not even marry without consent of the Elders; they lived in the same house as the Deacons and Acoluths, and exercised a kind of patriarchal authority over them. Their congregations were divided into three classes—the Beginners, the Proficients and the Perfect, 'those so established in faith, hope and love as to be able to enlighten others'. There were codes of behaviour for workers of different kinds, not unlike those of the medieval Guilds, though the régime was stern and puritanical. The government of the Church was Presbyterian, the Synod being the final court, as it is today. Doctrine was simple and unpolemic—it is to be remembered that this was before the time of Luther—and was Johannine rather than Pauline. The Catechism drawn up by Luke of Prague and used as an authorized manual of instruction in the Brethren's homes reveals the divergence of doctrine from that of the Lutherans which was soon to show itself. The seventy-six questions and answers of which it consists include no specific reference to the doctrine of Justification by Faith. Indeed, from the very beginning as in their later history the Brethren emphasized almost exclusively the Person and teaching of Jesus Christ. There are few quotations from the Epistles, there are many from the Gospels. To Luther, faith was primarily trust in God; to the Brethren it covered more than trust—it included hope and love. Faith in God was 'to know God, to know his word; above all, to love him, to do His commandments, and to submit to His will', while faith in Christ—the distinction is interesting—was 'to listen to His word, to know Him, to honour Him, to love Him, and to join the company of His followers'.[7]

The Brethren's reluctance to be involved in theological controversy was shown in their doctrine of the Lord's Supper. At first, they refused to commit themselves to either of the conflicting views, viz. that it was a memorial or that the bread was really the body of Christ. 'We simply believe what He Himself said, and

[7] From the German edition of 1522, quoted in full in Müller's *Die deutschen Katechismen der Böhmischen Brüder*.

enjoy what He has given.'[8] Afterwards, when it was impossible to stand aside in this way, and when some more definite attitude was necessary, they denied the doctrines both of Transubstantiation and Consubstantiation, and took the whole passage in a spiritual sense. So too they differed from Luther in their doctrine of infant baptism; they rejected any idea of baptismal regeneration. To them, as to the Free Churches in general today, infant baptism was simply the outward and visible sign of admission to the Church. The Moravians of this time were united not by a common creed but rather by a common devotion to Christ, a common reverence for Holy Scripture, and a common desire to revive the customs of the early Christian Church. They were to change in many respects before the Revival by Zinzendorf, but it is not difficult to see why the Wesleys were so deeply impressed by them in Georgia.

B—THE REVIVAL UNDER ZINZENDORF

The story of the revival of this ancient Church, in the main through the instrumentality of two men, neither of whom was originally a Moravian, is a most romantic one. It begins with Christian David, a native of Moravia, but brought up a Roman Catholic. At first a shepherd, he afterwards became a carpenter, but his interests were primarily religious, and he sought, by reading, to find peace to his soul. At the age of twenty, he left Catholic Moravia and went to Berlin, where he became a Lutheran, but not yet was he satisfied; and after many vicissitudes, during which he served in the war against Charles XII of Sweden, he found fellowship and spiritual comfort with the Pietists. Not satisfied with keeping to himself his new-found peace, he sought to share it with others, and returned to his native Moravia, preaching with uncontrolled fervour. There he found a little group of German Protestants, the remnant of the Church of the Brethren, who, in spite of persecution, had kept their faith stable and their vision clear. To them in their distress Christian David appeared like an angel of light.

The time of his arrival seemed miraculously opportune. At this

[8] cf. Queen Elizabeth's attitude:

Christ was the Word that spake it,
He took the bread and brake it,
And what that Word did make it,
That I believe, and take it.

time there lived at Berthelsdorf, a village in Upper Lusatia, a young Count, Nicholas Ludwig of Zinzendorf. He had been brought up in Pietist circles, and through all his boyhood and youth had been deeply interested in religion. While still a boy at school, he had established little religious societies, and had founded a devotional club called 'The Order of the Mustard Seed', an order which was later extended to include men as diverse in origin and view as Archbishop Potter of Canterbury, Bishop Wilson of Sodor and Man, Cardinal Noailles, and Oglethorpe, Governor of Georgia. (The friendliness of Oglethorpe, so important to American Methodist history, persisted long after the breach between Zinzendorf and John Wesley.) The Count contemplated entering the State Church, and though this was impracticable he held a public meeting in his own rooms every Sunday, and there, as a layman, he preached. But his fellow-worshippers were men of his own social rank, and he wished to share his faith with humbler folk. He therefore purchased the little estate of Berthelsdorf, near Hennersdorf, installed there his friend Johann Andreas Rothe, a Pietist, as Pastor of the little flock, and sought to build up a Christian community. Rothe will be remembered for his magnificent hymn, *Ich habe nun den Grund gefunden*, best known in one of John Wesley's most successful translations, *Now I have found the ground.*[9]

It must not be forgotten that Zinzendorf was a Lutheran; indeed, all through his life he held sternly to Lutheran doctrines, as he conceived them; and there was no intention in his mind at that time to found another Church. Indeed, it is doubtful if he had ever heard of the Church of the Brethren. And yet, at Rothe's induction service, the text chosen by Schäfer, the Pietist pastor of Görlitz, was prophetic: 'God will light a candle on these hills which will illuminate the whole land.'[10] He was accused of untruthfulness by his enemies, and even his friends found in him a certain want of candour. It is difficult to believe that a man of such vision and courage deliberately told untruths, yet on more than one occasion he alternated the imaginative adornment of a tale with a reticence which invited a false conclusion. 'The cruellest lies are often told in silence.'[11] One of the most frequent charges made against him by John Wesley was that he used 'guile

[9] *Methodist Hymn-book* (1933), No. 375; and see pp. 202-3, *infra*.

[10] J. E. Hutton, op. cit., p. 191. [11] R. L. Stevenson, *Truth in Intercourse*.

and dissimulation', a charge he extended to the Moravians in general. In the letter, written but not sent, and addressed to the Moravians at Marienborn and Herrnhut, he asked: 'Do you not use cunning, guile, or dissimulation in many cases?' 'Are you not of a close, dark, reserved temper and behaviour?' 'Is not the spirit of secrecy the spirit of your community?' 'Have you that childlike openness, frankness, and plainness of speech so manifest to all in the Apostles and first Christians?'[12] And on 21st April, 1741 he wrote to his brother Charles: 'There is darkness and closeness in all their behaviour, and guile in almost all their words.'[13]

John Wesley on one occasion scoffed at the rather extravagant names Zinzendorf used when travelling incognito, and there is more than a suggestion of vanity, if not of arrogance, in his description of himself in a letter sent to the Archbishop of Canterbury in June 1749:

> We, Lewis, by Divine Providence, Bishop, Liturgus, and Ordinary of the Churches known by the name of the Brethren; and, under the auspices of the same, Advocate during life, with full power over the hierarchy of the Slavonic Unity; Custos Rotulorum, and Prolocutor both of the general Synod and of the Tropus of instruction.[14]

Zinzendorf cannot be totally exonerated from responsibility for the scandals of Herrnhaag;[15] and his hymns, which often reached great heights of eloquence and power, at other times fell into the depths of sentimentality and ineptitude. Even his warm admirer, August Gottlieb Spangenberg, felt constrained to say: 'I cannot deny that his speeches have often appeared to me paradoxical and his business methods extraordinary. I must confess that I have many a time had some hesitation about this';[16] and John Gambold, the first Bishop of the Moravians in England, in a spirited defence of his leader, has to admit: 'He is an extraordinary person or genius, and, as such, requires to be looked at in a particular point of view, if one will avoid error.'[17]

But the Count's weaknesses must not be allowed to obscure his outstanding qualities. The frequent practice of comparing him

[12] *Letters*, I.258. [13] ibid., p. 353.

[14] Benham, *Memoirs of James Hutton*, p. 237; see p. 131, *infra*.

[15] See pp. 129, 148, *infra*.

[16] *Declaration über die zeither gegen uns ausgegangene Beschuldigen, sonderlich die Person unsers Ordinarii betreffend* (1751).

[17] *Letter to Spangenberg*, 4th June, 1750.

with John Wesley does justice to neither, for it introduces an emotional and even a combative note into the assessment. It may be suggested that personalities so vivid and yet so unlike were bound to clash, and that neither was at his best in dealing with the other. What neither Zinzendorf's admirers nor his critics can deny is his unselfish devotion to one grand ideal, the cause of Christian fellowship. To this cause he gave his whole life; on it he pledged his whole fortune. If he had been more practical, he would have been less of a poet; if he had been less of an autocrat, he would have been less able to keep within bounds the centrifugal tendencies of a growing Church. The same, of course, may be said of John Wesley. Certainly, by his fellow-Brethren, who were indebted to him not only for leadership but for rescue from financial disaster, he was regarded with an admiration amounting almost to idolatry. James Hutton, for example, in three long letters written in 1750 and 1754, calls him 'a man whom my soul blesses when it sees him, a man of the noblest, most generous and exalted, and yet most natural and simple sentiments', and sees in him one 'whom every spectator cannot but reckon among the foremost of Christian heroes'. Later in the same letter he declares, 'Uprightness is at the bottom of the man, and sound sense accompanies all his actions, when they are looked upon with exactness', and ascribes to him 'a constant regard for what is proper and decent in the eyes of all men, and the most lively aversion to absurdity and extravagance of every sort, which he supposes to be always very much resembling immorality in its very nature'[18] —a tribute which it is difficult to reconcile with the excesses of Herrnhaag and the 'Blood and Wounds' hymns. So, too, in the same declaration in which he speaks of the Count's paradoxical speeches and extraordinary business methods, Spangenberg adds:

> Yet his bedrock has remained with me, and his pure motives and his burning zeal for the Saviour have justified him in my sight no less than his orthodox, high-Church, zealous care for the Lutheran Church. He is a knight of Jesus Christ. If only his Lord is satisfied with him, he need not depend upon man.

Gambold, too, after his plea that special standards of judgement are necessary for men of genius—a plausible but dangerous argument—goes on to say:

[18] Benham, op. cit., pp. 580-3.

He is a plain man, who proceeds straightforward; and, amidst all the richness of his active and extensive genius, will always be serving and inculcating one only point, namely, the meritorious sufferings of our Creator.

One who was neither Moravian nor Methodist, but who had friends in both camps, Philip Doddridge, referred to Zinzendorf as 'that blessed herald of our Redeemer'.[19]

If Zinzendorf was at times reckless and improvident, his fundamental loyalty to Christian principle saved him from disaster. If he had been more circumspect, he might have lacked that spark of genius which made him a born leader and assured him of the devotion of his followers when he was most bitterly attacked. He was, in fact, a many-sided personality, a mixture of strength and weakness, of insight and of folly. His enemies saw only his mistakes and made the most of them; his supporters loved him in spite of his failings. Both friends and critics exaggerated, but the story of eighteenth-century Christianity, and of evangelism in particular, is not complete without him.

Such was the man to whom the Revival of the Church of the Brethren was primarily due, primarily in importance if not in point of time; and the organization of the renewed Church, as well as its spirit, reveals his driving influence and singleness of aim at every turn. In a subsequent chapter, the debt of Methodism to Moravianism will be discussed, and it is necessary therefore to give some account of the arrangements of Moravian polity and practice, central and local. Zinzendorf, though a Lutheran, saw no inconsistency in encouraging the renewal of a Church which, though it had some similarities with Lutheranism, was an independent Church. He certainly asked the settlers at Herrnhut to sign a 'Brotherly Agreement', by which they agreed to live in friendship with Christians of other denominations, and also to regard themselves as members of the Lutheran Church. This was in accord with his general idea of '*ecclesiola in ecclesia*', and was intended to secure a common ground of Christian conduct rather than a unified theology. As will be seen, however, the highly specialized organization of Moravian life at Herrnhut and elsewhere made it difficult to preserve the conception of 'a church within a church', and encouraged ultimate separation. The Moravians laid great stress on meetings for worship and prayer.

[19] In a letter to Benjamin Ingham, 8th March, 1741.

Every day three meetings for the whole congregation took place, the first as early as five o'clock in the morning. At an early period the whole congregation was divided into ninety unions for prayer, and each 'band' met two or three times a week. In view of the claim made in the *Methodist Hymn-book* of 1933, 'Methodism was born in song', it is interesting to note that singing from the earliest times had played a large part in the life of the Moravian Church and that the singing of hymns was one of the customs of the Ancient Church soonest recaptured. At nine in the morning, for example, the young men marched round the settlement singing hymns. Hymns today are generally an approach to God, but many of the Moravian hymns were didactic, and indeed seem to have been used antiphonally in debate. In *A Collection of Hymns*, published in 1754 (which Gambold produced under the guidance of Zinzendorf) one hymn begins:

Should an Historiographer
Arise some future day,
Who all events and men with care
Would in just light display,
And should this theme Church Matters be
Of the now-current century,
And at last Fratrum Unitas;
How shall he paint their case?

Many of the hymns were of high quality, as will be seen later,[20] and are in regular use today; but a good many others differed in conception of function from those in general use at the present time. Instead of being addressed to God, they were addressed to fellow-worshippers, and were *about* God.

One interesting practice arose from Zinzendorf's desire for variety in worship. At the regular evening singing-meeting he gave a short address on a verse of Scripture or of a hymn, and this developed into a normal procedure, by which texts for meditation were chosen by the Elders from a box. The *Moravian Text-book* began in 1731 has lasted until today. Once a month, too, on 'Congregation Day', reports were given of evangelical work in other districts. This has some similarity to the 'Conversation on the Work of God' which is a characteristic feature of Methodist Quarterly Meetings, Synods, and Conferences.

[20] See p. 200, *infra*.

The Brethren at Herrnhut regarded themselves as part of the historic Church, and though they knew little of their early history and customs they sought to recapture and preserve the traditions of Apostolic times. They met, for example, in one another's houses, and attempted to revive the *Agape* of the early Church. In this Love-feast (an institution which is still preserved by Moravian congregations), they partook of a simple meal of rye-bread and water, and wished one another the wish: 'Long live the Lord Jesus in our hearts.' In course of time, the Love-feast became a meeting for the whole congregation. The ceremony of feet-washing, which immediately preceded the Lord's Supper, has not been preserved. It was abandoned in 1818, but had lost its popularity for some time before that. They also revived the *vigiliae* of the Primitive Church in the Watch-night services which were held at 'the noon of night', generally on New Year's Eve.[21]

One of the most interesting features of the life at Herrnhut was the division of the community into 'choirs'. Not only were the sexes kept strictly apart in the services, but in its ordinary life the settlement was divided into 'choirs'—the Married Choir, the Single Brethren, the Single Sisters, the widowers, the children, and so on. In times these unions, which were at first voluntary, became official, and the whole congregation was divided into ten companies, each with its own president or 'Helper', its own special services, its own festival day, and its own Love-feasts. Certain of the buildings at Fulneck, the Moravian settlement at Pudsey, near Leeds, still bear the names of these 'choirs'. Each choir consisted of 'bands' of from five to seven persons each, who met every week under their president to exchange their religious experiences and encourage one another in the faith. It is important to differentiate between the 'bands' and the 'choirs'. Not only were the former smaller and more intimate than the latter: their functions were different. The general meetings of the choirs were not intended for mutual help and satisfaction so much as for receiving instruction. It will be seen, therefore, that they have some kinship with, and some differences from, the English Religious Societies.

The Brethren were convinced of direct answer to prayer, either in their own hearts or through the medium of their recognized readers. This explains their continued use of the 'Lot', by

[21] See p. 216, *infra*.

which they believed that God made His wishes known to them. Strange as this may appear to modern thought, it was based on a definite theological attitude. It was not a mere appeal to chance: the Lot was not used except after earnest prayer to God. It was not used on every occasion when a choice was necessary—they found the answer to most of their problems in the workings of their own conscience or in the words of Holy Scripture—but in cases of doubt they regarded the decision of the Lot as the voice of God, especially when through it they were called to some form of Christian work. Something similar is seen today in the procedure of certain small Protestant communions, the leaders of which 'speak with tongues' which other leaders interpret whenever a call is made to the ministry.

The Lot was always used in matters of major importance, and sometimes in those of less concern. It was used by a sister in determining her answer to an offer of marriage, and it will be remembered that John Wesley acted under Moravian advice in consulting the Lot about his contemplated marriage to Sophia Hopkey.[22] If Wesley, the pupil, could accept so loyally a decision which meant so much to him, it is hardly likely that his Moravian teachers would set less store upon similar decisions.

The constitution of the young Church had a democratic basis, but one which, like that of most democracies, gave ample opportunity for a dictatorship. It was governed by twelve Elders, chosen by vote of all male adults in Herrnhut, and these Elders had enormous power and exercised control over every department of life. Later on, the Elders were assisted by voluntary 'Helpers'. At first, preachers might be either ministers or laymen, but after the consecration of David Nitschmann in 1737 by Bishop Daniel Ernest Jablonsky, who was linked through his grandfather John Amos Comenius to the Ancient Church of the Brethren, ordination became the rule. A Bishop had a purely spiritual office, with power to ordain, but ruling over no diocese and receiving no additional emolument. Even today Moravian Bishops receive the same stipends as other ministers. Disputes between individual Brethren were decided by a Board of Arbitrators, and litigation was discouraged. There had been a Synod, or General Conference, as early as 1464: Zinzendorf revived this institution in a Synod which met at Ebersdorf in 1738, anticipating the first

[22] See p. 42, *infra*.

Methodist Conference by six years. This constitution was to change, but some of its features have lasted till today.

SUMMARY

In this account of the history and constitution of the Ancient Church of the Brethen and its Revival under Zinzendorf, there are already indications of features which were likely to exercise a profound influence over John Wesley.

(1) The Brethren had always sought to preserve the spirit and practice of the early Christian Church. John Wesley, though not, as he insisted, 'bigoted either to the Ancient Church or the Church of England', claimed that the Primitive Church should be reverenced 'as faithfully delivering down for two or three hundred years the discipline which they received from the Apostles and the Apostles from Christ'.[23]

(2) The Church of the Brethren was an Episcopal Church, acknowledged as such by the Church of England. In 1737 Archbishop Potter of Canterbury declared the validity of their orders to be beyond doubt, and was always friendly to them. This would attract the goodwill of Wesley, who had little sympathy with Dissent and would never admit that Methodists were Dissenters, even when such refusal involved his people in legal difficulties.

(3) For the same reason, Zinzendorf's conception of the Brethren as *ecclesiola in ecclesia* would be likely to impress Wesley, who wished his Societies to remain within the bosom of the Established Church.

(4) It was too early to talk of co-operation on the Mission field; for though the Moravians had begun their overseas work (in 1731) there was to be no organized missionary work by the Methodists for many decades. Yet John Wesley's first meeting with the Brethren took place when both he and they were on a missionary expedition, and it is possible that this identity of aim established an early link.

It would seem, therefore, that even before he had met them, John Wesley was predisposed in favour of the Brethren, and that the way was prepared for Peter Böhler, Spangenberg, and the rest to deepen the impression.

[23] *Letters*, I.274.

CHAPTER THREE

WESLEY THE PUPIL

THE IMPRESSION was soon deepened. The attitude of the Moravians on board the *Simmonds* during a terrifying storm revealed to John Wesley that they possessed a quiet assurance denied to himself. The connexion of the Brethren with England began as early as 1728, when a conference of the Elders decided to send Johann Töltschig to this country. He was accompanied by David Nitschmann and Wenzel Neisser, and these three, all natives of Moravia, carried with them letters from Zinzendorf to the University of Oxford, the Society for Promoting Christian Knowledge, Ziegenhagen, Chaplain to George I, and the Countess of Schaumberg-Lippe, a Lady-in-Waiting at the English Court, who had shown some interest in Zinzendorf's work. The three emissaries came with a message of good will, but their visit had something of a missionary character, for they intended 'to tell such as were not blinded by their lusts, but whose eyes God had opened, what God had wrought'. They do not appear to have effected much beyond establishing some useful contacts.

A second visit was more fruitful. Amongst the many persecuted Protestants to whom Zinzendorf had given shelter were some followers of the sixteenth-century Anabaptist mystic, Caspar Schwenkfeld. When, by the decrees of the King of Saxony, they were banished from their new home, Zinzendorf negotiated with General Oglethorpe, the Governor of Georgia, who was glad to allow them to settle in his colony. For some reason, the Schwenkfelders went on to Pennsylvania, and as Zinzendorf feared that the Herrnhut Moravians might also be expelled, he sent August Gottlieb Spangenberg, a Professor of Jena University, who had attached himself to the Count, to negotiate with Oglethorpe for the admission of a band of Moravian immigrants into Georgia. The negotiations were successful, and the little company, only ten in number, duly reached the colony, where they set about with evangelistic zeal to preach to the Indians. Oglethorpe's close connexion with the Moravians, at this time and afterwards, was so intimate, and his friendship with the Wesleys so lasting, that he ought not to be ignored in any account of the relations between the Methodists and the Moravians.

Encouraged by the welcome given to the first batch, a further group set out in the *Simmonds* on 21st October 1735. They were twenty-six in number, and their purpose in emigrating was two-fold—to find a refuge from a *possible* persecution and to preach the Gospel.[1] John Wesley, who, with his brother Charles, Benjamin Ingham, and Charles Delamotte, was on the same boat, John as a missionary sent by the Society for the Propagation of the Gospel, Charles as secretary to Oglethorpe, and the other two as Christians seeking to serve God and to save their own souls, was warmly attracted by their adherence to the customs of the Primitive Church, by their Episcopal orders, but most of all by their simple faith and sublime cheerfulness. The story of their behaviour during the famous storm is familiar, but has such charm that it loses nothing by repetition. Here is John Wesley's own account:

> At seven I went to the Germans. I had long before observed the great seriousness of their behaviour. Of their humility they had given a continual proof, by performing these servile offices for the other passengers which none of the English would undertake; for which they desired and would receive no pay, saying, 'it was good for their proud hearts', and 'their loving Saviour had done more for them'. And every day had given them occasion of showing a meekness which no injury could move. If they were pushed, struck or thrown down, they rose again and went away; but no complaint was found in their mouth. There was now an opportunity of trying whether they were delivered from the spirit of fear, as well as from that of pride, anger, and revenge. In the midst of the psalm wherewith their service began, wherein we were mentioning the power of God, the sea broke over, split the main-sail in pieces, covered the ship, and poured in between the decks, as if the great deep had already swallowed us up. A terrible screaming began among the English. The Germans looked up, and without intermission calmly sang on. I asked one of them afterwards, 'Was you not afraid?' He replied mildly: 'I thank God, no; . . . our women and children are not afraid to die.'[2]

It may be suggested here that John Wesley's warm tribute to the Moravians' humility is hard to reconcile with his letter of 1740

[1] Canon Overton (*John Wesley* (1891), p. 48) says that they had already been driven out of their own country, but this is open to question.

[2] *Journal*, I.142.

to the Rev. Thomas Church,[3] in which he charged the Brethren with 'exalting themselves and despising others', declaring that 'he scarce had heard a Moravian owning his Church or himself to be wrong in anything'. This may have been a lapse of memory; more probably his recollections were coloured by his more recent and less happy experiences. Several years later, in an account of his relationships with the Brethren, he wrote: 'Being with many of them in the same ship, I narrowly observed their whole behaviour, and I greatly approved all I saw.'[4]

This incident has made a great impression upon Methodist historians, who are perhaps inclined to exaggerate its importance. In a letter to Dr Burton on 20th January 1736,[5] for example, Wesley spoke of the storm, but did not mention the Moravians—and this, be it noted, was long before the breach; nor does Ingham[6] on whom the impression made was much more lasting. It is possible that Wesley's prepossession on behalf of the Brethren made him very ready to see good in them, and that later he saw their behaviour in the storm in a different perspective. It has been suggested that the 'psalm' with which their service began may have been Rothe's *Ich habe nun den Grund gefunden.* Certainly one verse (in John Wesley's magnificent translation) seems more than a little appropriate:

Though waves and storms go o'er my head,
Though strength, and health, and friends be gone,
Though joys be withered all and dead,
Though every comfort be withdrawn,
On this my steadfast soul relies—
Father, Thy mercy never dies![7]

It is more likely, however, that what they sang was actually a psalm.

It is possible, as some Moravians think, that the storm was only an incident, a stage in John Wesley's spiritual progress. It must be remembered that the voyage had already lasted three months, and that Wesley had come to admire the Moravians and to seek their company. On 17th October, only three days after the voyage had begun, he had set out to learn German in order to

[3] *Letters,* II.179. [4] *Journal,* II.495. [5] *Letters,* I.193.
[6] Tyerman, *The Oxford Methodists,* p. 68.
[7] *Methodist Hymn-book* (1933), No. 375.

converse with 'men who have left all for their Master, and who have indeed learned of Him, being meek and lowly, dead to the world, full of faith and of the Holy Ghost'.[8] Three days later, on the 20th, he was so much impressed by their demeanour that he could say, 'Oh may we be not only of one tongue, but of one mind and of one heart!'[9]—and a week later he had already begun to translate some of the German hymns. No doubt, as has been suggested, John Wesley, a High Churchman, was drawn towards the Moravians because they seemed to him so closely allied in spirit and practice to the Christians of the first three centuries. They were, as Ingham wrote,

> more like the Primitive Christians than any other Church now in the world; for they retain both the faith, practice and discipline delivered by the Apostles. They have regularly ordained bishops, priests, and deacons. Baptism, Confirmation, and the Eucharist are duly administered. Discipline is strictly exercised without respect of persons. They all submit themselves to their pastors, being guided by them in everything. They live together in perfect love and peace, having, for the present, all things in common. They are more ready to serve their neighbours than themselves. In their business they are diligent and industrious; in all their dealings strictly just and conscientious. In everything, they behave themselves with great sweetness and humility.[10]

It is not difficult to see how John Wesley, with his love for the historic Church and his emphasis on 'doing all the good you can' was warmly attracted by the Moravians.

Wesley had written to Zinzendorf as early as 15th March 1736[11] in a letter of which the Count said afterwards, in the historic interview in Gray's Inn Gardens on 3rd September 1741: '*Ego, cum ex Georgia ad me scripsisti, te dilexi plurimum.*'[12] In that letter Wesley asked, as of a father in God, for Zinzendorf's prayers, and especially that he might utter on his behalf a verse[13] from Freylinghausen's hymn, *Wer ist wohl wie Du, Jesu, süsse Ruh* (a verse which Wesley afterwards translated as

[8] *Journal*, I.110. [9] ibid., p. 112.
[10] Ingham's *Journal*, in Tyerman's *Oxford Methodists*, p. 68.
[11] *Letters*, I.195. [12] *Journal*, II.488.
[13] *Einen Helden muth*
Der da Gut und Blut
Gern um deinetwillen lasse
Und des Fleisches Lüste hasse,
Gieb ihm, Höchstes Gut,
Durch dein theures Blut.

A patient, a victorious mind,
That life and all things casts behind,
Springs forth obedient to Thy call,
A heart that no desire can move,
But still to adore, believe, and love,
Give me, my Lord, my Life, my All![14]—

a prayer which, he said, 'I have heard frequently offered by your brethren at Savannah (and would they were mine also!)'.

The Count referred to the same hymn in a letter which he wrote in Latin to Wesley in October of the same year, altering it to:

Einen Heldenmuth
Gib dem Westley ein,
Durch dein Blut allein![15]

It seems clear that at this time, at any rate, there was no incipient hostility or even coolness between the leading figure of Moravianism and the future prophet of Methodism; for Zinzendorf went on to assure Wesley, in the friendliest terms, of his prayers for him. He encouraged him by emphasizing our Lord's concern about the sorrows of His children, and then submitted a series of theological questions which showed that his friendship was based not on mere personal amiability, but on objective agreement.

In any case, whether the influence was the specific result of the behaviour of the Moravians in the storm, whether it arose from Wesley's recognition of his own unsatisfied need, or whether it sprang from admiration of Zinzendorf, Böhler, and Spangenberg, or from a more diffused regard for a saintly little company, it is plain that John Wesley was deeply impressed. This is borne out by the fact that only two days after landing in America he consulted about his own conduct August Gottlieb Spangenberg, who had led the first company of the Brethren to Georgia in 1735, and whom General Oglethorpe had brought to see Wesley on the previous day.[16] There is no indication in Wesley's *Journal* or correspondence of the reason for Oglethorpe's action, but it is to be presumed that he already knew of the English clergyman's lively interest in his German ship-fellows. Spangenberg was the son of a Lutheran pastor, and had been born at Klettenberg in

[14] *Methodist Hymn-book* (1904), No. 571.
[15] *Moravian Archives at Herrnhut.*
[16] *Journal*, I.151.

1704. While studying at Jena, he was deeply affected by the religious revival there, and his contacts with the Brethren as they passed through Jena on the way to England made an impression upon him similar to that which he himself was to make upon the Wesleys. His somewhat unorthodox views (which were ascribed to his close connexion with Zinzendorf) led to his expulsion from the University and Orphanage of Halle, where he had been appointed Professor, and for the rest of his life he was closely associated with the Church of the Brethren, mainly in America. He was a man of great devoutness and wisdom, a statesman in his utterances and his arrangements, and it is probable that the Renewed Church of the Brethren owed more to him than to any other single individual, more (after the beginnings) than to the Count himself. Indeed, it is not unlikely that had Spangenberg and not Zinzendorf been the leader of the Brethren during the stormy middle years of the eighteenth century the rift between Moravian and Methodist might never have occurred or would have been swiftly healed. It has indeed been suggested[17] that Wesley owed more to Spangenberg than even to Peter Böhler, but the recorded entries in Wesley's *Journal* do not bear this out. Wesley's relations with him were always friendly, and their discussions were carried on in good spirit; and though for a time, perhaps out of loyalty to a fellow-Moravian, he supported Molther's doctrine of 'stillness', his remarkable account of Moravian theology, *Idea Fidei Fratrum*,[18] departed very little from current Methodist beliefs.

Wesley's interest in him had been revealed in a conversation on Saturday 7th February 1736, the day after the *Simmonds* had reached Georgia. 'He told me', says Wesley, 'several particulars relating to their faith and practice and discipline, all of which were agreeable to the plan of the first ages, and seemed to show that it was their one care, without desire of pleasing or fear of displeasing any, to retain inviolate the whole deposit once delivered to the saints.'[19]

The *Journal* for the following day, Sunday 8th February, runs thus:

I asked Mr Spangenberg's advice with regard to myself. . . . He told me he could say nothing till he had asked me two or three questions.

[17] By Nehemiah Curnock, Wesley's *Journal*, II.60 n.

[18] 1778.

[19] *Journal*, I.150-1.

> 'Do you know yourself? Have you the witness within yourself? Does the Spirit of God bear witness with your spirit that you are a child of God?' I was surprised, and knew not what to answer. He observed it, and asked, 'Do you know Jesus Christ?' I paused, and said, 'I know He is the Saviour of the world'. 'True,' replied he, 'but do you know He has saved you?' I answered, 'I hope He has died to save me'. He only added, 'Do you know yourself?' I said, 'I do'. But I fear they were vain words. After my answering, he gave me several directions, which may the good God who sent him enable me to follow![20]

Spangenberg's own comment is worth recording: 'I noticed that true Grace reigns and dwells in him.'[21]

Canon Overton writes somewhat pungently about this interview, which, he says, 'considering the position and attainments of the respective parties, seems to an outsider rather impertinent'.[22] But this is to undervalue the status and quality of Spangenberg, who had already achieved distinction in his academic career and whose high intellectual grasp is revealed in his *Idea Fidei Fratrum.* His questions to Wesley on this occasion presented a new point of view, very different from the arguments of Law. They revealed to him, if only in part, a way of life and the power by which that way could be ensured; and they throw some doubt on the claim, often made, that Wesley's Doctrine of Assurance, or the Witness of the Spirit, was original to himself. In any case, it is plain that Wesley himself placed considerable confidence in the wisdom and integrity of his new friends. Only the next day, he asked Spangenberg's advice about Mrs Hawkins, whose behaviour on board the *Simmonds* had given him great concern:

> I asked Mr Spangenberg of Mrs Hawkins's case, and desired his advice how to behave towards her. He answered: 'My dear brother, I believe our friend Kempis advises well, *Omnes bonas mulieres devita, easque Deo commenda.* Not that I would advise you to give her up quite, but to converse much may be dangerous either to her or to you. It may be best to speak to her seldom, and in few words, and earnestly pray God to do the rest.'[23]

For their first few weeks in America, Wesley and Delamotte lodged with Spangenberg, Nitschmann, Dober, and other Moravians, and the good impression was strengthened. John Wesley wrote in his *Journal*:

[20] *Journal*, I.151. [21] *Diary*, *Moravian Archives at Herrnhut.*
[22] *John Wesley*, p. 55. [23] *Journal*, I.155.

We had now an opportunity, day by day, of observing their whole behaviour. For we were in one room with them from morning to night, unless for the little time I spent in walking. They were always employed, always cheerful themselves, and in good humour with one another; they had put away all anger, and strife, and wrath, and bitterness, and clamour, and evil-speaking; they walked worthy of the vocation wherewith they were called, and adorned the gospel of our Lord in all things.[24]

He was present at the ordination of Anton Seiffart as Moravian Bishop of Georgia, and his unquestioning acceptance of this ordination is evidence of his recognition as a High Churchman of the validity of Moravian orders. As has been stated, Potter, Archbishop of Canterbury, who as Bishop of Oxford had ordained Wesley, Ingham, Gambold, and other members of the Holy Club, expressed similar satisfaction in a conversation with Zinzendorf. 'Only those', he said, 'who are ignorant of Church history would doubt the validity of the Moravian episcopal succession.'[25] It is interesting to note, however, that James Hutton, who afterwards became so sturdy a defender of the Brethren, needed some reassurance on this matter. Writing to John Wesley in September 1736 he wrote: 'Take care to inquire carefully and strictly concerning the mission of the Moravian Bishop. I will make what inquiries I can. A great deal depends upon the validity of ordinations.' Wesley was moved by this ceremony:

The great simplicity, as well as solemnity, of the whole, almost made me forget the seventeen hundred years between, and imagine myself in one of those assemblies where form and state are not, but Paul the tent-maker or Peter the fisherman presided, yet with the demonstration of the spirit and of power. . . . God hath opened me a door into a whole Church.[26]

John Wesley's relations with the Moravians continued to be intimate, and his confidence in their judgement is revealed in the painful and difficult incident of Sophia Hopkey. It is not easy to exonerate Wesley from some indiscretion in this affair. However great his wisdom in other directions, his attitude toward women led him into more than one difficulty. In all probability, he had an indefinable charm of which he was not always conscious, and the unwitting exercise of which gave the impression of a

[24] *Journal*, I.168-9. [25] *Büdingische Sammlung*. [26] *Journal*, I.170-1.

feeling deeper than he actually felt. His early connexion with this young lady, the niece of Mr Causton, chief magistrate of the place, seems to have been of a purely pastoral character; but their close intimacy led to a deeper feeling, probably deeper on her side than on his. Wesley appears to have been less certain of Miss Hopkey's unsuitability than of the instability of his own feelings, for though he was very much attracted by her—'her words, her eyes, her air, her every motion and gesture', he wrote, 'were full of such a softness and sweetness'[27]—yet he rejoiced that he had been strong enough to refrain from touching her hand. A little later he was not quite so strong, but took her by the hand, and then reproached himself for so doing. After assuring his friend Delamotte that he had no intention of marrying her, he appealed to 'the Searcher of hearts' by casting lots,[28] and discovered not only that he ought not to marry, but that he ought not even to converse with her any more, except 'in presence of Mr Delamotte'. This may appear something of an anticlimax, but, as has been said earlier,[29] this entire separation from Sophia Hopkey was a costly sacrifice. Wesley's resolution, however, failed, and he soon found himself in the toils again. It is not clear from his *Journal* when he consulted the Moravians and asked their advice. Apparently he had already (on 3rd February) discussed the matter with Töltschig and Seiffart, but, according to Henry Moore,[30] he submitted the question to David Nitschmann, the Moravian Bishop, who answered: 'Marriage is not unlawful; but whether it is now expedient for you, and whether this lady is a proper wife for you, ought to be maturely weighed.' This was not very helpful, and Wesley decided to ask the advice of the Elders of the Moravian Church, by whose decision he agreed to abide. 'Then', said Nitschmann, 'we advise you to proceed no further in the matter.' Wesley answered: 'The will of the Lord be done.' As these were the words used by Wesley on 27th February to Delamotte, who is mentioned as having been present when the Moravian Elders were consulted, it is probable that these two narratives refer to one and the same incident.

John Wesley has been much criticized, not least by his admirers, for consulting the Brethren on so delicate and intimate a matter. Certainly, in this consultation, and in his ready acceptance of

[27] *Journal*, I.323. [28] ibid., p. 325. [29] p. 33, *supra*.
[30] Henry Moore, *Life of Wesley*, I.312.

somewhat conflicting advice, he showed a simplicity at variance with his usual strong common sense; but his scrupulous anxiety to say and do no more than his conscience could support does credit to his sincerity. What is relevant here is his obvious confidence in the competence of the Moravians to advise him. If they are to be blamed for giving the wrong advice, it must be pointed out that Wesley's subsequent unhappy marriage has somewhat sharpened the criticism. It is easy to be wise after the event. In any case, it was not John Wesley's decision not to marry Sophia Hopkey which involved him in disaster, except indirectly, but his indiscreet actions after she had married someone else. Besides, it was a Moravian, Töltschig,[31] who, on 4th February, had seen no reason why he should not marry her, and Ingham and Delamotte, who were *not* Moravians, who had strongly opposed the marriage.

There is little evidence that Charles Wesley was as attracted by the Brethren as his brother was. Unfortunately, his published *Journal* was not begun until several months after the *Simmonds* set out for Georgia, not indeed until a month after his arrival, and there is therefore no means of discovering the impression made upon him. But from his letters written at that time it is evident that he was in a mood of black depression, concerned with his own misery—and with not much else! Like his brother he had serious trouble with one or two women—Mrs Hawkins and Mrs Welch—and his *Journal* records under date 31st May 1736 that he was advised by Spangenberg 'never to talk to a woman without a witness, or in the face of the sun'. Charles Wesley adds: 'I followed his directions; but did not see the providential reason of it until now.'

Charles Wesley makes no further reference to the Brethren until January 1737,[32] when he visited Zinzendorf, who had just arrived in England and who gave the younger brother a warm welcome. He must have made a deep impression, for on the very next day Charles Wesley wrote to the Count about his own spiritual condition. A day or two later, he attended a service at the Count's house, and thought himself 'in a quire of angels'.[33] Whether this is a tribute to their spiritual character or to the quality of their singing is not quite clear. He even considered going with Zinzendorf to Germany. In one of their conversations, the Count made an interesting and apposite revelation. Speaking of the Christian's

[31] *Journal,* I.315. [32] op. cit., 19th January 1737. [33] ibid., 23rd January.

duty to fight against sin, whatever the cost, he told Charles that 'he and a lady were in love with each other; till, finding something of nature, he resolved to renounce her; which he did, and persuaded her to accept of his friend'. 'From that moment', he said, 'I was freed from all self-seeking; so that for ten years past I have not done my own will in anything, great or small!'[34] The Brethren therefore had some sort of precedent for the advice they gave to John Wesley.

Wesley's confidence in his Moravian mentors, however, arose not merely from his admiration for their wisdom and goodness, but from his dissatisfaction with himself. But for this he would not have realized his need of a deeper, richer experience. But for Georgia there would have been no Aldersgate Street. But for Spangenberg it is doubtful if Peter Böhler would have found so fertile a soil.

There is no need here to recount the unhappy story of Wesley's remaining stay in Georgia, his prosecution by Sophia Hopkey's husband, the long list of grievances on which he was arraigned. and his virtual expulsion. Disappointed and dispirited he was. His frank confession—'I, who went to America to convert others, was never myself converted'—need not be taken too seriously: he himself afterwards commented. 'I am not sure of this.'[35] But there is no doubt that he had begun to realize the inadequacy of his scholarship, his almsgiving, his Churchmanship, and that the Moravians had aroused in him a divine discontent which had yet to be removed. His confidence in Spangenberg continued until his departure for England. On Wednesday 27th July 1737, for instance, he records: 'I rejoiced to meet once more that good soldier of Jesus Christ, August Spangenberg'[36]—and four days later, 'at Mr Spangenberg's desire', he propounded to his Moravian friends a series of questions on the nature of conversion, the meaning of Scripture, the Church, faith, the Creeds, the religious education of children, attendance at public worship, forms of prayer, and other related matters.[37] Some of the answers are extremely interesting in view of later events. According to Moravian beliefs, it was not lawful to bear arms, even in self-defence, or to go to law, or to swear when required to do so by a magistrate. To the question 'Are the ministrations of a man not

[34] op. cit., 6th February.
[35] *Journal*, I.422.
[36] ibid., p. 371.
[37] ibid., p. 372.

episcopally ordained valid?' no answer was given. Apart from hymn-singing, which they regarded as prayer,[38] extempore prayer was encouraged: 'Every one speaks as he is moved by the Holy Ghost'—a practice which has not been maintained in recent years. It is noticeable that Wesley was already less enthusiastic about Zinzendorf than about Spangenberg. On the same day (1st August 1737) on which he asked the latter's advice and expressed his intention of following it, he commented on 'the Count's exposition of Scripture and method of prayer', which fully convinced him that 'he likewise is but a man'.[39]

There is an interesting report in the *Moravian Archives at Herrnhut* in which Spangenberg speaks frankly of John Wesley, and especially of his ecclesiastical orthodoxy.[40] It is dated 1737, and includes the following:

> Wesley has long been accustomed to hold that the Holy Communion is a means of grace, and has thought that a man can be converted thereby. He has therefore admonished all men to attend communion, and weekly not once but more often he has made use of it. . . . I have asked the Brethren to receive him in love, and to wait in patience to see how he gets along. If the English cast him out, they will take him in our house. He thinks that no one is properly baptized who has the baptism from a Lutheran or a Calvinist pastor. . . . Nitschmann's and Anton's[41] baptism he considers proper, for the reason that they have the episcopal order from the Apostolic Church.

This report is of particular interest:

(1) It makes it clear that Wesley recognized the validity of Moravian orders, and suggests that he denied such validity to 'dissent'.

(2) It bears out the contention that it was this episcopal validity which attracted Wesley to the Brethren in the first instance.

(3) It emphasizes Wesley's belief that the Sacrament of Holy Communion was 'a converting ordinance'. By mentioning it, Spangenberg seems to imply that he had different views. This report therefore foreshadows Molther's doctrine of 'stillness',[42] with its corollary that 'the ordinances' were of no avail unless faith

[38] It was not always so; see p. 31, *supra*.

[39] *Journal*, I.375.

[40] *Moravian Archives at Herrnhut*, translated by Douglas L. Rights, *South Atlantic Quarterly*, Vol. XLIII, No. 4 (1944).

[41] Seiffart.

[42] See p. 84, *infra*.

is complete. This therefore is the first hint of a possible cleavage between Wesley and the Moravians.

Though Charles Wesley was apparently slower in reaching a full appreciation of the Brethren, his admiration lasted longer, and he sought friendship with them until the end of his days. A letter believed by Professor Helfield of Chicago to have been written (in Latin) by Kinchin was probably written, as Dr Henry Bett maintains, by the younger Wesley. If so, it indicates that Charles Wesley had as much confidence in the Count as his elder brother had in Spangenberg. Here is part of it:

LONDON, 26*th November* 1737

To the Reverend Superintendent Nicolaus von Zinzendorf, unending Salvation in Christ.

After wandering through all the miseries of passion, I would fain turn at last to thee, to myself, and to God. It would be superfluous to write of my affection. But I send a few words on the matter. . . . May thy prayers and the prayers of the community at Herrnhut accompany me, as I return to Georgia. I take with me a young man named George Whitefield, a minister of fervent spirit—if I may say so, a second Timothy. God has wonderfully aroused by his means this twice dead populace. The Churches will not contain the hearers. For indeed his word and his preaching is not in persuasive words of human wisdom but in the manifestation of the spirit and of power. . . .[43]

Charles Wesley's authorship of this letter is only conjectural, but it is very probable. In view of the fact that both Charles and John Wesley were closely involved in the Whitsuntide experience, it strengthens the contention that their Moravian contacts were largely responsible for that experience.

It was left to Peter Böhler, so often referred to in Moravian letters as 'Petrus', to bring matters to a head. Böhler is probably the most attractive figure in this period of the history of the Brethren. Though he was not a born leader, like Zinzendorf and Spangenberg, and though for a time he too was affected by the extravagances of the 'Time of Sifting', he possessed a certain charm which disarmed even those who disagreed with him; and the affection of the Wesleys for him persisted when their regard for other Moravian leaders wavered. There is no suggestion in

[43] *W.H.S. Proceedings*, XV.166 and *Letters*, I.227-8.

the *Journals* or correspondence of the two Wesleys of any hostility or indeed criticism, a rare distinction in a time of acute controversy, and it will be remembered that, in the quarrel between John Wesley and William Law, the elder brother stoutly defended Böhler against Law's attack.[44]

Böhler had been brought up in Pietistic circles, and at Jena had experienced 'instantaneous conversion', and ever after held that sudden conversion was the normal kind, a view which he was, for a time at any rate, to implant in John Wesley. After being received into the Moravian Church at Herrnhut in 1737, he visited England, staying chiefly in London and Oxford. In both places he was warmly received, and in Oxford his simple sincerity and his single-mindedness attracted his hearers, especially those in the Religious Societies, to the doctrine and the practice of the Brethren.

This was the man to whom, more than to any other single person, John and Charles Wesley owed that change of mind and heart which brought about the Methodist Revival. The story is one of entrancing interest. Böhler who, after several years of friendliness with Zinzendorf, had just been ordained by him, and was on his way as a missionary to Carolina, had arrived in London only a few days before John Wesley, weary and dispirited, had reached this country. They met in the house of Weinantz, a Dutch merchant, on 7th February 1738. John Wesley's *Journal* makes only a passing reference to the meeting,[45] and merely includes Böhler's name in a list of German brethren, with those of Schulius, Richter, and Wenzel Neisser. Charles Wesley's *Journal*, which is generally much briefer, makes no mention of Böhler until Monday 20th February, when he began to teach him English. By this time, John had already found these German visitors a lodging near the house of James Hutton, where he himself was at the time staying, and had set out with Böhler for Oxford. This meeting of Böhler and Hutton was to be of immense importance to the Moravian Church in this country, and John Wesley's part in this association has not generally been accorded full recognition. James Hutton was the son of the Rev. John Hutton, who lived next door to the house formerly occupied by Samuel Wesley, John's elder brother, in Great College Street, Westminster. Like his neighbour, he took boarders from Westminster School, where

[44] *Letters*, I.241. [45] I.436.

he himself had been a pupil. While still a bookseller's apprentice, he journeyed to Oxford, probably on business bent, but also to renew his acquaintance with former school companions. There he met the two Wesleys, and was as much attracted by them and their companions as they themselves were to be later by the Moravians. A close friendship was soon established. John and Charles Wesley spent a couple of days where, according to Benham, Hutton was converted under the preaching of the elder brother.[46] The importance of this will be discussed in a later chapter. Hutton spent some time on the *Simmonds* before it set out on its voyage to Georgia. There, for the first time, he met the Moravians, but at this time they occupied a lower position in his life than did the elder Wesley. He set up business for himself, founded a Religious Society in his own house, and there read to its members the thrilling story which John Wesley had already begun to recount in his *Journal.* He became deeply interested (again through reading about them in Wesley's pages), and it was Charles Wesley who introduced him to Zinzendorf. And thus another link in the chain was forged. James Hutton, who became in time the first English member of the Moravian Church, was of exceptional importance in the early history of the Renewed Church of the Brethren. It was at his house that the first meeting of the evangelical group from which were to spring both the English Moravians and the Methodists; he was the official publisher of Moravian propaganda; and he lived so long that he became a link between the foundation days and the days of settlement later in the century. The debt of Methodism to Moravianism has often been acknowledged, and rightly so; but any assessment of mutual interaction ought not to ignore the fact that James Hutton, the first English Moravian, was deeply indebted to the Wesley brothers. By John he was converted, by Charles he was introduced to Zinzendorf, by John again he was brought under the influence of Böhler, and at the hands of both brothers, in the impressionable days of his youth, he came under the impress of their faith and practice.

It was on 17th February 1737 that John and Charles Wesley set out for Oxford with Peter Böhler, and Böhler's own account of the two brothers, in a letter to Zinzendorf, is particularly interesting.

[46] op. cit., p. 11.

> On February 28th [this is the same date, allowing for the difference between the Calendars] I travelled with the two brothers, John and Charles Wesley, from London to Oxford. The elder, John, is an amiable man; he acknowledges that he does not yet rightly know the Saviour and suffers himself to be instructed. He loves us sincerely. His brother, with whom you conversed frequently in London a year ago is greatly troubled in spirit and knows not how he shall begin to know the Saviour.[47]

It was indeed upon Charles rather than upon John that Böhler's conversation had the greater effect, possibly because the elder brother was more argumentative, more probably because Charles was in poor health and in more obvious need of comfort. But it would be a mistake to regard the impression as less important because it was encouraged by the immediate circumstances. It is probable that more people have been influenced by Charles Wesley's hymns than by John's sermons, and that 'Jesu, Lover of my soul' will be cherished when the sermon on 'Christian Perfection' is little more than the battleground for the theologians. Charles Wesley was, of course, a theologian too, and his hymns, as will be seen, played a valiant part in the Calvinistic and Quietistic controversies.

How ill Charles Wesley was it is difficult to determine. Böhler uses the words 'very dangerously', and Charles's doctor expected to find him dead at his second visit. He appears to have been suffering from pleurisy, aggravated by acute toothache, and to have felt so ill that he almost expected to die. Here is his own account of Böhler's visit on 24th February:

> At eleven I waked in extreme pain, which I thought would quickly separate soul and body. Soon after, Peter Böhler came to my bedside. I asked him to pray for me. He seemed unwilling at first, but, beginning very faintly, he raised his voice by degrees, and prayed for my recovery with strange confidence. Then he took me by the hand, and calmly said, 'You will not die now'. I thought with myself, 'I cannot hold out in this pain till morning. If it abates before, I believe I may recover'. He asked me, 'Do you hope to be saved?' 'Yes.' 'For what reason do you hope it?' 'Because I have used my best endeavours to serve God.' He shook his head, and said no more. I thought him very uncharitable, saying in my heart, 'What, are not my endeavours a

[47] *Moravian Archives at Herrnhut*, reproduced in *World Parish* (November 1949).

sufficient ground of hope? Would he rob me of my endeavours? I have nothing else to trust to.'[48]

Charles Wesley had a long way to go before he could sing:

The mansion for Thyself prepare,
Dispose my heart by entering there;
'Tis this alone can make me clean,
'Tis this alone can cast out sin;[49]

Or:

Just and holy is Thy name,
I am all unrighteousness;
False and full of sin I am,
Thou art full of truth and grace.[50]

Great as was the difference, it was soon to be bridged, for within two years both these hymns had been written.

Böhler's account of this visit is simpler and shorter, and is written with modesty:

Charles Wesley had become very ill during the night; therefore at break of day he sent for me and begged me that I might pray for him that God would grant him patience in his sufferings and would ease them. I prayed with him for the salvation of his soul and body. He got some sleep and the pains were lessened. He recognizes that it comes from God, the pain as well as the relief from the same.[51]

On 9th March (26th February, O.S.) Charles was ill again, and Böhler spent some time with him.

The night I watched with Charles Wesley, who unfortunately is still very dangerously ill. On the following day, I met Pastor Gambold with him, who was about to administer the Lord's Supper. Wesley asked me to partake of it with him, and I did so. Several others were present. He was very happy and said that if he should die, he would go to the Saviour, at least as one who hungers and thirsts.[52]

Meanwhile, John Wesley's friendship with Böhler was growing apace. It is said that when they walked through the college

[48] Charles Wesley, *Journal.*
[49] *Methodist Hymn-book* (1933), No. 344.
[50] ibid., No. 110.
[51] *Moravian Archives at Herrnhut,* in *World Parish* (November 1949).
[52] ibid.

squares they were mocked. Wesley was troubled at this inhospitable treatment of a stranger, Böhler said philosophically. 'My brother, it does not even stick to our clothes'.[53] The story does credit to Wesley's courtesy and to Böhler's good humour. But the two were still far apart in theological views.

All this time [wrote Wesley], I conversed much with Peter Böhler; but I understood him not, and least of all when he said, *Mi frater, mi frater, excoquenda est ista tua philosophia.* 'My brother, my brother, that philosophy of yours must be purged away.'[54]

There was surely some truth in Canon Overton's witty statement, 'and forthwith commenced the process',[55] if by 'purging' is meant the correction of a false attitude; for the conversation continued with a gradual change in Wesley's views. A crucial meeting took place on 5th March. On the previous day, he returned to Oxford and found his brother recovering, and with him, he says: 'Peter Böhler, by whom (in the hand of the great God) I was, on Sunday . . . clearly convinced of unbelief, of the want of that faith whereby alone we are saved.'[56] Böhler mentions the same conversation:

I went walking with the elder Wesley, and asked him about his spiritual state. He said that sometimes he felt quite certain, but sometimes very fearful; he could say nothing further than 'If that is true which stands in the Bible, then I am saved'. On this matter I talked with him very fully and besought him heartily that he might go to the opened fountain and not spoil the matter for himself[57]—

advice which was accepted more eagerly than Böhler seems to have realized. Here are John's own words:

Immediately it struck into my mind, 'Leave off preaching. How can you preach to others, who have not faith yourself?' I asked Böhler whether he thought I should leave it off or not. He answered, 'By no means'. I asked, 'But what can I preach?' He said, 'Preach faith *till* you have it; and then, *because* you have it, you *will* preach faith!'

At first sight this might seem dangerous advice, for it might lead either to self-deception or even to pretence, but Böhler's

[53] J. P. Lockwood, *Memorials of Peter Böhler*, p. 67.
[54] *Journal*, I.440. [55] *John Wesley*, p. 60. [56] *Journal*, I.442.
[57] *Moravian Archives at Herrnhut*, in *World Parish* (November 1949).

meaning is clear: 'If I have convinced you of the need for faith, preach it until it is no longer a mere intellectual conviction, but your own spiritual certainty.' There is an interesting parallel to this conversation in a story told by William Darney, the eccentric Scottish preacher, about the Rev. William Grimshaw of Haworth:

> Mr Grimshaw was greatly distressed about preaching. 'How can I', says he, 'preach justification and the new birth, when I am a stranger to these things and under the wrath of God myself?' 'Oh!' [said Darney], 'you must preach them till you experience them; and then preach them because you know and enjoy them.'[58]

It seems likely that Darney said this with a recollection of Böhler's words.

It will be noticed that in giving this advice Böhler was far removed from Molther's teaching on 'stillness' which was afterwards to prove so divisive. He was not only regarding preaching as a 'converting ordinance', but he was implying degrees of faith, an implication against which Molther (and Spangenberg at one time) would have revolted. It will be found that this was not the only doctrinal issue on which Moravian leaders differed.

John Wesley met Böhler again on 23rd March, and was 'more and more amazed by the account he gave of the fruits of living faith—the holiness and happiness which he affirmed to attend it'. According to Böhler, both Wesleys were present at this interview:

> I had [he wrote to Zinzendorf] a very full conversation with the two Wesleys, in order to impress upon their minds the Gospel, and in order to entreat them to proclaim the same to others as they had opportunity, at Oxford and elsewhere. Thereupon they confessed their doubts respecting the truth of the doctrine of free grace, through the merits of Jesus, whereby poor sinners receive forgiveness, and are set free from the dominion of sin. The Saviour, however, granted me grace to convince them from the Scriptures; and they had no way of escape, except to ask to see and converse with persons who had made the experiences of which I spoke. I told them that in London I hoped to be able to show them such Christians.[59]

Perhaps the crucial conversation took place on 22nd April.

[58] William Miles, *The Life and Writings of the late Reverend William Grimshaw* (1806), p. 18.

[59] Lockwood, op. cit., pp. 74-5.

I met Peter Böhler once more [says Wesley]. I had now no objection to what he said of the nature of faith; namely, that it is (to use the words of our Church) 'a sure trust and confidence which a man hath in God, that through the merits of Christ his sins are forgiven and he reconciled to the favour of God'.[60] Neither could I deny either the happiness or holiness which he described as fruits of this living faith. 'The Spirit itself beareth witness with our spirit that we are the children of God' and 'He that believeth hath the witness in himself' fully convinced me of the former; as 'Whatsoever is born of God doth not commit sin' and 'Whosoever believeth is born of God' did of the latter. But I could not comprehend what he spoke of an *instantaneous* work. I could not understand how this faith should be given in a moment; how a man could *at once* be thus turned from darkness to light, from sin and misery to righteousness and joy in the Holy Ghost. I searched the Scriptures again touching this very thing, particularly the Acts of the Apostles: but, to my utter astonishment, found scarce any instances there of other than *instantaneous* conversions: scarce any so slow as that of St Paul, who was three days in the pangs of the new birth.

He goes on:

I had but one retreat left: namely, '*Thus*, I grant, God wrought in the *first* ages of Christianity; but the times are changed. What reason have I to believe He works in the same manner now?'

But on Sunday the 23rd, I was beat out of this retreat too, by the concurring evidence of several living witnesses; who testified God had thus wrought in themselves, giving them in a moment such a faith in the blood of His Son as translated them out of darkness into light, out of sin and fear into holiness and happiness. Here ended my disputing. I could now only cry out: 'Lord, help Thou my unbelief!'[61]

Compare this with Böhler's own account, as written in a letter to Zinzendorf:

I took with me four of the English brethren to John Wesley, that they might relate to him their guidance, how the Saviour so quickly and so mightily has mercy on sinners and accepts them. They related one after the other how it had gone with them, particularly Wolf ('our other English brother'), for whom it was still quite new. He spoke very heartily, forcefully, introspectively, concerning his experience of grace. John Wesley and the rest who were with him were as though struck dumb at these narratives.

I asked Wesley what he now believed? He said, four examples did

[60] Homily, '*Of Salvation*'.

[61] *Journal*, I.454.

not settle the matter and could not convince him. I replied that I would bring him eight more here in London. After a short time he arose and said: 'We will sing the hymn, *My soul before Thee prostrate lies.*'

During the singing he frequently dried his eyes and immediately afterward he took me alone with him into his bedroom and said that he was now convinced of that which I had said concerning faith and that he would ask nothing further, that he saw very well that it was not yet anything with him, but how could he now help himself and how should he attain to such faith? He was a man who had not sinned as grossly as other people. I replied that not to believe in the Saviour was sinning enough; he should only not go away from the door of the Saviour until He had helped him. I was strongly moved to pray with him; therefore I called upon the blood-covered name of the Saviour for mercy on this sinner. He said to me if he once had *this* he would certainly preach about nothing other than faith.[62]

Apparently John was deeply impressed, but Charles was less open to persuasion. Acting on Böhler's advice, the elder brother, two days later, spoke to a little company on the nature and fruits of faith.

My brother [he writes] was very angry, and told me I did not know what mischief I had done by talking thus. And, indeed, it did please God then to kindle a fire which I trust shall never be extinguished.[63]

According to Charles, whose admiration for Böhler was undiminished—he refers to him as 'that man of God'—the dispute was not about the nature of faith but about 'whether conversion was gradual or instantaneous'.[64]

My brother [says Charles] was very positive for the latter, and very shocking; mentioned some late instances of gross sinners believing in a moment. I was much offended at his worse than unedifying discourse.

April 26th brought Böhler and John Wesley even closer together. In an hour's walk they talked earnestly together—Böhler calls it '*ein recht herzliches gesprach*'—and relates that Wesley wept heartily and bitterly.[65] 'This I can say of him', he adds; 'he is truly a poor sinner, who has a broken heart and who hungers after a better righteousness than he has had until now, namely the righteousness of Jesus Christ.' In spite of this, or

[62] *Moravian Archives at Herrnhut*, in *World Parish* (November 1949).

[63] *Journal*, I.456.

[64] Charles Wesley, *Journal*, 25th April 1738.

[65] *Moravian Archives at Herrnhut*, in *World Parish* (November 1949).

perhaps because of it (following Böhler's advice of 5th March), and on the same day preached so effectively that 'all people were astounded' (this is Böhler's account) 'because one never heard like that from him. His first words were: "I feel myself heartily unworthy to preach about the crucified Jesus." . . . Many were awakened thereby.' Wesley's account is modestly worded: 'At Gerrard's Cross I plainly declared to those whom God gave into my hands the faith as it is in Jesus.'[66]

Böhler seems to have convinced Wesley of three things: the truth of the doctrine of Justification by Faith and of the paramount necessity of a *personal* faith in Christ, the need for and the fact of instantaneous conversion, and the assurance which converted sinners have through faith in Christ. It would not be true to say that Wesley was ignorant of the doctrine of Justification by Faith until he met the Moravians. In the entry in his *Journal* for 24th January 1738 he shows how dissatisfied he is with his own works. 'I was early warned', he writes, 'against laying, as the Papists do, too much stress on outward works . . . having from the very beginning valued both faith, and the means of grace, and good works.'[67] He then refers, rather critically, to 'some Lutheran and Calvinist authors, whose confused and indigested accounts magnified faith to such an amazing size that it quite hid all the rest of the commandments.'[68] But the qualifications he attaches to the doctrine show that in so far as he accepted it he did so with an intellectual affirmation and with little spiritual conviction. It was not until 4th March, when he met Peter Böhler, that he was 'clearly convinced of unbelief, of the want of that faith whereby alone we are saved'. This is confirmed by the entry for 3rd May:

My brother had a long and particular conversation with Peter Böhler. And it now pleased God to open his eyes; so that he also saw clearly what was the nature of that one true living faith, whereby alone 'through grace we are saved'.[69]

Strangely enough, Charles has no reference to this date, though it is plain that his mind was working in this direction. On 28th April he refers to

a better physician, Peter Böhler, whom God had detained in England for my good. I immediately thought it might be (i.e. the divine intention in this and my late illness) that I should again consider Böhler's

[66] *Journal*, I.457. [67] ibid., I.419. [68] ibid. [69] ibid., p. 459.

doctrine of faith; examine myself whether I was in the faith; and if I was not, never cease seeking and longing after it until I attained it. . . . For some days following I felt a faint longing for faith; and could pray for nothing else;[70]

while on 6th May he says: 'I seemed determined to speak of, and wish for nothing but faith in Christ.' Böhler, in his letter to Zinzendorf, corroborates this in his entry for 11th May (30th April, O.S.):

I came to the younger Wesley, who . . . spoke with me about his faith. He knew well that he was not of the same mind as I, but said he did not wish to dispute with me, but I should pray with him, that the Saviour might give him the assurance of faith.[71]

On the following day Böhler writes:

The younger Wesley now also believes that he is a poor sinner and seeks grace in the bloody wounds of the Redeemer. . . . At nine o'clock in the evening I met the older Wesley at Hutton's. *He feels himself justified* and is a seeking poor sinner. His heart is quite broken;

and on 19th May (8th May, O.S.—Wesley says 4th May) he makes this striking comment:

I talked once more with John Wesley and his brother Charles and brother-in-law Mr Hall. Grace is working mightily in him but has yet to prove itself fully in the younger Wesley. The elder one is entirely convinced and now knows nothing more than: I want to believe. The Saviour has done very much.

John Wesley's own entry for 1st May declares that Charles was 'strongly averse from what he called "the new faith" '.[72]

In view of the substantial agreement of these records—the slight discrepancy in dates is not important—it is difficult to support the view of Dr Piette that what Wesley learned from Böhler was not so much the necessity of faith in God as the importance of 'the intense practice of the love of God'. He maintains[73] that the part Böhler played in his fellowship with John Wesley was not to introduce him to the Lutheran doctrine of 'faith without works' (the phrase is Piette's, and begs the question), but to impress upon him the paramount importance of cultivating the love of

[70] Charles Wesley, *Journal*, 28th April and 1st May 1738.

[71] *Moravian Archives at Herrnhut*, in *World Parish* (November 1949).

[72] *Journal*, I.458. [73] *John Wesley in the Evolution of Protestantism*, p. 307.

God; and he adduces, in support of this contention, the letter sent by Böhler to Wesley on 8th May 1738. This interpretation seems somewhat strained, not only because it ignores all the other comments made by Böhler in his diary-letter to Zinzendorf, but because the letter of 8th May, though it speaks of God's love, speaks even more of the necessity of faith:

> . . . that you may continually trust in Him. Beware of the sin of unbelief; and if you have not conquered it yet, see that you conquer it this very day, through the blood of Jesus Christ. Delay not, I beseech you, to believe in *your* Jesus Christ. . . . Nothing can offend him but our unbelief. Believe therefore.[74]

The order of the words in the final sentence is perhaps significant: 'Abide in *faith*, love, teaching, the communion of saints.' Böhler's emphasis on saving faith was certainly new to many who heard him, even to those of his own Communion; but its novelty did not make it less welcome, and there can be no doubt that the Brethren embraced it with joy. What is clear is that something happened to Wesley in 1738, an event or an influence which altered the whole current of his life. It could hardly be a new idea, a new intellectual attitude, which effected this mighty change so much as a new experience; and though, as has already been indicated, other factors played their part, it seems probable that it was to the Moravian teaching and example in general, and to that of Peter Böhler in particular, that Wesley owed his transforming experience.

John Wesley's own testimony surely puts the matter beyond doubt:

> In my return to England, January 1738, being in imminent danger of death, and very uneasy on that account, I was strongly convinced that the cause of that uneasiness was unbelief; and that the gaining a true, living faith was the 'one thing needful' for me. But still I fixed not this faith on its right object: I meant only faith in God, not faith in or through Christ. Again, I knew not that I was wholly void of this faith; but thought only I had not enough of it. So that when Peter Böhler, whom God prepared for me as soon as I came to London, affirmed of true faith in Christ (which is but one) that it had those two fruits inseparably attending it, 'dominion over sin and constant peace from a sense of forgiveness', I was quite amazed, and looked upon it as a new gospel. If this was so, it was clear I had not faith. But I was not

[74] *Journal*, I.461-2.

willing to be convinced of this. Therefore I disputed with all my might, and laboured to prove that faith might be where these were not; for all the Scriptures relating to this I had been long since taught to construe away; and to call all Presbyterians who spoke otherwise. Besides, I well saw no one could, in the nature of things, have much of a sense of forgiveness, and not *feel* it. But I felt it not. If there was no faith without this, all my pretensions to faith dropped at once.

When I met Peter Böhler again, he consented to put the dispute upon the issue which I desired, namely, Scripture and experience. I first consulted the Scripture. But when I set aside the glosses of men, and simply considered the words of God, comparing them together, endeavouring to illustrate the obscure by the plainer passages, I found they all made against me, and was forced to retreat to my last hold, 'that experience would never agree with the *literal interpretation* of those scriptures. Nor could I therefore allow it to be true, till I found some living witnesses of it.' He replied, he could show me such at any time; if I desired it, the next day. And accordingly the next day he came again with three others, all of whom testified, of their own personal experience, that a true living faith in Christ is inseparable from a sense of pardon for all past and freedom from all present sins. They added with one mouth that this faith was the gift, the free gift of God; and that He would surely bestow it upon every soul who earnestly and perseveringly sought it. I was now thoroughly convinced; and, by the grace of God, I resolved to seek it unto the end, (i) by absolutely renouncing all dependence, in whole or in part, upon *my own* works or righteousness; on which I had really grounded my hope of salvation, though I knew it not, from my youth up; (ii) by adding to the constant use of all the other means of grace, continual prayer for this very thing, justifying, saving faith, a full reliance on the blood of Christ shed for *me*; a trust in Him, as *my* Christ, as *my* sole justification, sanctification, and redemption.[75]

This emphasis Wesley never forsook. Though he believed that good works were the necessary implication of the Christian faith, he rigorously adhered to his resolution not to depend upon them for salvation; and though he seems to have believed, before meeting with Böhler, that dominion over sin was accompanied or followed by a sense of assurance, he was not fully convinced until his meeting with the Brethren.[76] It would be an exaggeration, or rather an anticipation, to claim that the Doctrine of Assurance, which was to play so large a part in the development of Methodism,

[75] *Journal*, I.471.

[76] See p. 56, *supra*, and *Letters*, I.20.

was formulated at this time. Indeed, Wesley's prime and immediate concern was to establish a right relationship with God, and to clarify his own ideas rather than to instruct others. Moreover, to believe in Assurance is not the same thing as to be assured, and Wesley's experience of Assurance had to wait for Whitsuntide 1738. In his account of that experience he wrote:

> An assurance was given me that He had taken away *my* sins, even *mine*, and saved *me* from the law of sin and death;[77]

and in 1767, writing of that experience, he said:

> It is confirmed in your experience and mine. The Spirit Himself bore witness to my spirit that I was a child of God, gave me an evidence thereof; and I immediately cried: 'Abba, Father.'[78]

Both to Wesley's intellectual conviction and to his heart-warming experience the Moravians, and Böhler in particular, made a vital contribution.

It is to be observed, however, that Zinzendorf's ideas on Assurance were not identical with those of Böhler. On 12th July 1738 Wesley records in his *Journal* an address by the Count,[79] in which he states that Assurance may not come until long after justification, a declaration which may have given Wesley some comfort, for in the pages of the *Journal* immediately following 24th May 1738 frequent references are made to the lack of joy in his religious life —a deficiency which greatly troubled him. Apparently, at this time, most of the Moravian teachers agreed with this view, namely that there is usually an interval between justification and the witness of the Spirit, an example of the differences of opinion which were frequently to exist between the Moravian leaders, and which are not surprising in a growing Church. Michael Linner, for example, said to Wesley:

> The leading of the Spirit is different in different souls. His more usual method, I believe, is to give, in one and the same moment, the forgiveness of sins and a full assurance of that forgiveness. Yet in many He works as He did in me—giving first the remission of sins, and, after some weeks or months or years, the full assurance of it.[80]

David Nitschmann had a different experience:

[77] *Journal*, I.476.
[78] Sermon XLV, 'The Witness of the Spirit'.
[79] *Journal*, II.13.
[80] *Journal*, II.37-40.

I delivered myself wholly into His hands, to dispose of according to His good pleasure. *In that hour*, I saw that all who believe in Him are reconciled to God through His blood; and was assured that I was thereby reconciled, and numbered among the children of God; and from that hour I have had no doubt or fear, but all peace and joy in believing.[81]

If Benham's story of the refusal of the Sacrament to John Wesley is true, it was probably because of his own lack of assurance at the time, for, as Christian David said, this issue was regarded as of first-class importance:

Our constant inquiries were, . . . 'Are you fully assured, beyond all doubt and fear, that you are a child of God? In what manner, and at what moment, did you receive that full assurance?' If a man could not answer all these questions, we judged he had not true faith. Nor would we permit any to receive the Lord's Supper among us till he could.[81]

With this background, the description of Wesley as *homo perturbatus* may signify 'a man without full assurance'. Apparently, Benjamin Ingham had no such doubts!

The influence of the Brethren upon John Wesley, therefore, both generally and specifically, cannot be denied. It was not merely, or mainly, a matter of theological opinion. In all the three directions indicated—Justification by Faith, instantaneous conversion, Assurance—John Wesley departed far from his teachers. Theology cannot of course be divorced from the religious life, nor is it wise to separate, as some writers have tried to do, the intellectual from the emotional change in Wesley's outlook. But it is clear that the influence of the Moravians—Böhler, Spangenberg, David Nitschmann and others—upon the Wesleys was primarily a personal one. The tributes paid by both brothers to their German friends are a recognition of their goodness rather than of their ability. For example, when, on 28th April 1738, Charles Wesley described Peter Böhler as 'a better physician' (than his own doctor) he was obviously not referring to his medical knowledge; and John Wesley's description of Spangenberg as 'the good soldier of Jesus Christ'[82] suggests no connexion with his controversial powers. Spangenberg's formulation of Moravian theology in *Idea Fidei Fratrum* was to come forty years later. Wesley's eulogy of

[81] *Journal*, II.35. [82] ibid., I.371.

Böhler, 'Oh, what a work hath God begun, since his coming into England! Such an one as shall never come to an end till heaven and earth pass away',[83] was, according to Curnock, added many years after the date under which it appears in the *Journal*, when the theological rift had widened, but when his affection had not waned. The crucial fact was that these men had a secret which Wesley did not possess, and that what impressed the Wesleys most was not so much the Christianity which the Brethren preached as the Christianity which they lived.

At any rate, the stage was now set for what Charles Wesley calls 'The Day of Pentecost'; but some details had still to be arranged before the drama could be presented, and in that arrangement the Moravians took no small part. Böhler had left London on the way to Carolina, but his letter of 8th May 1738,[84] written in Latin, cheered Wesley, who was 'sorrowful and very heavy, being neither able to read, nor meditate, nor sing, nor pray'. Perhaps the most interesting part of the letter (apart from its emphasis on the need for faith) is the somewhat didactic language. Wesley, though a clergyman in Holy Orders and a graduate of Oxford, apparently still regarded the Moravians as his teachers, and willingly accepted advice from them.

Thus encouraged, John Wesley continued to preach his 'new gospel'—at St Ann's, Aldersgate, and at the Savoy Chapel—on 'Free Salvation by Faith in the Blood of Christ'. At St Ann's, as previously at St Lawrence's, St Katherine Cree's, and at Great St Helen's, he was forbidden to preach again.

An important event with which both Böhler and Wesley were associated had taken place on 1st May. On that day the little Society was formed which afterwards became the Fetter Lane Society, the centre of Moravian activities in England. It was not originally either a Moravian or a Methodist Society, though from it eventually sprang both the organized Methodism of the 'United Societies' and the Moravian Church in England. The Society was formed at James Hutton's bookshop, Little Wild Street; it was a Church of England Society, and its founders were 'John and Charles Wesley, Piers, Vicar of Bexley, and a few others'.[85] The proportionate part played by the Wesleys and Böhler is not clear. According to John Wesley's own account, the Society was formed 'in obedience to the command of God by St James and by the

[83] *Journal*, I.459-60. [84] ibid., p. 461. [85] ibid., p. 458.

advice of Peter Böhler'.[86] A Committee which was set apart by the Moravian Synod held at Herrnhaag in 1747 to consider the 'awakening' in England says 'John Wesley was the beginner of the Fetter Lane Society', but a second Committee, meeting a day or two later, corrects this:

> The taking Fetter Lane Society Room mentioned in the Minutes of the first Committee cannot so positively be ascribed to John Wesley, it being probable that it was done by P. Böhler's advice and with the concurrence of many other Methodist brethren.[87]

The Rules ordain weekly meetings—'to confess our faults one to another, and pray one for another'—and enjoin the formation of 'bands', testimony meetings, conditions of admission, days of intercession, a monthly Love-feast, and the exclusion of recalcitrant members. J. E. Hutton[88] points out that Wesley's account omits the rule that 'every one, without distinction, submit to the determination of the Brethren', and suggests, perhaps a little unkindly, that he did so because it interfered most with his own liberty. But surely Rule 11, as given by Wesley, covers this—'That no particular member be allowed to act in anything contrary to any other of the Society'—unless the term 'Brethren' refers exclusively to the Moravians, in which case Wesley's hesitation is not surprising. But as Wesley prints only eleven of the full later number of thirty-three rules, it is probable that Wesley made the original draft, which Böhler and others afterwards amplified.

Within five months the Society moved to a room in Fetter Lane. Here is Böhler's account:

> A certain Englishman also particularly wanted to speak with me and invited me to a certain house. But as this became generally known many Englishmen gathered at that place and I had to keep prayer-meetings. I spoke on the new birth.... At nine o'clock in the evening I met the older Wesley at Hutton's. He feels himself justified and is a seeking poor sinner.... These brethren had been invited who were of the same mind and who seek closer fellowship with each other and therefore wish to organize with each other a band; eleven persons were present, among them the older Wesley and Hutton. I spoke to them of the fellowship of the children of God among each other. They received the word with joy and all of them who are of one mind gradually want to join their band; they will then divide into two companies

[86] *Journal*, I.458. [87] See p. 132, *infra*. [88] op. cit., p. 294.

and the single and the married men will meet separately. But every four weeks both classes will have a common meeting.[89]

The importance of this Society in relation to subsequent Methodist organization will be seen in Chapter 7, but for the present it is enough to point out the friendly relations which existed between the Wesleys and the Brethren, and to emphasize that *at this time* all the members claimed to belong to the Church of England. They went in a body to St Paul's Cathedral, headed by Charles Wesley and George Whitefield, to receive the Lord's Supper.

There is no further reference in John Wesley's *Journal* to Böhler, or indeed to any of the Moravians, until after 24th May, but one or two of the entries in his brother's *Journal* are of particular interest. After Böhler's departure to Carolina, his place in Charles Wesley's confidence was taken by Thomas Bray, 'a poor ignorant mechanic, who knows nothing but Christ; yet, by knowing Him, knows and discerns all things'.[90] It was in Bray's house that Charles was to undergo his Whitsuntide experience, and it was Bray who urged him to complete his great 'Conversion Hymn', *Where shall my wondering soul begin?*,[91] when he had been persuaded to break off, 'for fear of pride'. Though Bray was of great assistance in this emotional crisis, and was a kind and generous host, he was later to prove a stumbling-block, for he was a doughty and immoderate opponent of the Wesleys in the 'stillness' controversy, and, though never himself a Moravian, supported Molther and his fellows in the conflict which broke up the Society at Fetter Lane and sent the Wesleys to form another one at the Foundery in Moorfields.

Bray was a substitute for Böhler, but it was another Moravian who brought Charles Wesley very near to his Pentecost on 17th May. On that day, he tells us, he 'experienced the power of Christ rescuing him in temptation'. He was introduced to 'Luther on the Galatians' by William Holland, a member of the Church of England, but in union with the Brethren. He was a master-painter, and afterwards ranked in the Moravian Church as the first 'Congregation Elder'. Here is Charles Wesley's account:

[89] *Moravian Archives at Herrnhut*, in *World Parish* (November 1949).
[90] Charles Wesley, *Journal*, 11th and 23rd May 1738.
[91] *Methodist Hymn-book* (1933), No. 361.

> Today I first saw Luther on the Galatians, which Mr Holland had accidentally hit upon. We began, and found him nobly full of faith. My friend, in hearing him, was so affected as to breathe out sighs and groans unutterable. I marvelled that we were so soon and so entirely removed from Him that called us into the grace of God, unto another Gospel. Who would believe our Church had been founded on this important article of justification by faith alone? . . . I spent some hours this evening in private with Martin Luther, who was greatly blessed to me, especially his conclusion of the 2nd chapter. I laboured, waited, and prayed to feel 'who loved *me*, and gave himself to *me*'. When nature, near exhausted, forced me to bed, I opened the book upon 'For He will finish the work, and cut it short in righteousness, because a [illegible]hort work will the Lord make upon earth'. After this comfortable [illegible]rance that He would come, and would not tarry, I slept in peace.[92]

[illegible]nd's account is somewhat fuller:

> [illegible]y before Peter Böhler's departure for Georgia, he and Mr Wesley [illegible]n a band. I was gone at that time for a few days into the country. [illegible]er my return, in speaking with one of our Society on the doctrine [illegible] Christ, as preached by him, and reading the eighth chapter of the [illegible]pistle to the Romans, I was conscious that I was not in the state there [illegible]escribed. I became very uneasy, made a diligent search for books [illegible]ting of faith in Christ, and was providentially directed to Martin [illegible]uther's *Commentary on the Epistle to the Galatians*. I carried it [illegible]ound to Mr Charles Wesley, who was sick at Mr Bray's, as a very precious treasure that I had found, and we three sat down together, Mr Charles Wesley reading the Preface aloud. At the words, 'What, have we then nothing to do? No, nothing! but only accept of Him who of God is made unto us wisdom and righteousness and sanctification and redemption', there came such a power over me as I cannot well describe; my great burden fell off in an instant; my heart was so filled with peace and love that I burst into tears. I almost thought I saw our Saviour! My companions, perceiving me so affected, fell on their knees and prayed. When I afterwards went into the street, I could scarcely feel the ground I trod upon.[93]

It is interesting to compare with this account John Wesley's own comment on Martin Luther's *Epistle to the Galatians*, which he apparently did not read until three years later. In his *Journal* for 15th June 1741 he wrote:

[92] Charles Wesley, *Journal*, 17th May.

[93] *Account of the Beginning of the Brethren's Work in England, 1732-45, Rylands Eng. MSS*, 1076.

I read . . . that celebrated book, Martin Luther's *Comment on the Epistle to the Galatians*. I was utterly ashamed. How have I esteemed this book, only because I heard it so commended by others; or, at best, because I had read some excellent sentences occasionally quoted from it! But what shall I say, now I judge for myself, now I see with my own eyes? Why, not only that the author makes nothing out, clears up not one considerable difficulty; that he is quite shallow in his remarks on many passages, and muddy and confused almost on all; but that he is deeply tinctured with mysticism throughout, and hence often dangerously wrong. To instance only in one or two points: How does he (almost in the words of Tauler) decry reason, right or wrong, as an irreconcilable enemy to the gospel of Christ! Whereas, what is reason (the faculty so called) but the power of apprehending, judgin and discoursing? Which power is no more to be condemned i gross than seeing, hearing, or feeling. Again, how blasphemousl he speak of good works and of the law of God—constantly coupli law with sin, death, hell or the devil; and teaching that Christ us from all alike. Whereas it can no more be proved by Scripture Christ delivers us from the law of God than that He delivers us f holiness or from heaven. Here (I apprehend) is the real spring of grand error of the Moravians. They follow Luther, for better, fo worse. Hence their 'No works; no law; no commandments'. But who art thou that 'speakest evil of the law, and judgest the law?'[94]

This marked contrast to the attitude of Charles Wesley on 17th May 1738 cannot be explained by differences of temperament or of critical ability. How then is it to be explained? Probably by the date on which it was written. Not only did John Wesley write while still suffering from the bitterness engendered by his severance from the Brethren, but Molther's doctrine of 'stillness' presented Luther's words in a new light, and called Wesley's attention to dangers of interpretation which had not hitherto been apparent. This is borne out, not only by his disparaging reference to 'Moravian errors', but by the omission of any mention of the close connection of Luther with his own Aldersgate experience.

Charles Wesley's entry for 17th May is the last reference by either brother to any Moravian influence directly leading up to the events of 21st and 24th May. It has been suggested that William Holland was the 'one' who read Luther's *Preface to the Epistle to the Romans* at Aldersgate Street, but this is purely conjectural. There is no need, however, to base any argument on evidence so

[94] *Journal*, II.467.

flimsy: the cumulative evidence of Moravian impact is incontrovertible.

SUMMARY

From October 1736, when John and Charles Wesley embarked on the *Simmonds*, until May 1738, when both underwent an experience which changed their attitude to religion and the direction of their ministerial labours, they were in close touch with Moravians, abroad and at home. There is no indication at the beginning of this period that any change was taking place, or had taken place in the spiritual condition of either brother, and it is only logical to assume that the undoubted change which took place (and was recognized by both) at the end of the period was connected with the Moravian contacts. That this is an understatement is borne out in several ways:

(1) by the warm appreciation expressed by John and Charles Wesley of individual Moravians and of the Brethren in general;

(2) by the testimony of Spangenberg, Zinzendorf and, in particular, Böhler, corroborating the avowals made by the two brothers in their *Journals*; and

(3) by the close association of Wesley and the Moravians with the foundation of the Fetter Lane Society.

It may be held that the actual cause of John Wesley's conversion was the reading of Luther's *Preface to the Epistle to the Romans.* On the face of it, that is extremely improbable. What that reading did was to confirm a decision already made, to supply the spark to material which had become highly inflammable. Or, to adopt another image, to place a coping-stone on a building which had been for two years in course of construction. Indeed, it may be maintained that the vital change in the outlook of the elder brother took place as early as 23rd April, and that all that happened on 24th May was the culmination of a long process.

It may be taken as proved then that if, as is generally agreed, Whitsuntide 1738 was a decisive event in the spiritual development of the two Wesleys, the Moravians made a considerable and indeed preponderant contribution to that development, and that if, as Methodists at any rate believe, the Methodist Church began its life at that time, the 13,000,000 Methodists throughout the world are the spiritual heirs of a handful of German Christians.

CHAPTER FOUR

MORAVIAN AND METHODIST IN FELLOWSHIP

THIS CHAPTER will, unfortunately, be a brief one, for the fellowship begun so happily on board the *Simmonds* was to end in shipwreck four years later. An attempt will be made in another chapter to assess the factors which broke up a partnership which had begun with such high promise. In all probability, the prime reason is to be found in the conflicting personalities of the two leaders, John Wesley and Zinzendorf, and though there were differences of faith and practice, these were prolonged and exacerbated by the prepossessions arising from this conflict.

It has been maintained by writers on both sides[1] that the differences were fundamental, and that the continuance of fellowship was impossible. G. A. Wauer, indeed, maintains that these differences were manifest from the very beginning, and that they persisted after the Aldersgate experience.[2] Though that experience effected a striking change in Wesley's attitude, and though Böhler was an important factor in this change, this change was not a true conversion in the Moravian sense. Wesley, he says, merely added new knowledge to his previous views, and did not realize that conversion demanded a 'change of heart'. Benham makes the same distinction when he says that Wesley, in contradistinction to Benjamin Ingham, was ruled by his head rather than by his heart.[3]

This criticism begs the question. The head and the heart can never be exactly separated into compartments. Valuable as are 'right ideas', they could hardly suffice to keep Wesley's evangelical flame ablaze for fifty years. Preaching is either a passion or a nuisance, and there is no indication that Wesley ever became weary in well-doing.

There was, at any rate, no indication of fundamental differences immediately following 24th May 1738, nor, in John Wesley's

[1] e.g. G. A. Wauer and N. Curnock.

[2] *The Beginnings of the Brethren's Church in England*, p. 67.

[3] *Memoirs of James Hutton*, p. 40.

account of his visit to Herrnhut, is there any positive evidence of growing discomfort, in spite of the somewhat equivocal attitude of the Brethren there. Three weeks after his conversion he set out for Germany, in the hope, he said, that 'the conversing with those holy men who were themselves living witnesses of the full power of faith, and yet able to bear with those that are weak, would be a means, under God, of so establishing my soul that I might go on from faith to faith and "from strength to strength" '.[4] He was accompanied by Benjamin Ingham, Johann Töltschig, whom he had already asked for advice about his marriage, and who was to be one of the founders of Moravianism in Yorkshire, and Richard Viney,[5] at first an influential member of the Moravian Society, and indeed Spangenberg's successor as Superintendent of the work in Yorkshire, but afterwards a severe critic of the Brethren. They arrived at Marienborn, a Moravian settlement, on 4th July, and during their stay two events are said to have taken place, to neither of which does Wesley refer in his *Journal*, but which are sometimes said to have given birth to serious unrest. One, told by Benham, states that John Wesley was refused permission to partake of the Holy Communion. Here is Benham's account:

> On the 13th of June John Wesley and Benjamin Ingham went to Germany, in company with Töltschig, and reached Marienborn on the 4th of July, where Ingham was admitted to partake of the Holy communion. But when the congregation saw Wesley to be *homo perturbatus*, and that his head had gained an ascendency over his heart, and being desirous not to interfere with his plan of effecting good as a clergyman of the English Church when he should become settled—for he always claimed to be a zealous English Churchman—they deemed it not prudent to admit him to that sacred service.[6]

It is not clear whether the term *homo perturbatus* was applied to Wesley by the Marienborn congregation or by Benham. If by the latter, it must be pointed out that Benham wrote more than a century after the event, and that he produces no documentary evidence to support his statement; if by the former, it may possibly have been from a reluctance to interfere with his loyalty to the Church of England—though this would have applied equally to Ingham—or, as has been suggested, because at the time he himself had not a sense of assurance which the Moravians regarded as

[4] *Journal*, I.482-3. [5] See p. 144, *infra*. [6] op. cit., p. 40.

essential for participation in that Sacrament. Wesley had refused the Sacrament to his saintly friend Boltzius, pastor of the Salzburgers, who, as Wesley says, 'behaved with such lowliness and meekness as became a disciple of Jesus Christ',[7] and could hardly with consistency complain if he were similarly excluded by another Communion. In the report quoted earlier, Spangenberg says of Wesley, 'He thinks no one can partake of the Communion unless he has been previously baptized', and that he would not recognize as valid a baptism by Rothe, the Lutheran pastor of Berthelsdorf. It is probable therefore that he would not object to the erection of a similar fence by the Moravians. At the English Provincial Synod of 1754, Zinzendorf declared, 'Not every brother is at all times ready for the Communion',[8] which seems to indicate that not even the Brethren were certain of acceptability. The indulgence allowed to Ingham was probably due to the belief that he was rapidly advancing toward Moravianism, while Wesley was determined to remain 'a zealous English Churchman'. It must be conceded, however, that the Moravians at Herrnhut seem to have been less anxious for his friendship than he for theirs. The only reference in their records is: 'On August 12th the English Preacher came, and with him a wig-maker, and they stayed here some time.'[9] It would have been difficult to say less!

The other story is less credible. It is told by Hampson, who has no doubt of its authenticity:

> One day the Count had ordered his pupil to go and dig in the garden. When Mr Wesley had been there some time, working in his shirt and in a high perspiration, he called upon him to get into a carriage that was in waiting to pay a visit to a German Count; nor would he suffer him to wash his hands or to put on his coat. 'You must be simple, my brother', was a full answer to all his remonstrances; and away he went, like a crazed man, *in statu quo*.[10]

It is difficult to believe that Zinzendorf would have behaved with such rudeness to a guest, and the suggestion that he had acted thus in order to administer a merited reproof to Wesley's conceit is equally incredible. In any case, the fact remains that Wesley's own record testifies to his continued admiration for the Moravians and their ways. On 4th July, for example (the day of

[7] *Journal*, I.370. [8] *Rylands Eng. MSS*, 1054.
[9] *Moravian Archives at Herrnhut, Gemein-Diarium* (1738).
[10] *Life of Wesley* (*Memoirs*) (1791), I.218-19.

his supposed rebuff at Marienborn), he writes, 'Oh, how pleasant a thing it is for brethren to dwell together in unity', and his letters to his family speak with warm approval of his hosts, and of Zinzendorf in particular. On 6th July he writes thus to his mother:

The Count received us in a manner I was quite unacquainted with, and therefore know not how to express. I believe his behaviour was not unlike that of his Master . . . when He took the little children in His arms and blessed them. We should have been much amazed at him, but that we saw ourselves encompassed with a cloud of those who were all followers of him, as he is of Christ. . . .[11]

So too on the following day he writes to Charles, from the house of Zinzendorf's uncle:

The spirit of the Brethren is above our highest expectation. Young and old, they breathe nothing but faith and love at all times and in all places. I do not therefore concern myself with the smaller points that touch not the essence of Christianity [perhaps a hint that he had already discovered points of doctrinal difference], but endeavour (God being my helper) to grow up in these after the glorious examples set before me.[12]

A letter to his brother Samuel bears the same testimony:

God has given me at length the desire of my heart. I am with a Church whose conversation is in heaven, in whom is the mind that was in Christ, and who so walk as He walked. As they have all one Lord and one faith, so they are all partakers of one Spirit, the spirit of meekness and love, which uniformly and continually animates all their conversation.[13]

John Wesley gives a long and substantial account of his visit in his *Journal*. Dr Wauer is at some pains to show that Zinzendorf's theology (on Justification and Assurance) did not harmonize with Wesley's, and quotes the *Journal* for 9th July 1738 as evidence.[14] What Wesley actually records is that it was from Peter Böhler's theology that the Count differed, for though both agreed upon the fact of justification by faith in Christ and in its immediacy, Zinzendorf held that the assurance of such justification might be delayed, whereas Böhler (and presumably Wesley) held that a believer could not have peace with God without knowing it. This

[11] *Letters*, I.250-1. [12] ibid. [13] ibid. [14] op. cit., p. 70; and *Journal*, II.13.

F

can hardly be called the manifestation of fundamental differences between Methodist and Moravian. There is, at any rate, no suggestion of deep-rooted antipathies in Wesley's account of his conversations with Michael Linner, the eldest member of the Church, Christian David, the 'Bush Preacher', whom Wesley calls 'the first planter of it', David Nitschmann, one of the four public teachers of the Herrnhut community, Wenzel and Zacharias Neisser (the former of whom Wesley had met with Böhler at the house of Weinantz in February 1738), David Schneider, Christopher Demuth, and Arvid Gradin. Wesley faithfully reports their views, even when they did not entirely agree with his own, and makes no adverse criticism. Indeed, his only comment is: 'I believe no preface is needful to the account they gave of God's dealings with their souls; which, I doubt not, will stir up many through His grace, to "glorify their Father which is in heaven" '.[15] Elsewhere he exclaims: 'I would gladly have spent my life here; but my Master calling me to labour in another part of His vineyard . . . I was constrained to take my leave of this happy place.'[16]

A letter to Charles Wesley from his brother John on 28th June 1738 records what he conceived to be the general theological position of the Brethren, but expresses no hostility to it:

By the conversation I have had with the Brethren . . . I find the judgement of their Church is . . . (1) that we ought to distinguish carefully, both in thinking and speaking, between faith (absolutely speaking), which is one thing; justifying or saving faith, which is a second thing (and ought to be called, not faith absolutely, but always justifying or saving faith); the assurance of faith, where we know and feel we are justified; and the being born again, which they say is a fourth thing, and often distant in time (as well as in the notion of it) from all the rest; (2) that a man may have, and frequently has, justifying faith before he has the assurance that he is justified.[17]

It seems clear that until the very day of his departure John Wesley felt warmly disposed toward his Moravian friends, and that neither the differences of view nor the incompatibility of his own and the Count's temperaments had even suggested a separation. Perhaps there is a hint of anxiety in a letter which he sent to the Church at Herrnhut on 14th October 1738, and in which, after some expressions of regard, he writes:

[15] *Journal*, II.43. [16] ibid., II.28. [17] *Letters*, I.248.

O cease not, ye that are highly favoured, to beseech our Lord that He would be with us even to the end, to remove that which is displeasing in His sight. . . . And may the very God of peace fill up what is wanting in your faith, and build you up more and more in all lowliness of mind, in all plainness of speech, in all zeal and watchfulness.[18]

This reference to 'plainness of speech' echoes similar references in letters a month or two earlier to James Hutton and Charles Wesley. To the former he wrote on 4th August, 'If ye have, indeed, found mercy through His Blood, you must "use great plainness of speech" ';[19] and to his brother on the same date:

Salute our brethren in London and Oxford, and exhort them all, in the name of the Lord Jesus . . . that they work out their salvation with fear and trembling . . . never deceiving themselves; and that, above all things, they use great plainness of speech both with each other and toward all men.[20]

It is perhaps significant that both those letters were written from Herrnhut.

It is true too that in a letter to Zinzendorf on 30th October 1738, thanking him for his kindness, Wesley includes the somewhat cryptic comment:

I hope, if God permit, to see them [the Brethren at Herrnhut] at least once more were it only to give them that fruit of my love, the speaking freely on a few things which I did not approve, perhaps because I did not understand them.[21]

In his reply, Zinzendorf avows his inability to understand the letter, perhaps because of his limited knowledge of English, but that he would listen to specific complaints. Probably, he suggests, the differences between them were concerned with Church order, for, he adds: 'I find it difficult to draw a sharp line of demarcation between secular and ecclesiastical matters in the way our Saviour made the distinction in His day.'[22]

The differences, however, were not merely matters of Church order. In September 1738, soon after his return to England, Wesley began a letter to his friends in Marienborn and Herrnhut, which contained some frank criticisms. After his breach with the

[18] *Letters*, I.261. [19] ibid., I.253. [20] ibid., p. 252-3. [21] ibid., 266.
[22] *Moravian Archives at Herrnhut.*

Brethren in 1740 he published it. This is how it appears in his *Journal*:

My dear Brethren,

I cannot but rejoice in your steadfast faith, in your love to our blessed Redeemer, your deadness to the world; your meekness, temperance, chastity, and love of one another. I greatly approve of your conferences and bands; of your method of instructing children; and, in general, of your great care of the souls committed to your charge.

But of some other things I stand in doubt, which I will mention in love and meekness. And I wish that, in order to remove those doubts, you would on each of these heads, first, plainly answer whether the fact be as I suppose; and if so, secondly, consider whether it be right.

Do you not wholly neglect joint fasting?

Is not the Count all in all? Are not the rest mere shadows; calling him Rabbi; almost implicitly both believing and obeying him?

Is there not something of levity in your behaviour? Are you, in general, serious enough?

Are you zealous and watchful to redeem time? Do you not sometimes fall into trifling conversation?

Do you not magnify your own Church too much?

Do you believe any who are not of it to be in gospel liberty?

Are you not straitened in your love? Do you love your enemies and wicked men as yourselves?

Do you not mix human wisdom with divine; joining worldly prudence to heavenly?

Do you not use cunning, guile, or dissimulation in many cases?

Are you not of a close, dark, reserved temper and behaviour?

Is not the spirit of secrecy the spirit of your community?

Have you that childlike openness, frankness, and plainness of speech so manifest to all in the apostles and first Christians?[23]

This is disparaging enough, but it ought not to be judged apart from its context:

(1) It is by no means certain that the letter, *as a whole*, was written in September 1738. Wesley says in his *Journal* that he *began* it then, and it seems probable that part of it, at any rate, was added after his disagreement with the Moravians, and when his judgement was coloured by the animosities of that time.

(2) This view is supported by the marked difference in tone and temper between the first part of the letter and the later paragraphs.

[23] *Journal*, II.496.

(3) In spite of the criticisms contained in the letter, there is an evident wish for closer relations.

(4) Some of the questions are so trivial that it is difficult to resist the conclusion that Wesley was trying to strengthen his case by accumulation. Indeed, the last four questions cover much of the same ground, and seem directed more against Zinzendorf himself than against the Moravians as a whole. It is not easy to reconcile them with the unstinted praise given to them at the time at which the letter was begun.

It is worthy of note that in the version of this letter given by Wesley in his letter to the Rev. Thomas Church in February 1745,[24] only a few of these questions are included, as if Wesley himself had by this time realized their comparative unimportance.

It seems certain, however, that Wesley was somewhat uneasy, and that the letter, even if not dispatched, would hardly have been begun but for the growing doubts in his mind. But it seems equally clear that these doubts were not irremovable, in his judgement, nor were they sufficiently substantial to affect seriously his fellowship with Moravians at home and abroad. Perhaps his attitude had been prejudiced by the representations of Professor Francke, of Halle, who was somewhat hostile to the Brethren, and who had treated Wesley 'with the utmost humanity' on the journey home from Herrnhut;[25] but whatever change there was did not show itself for some time, and the suggestion that the prime cause of Wesley's separation from the Brethren was his recollection of his rebuff at Marienborn has no documentary support.

The seeds of disruption had been sown even before Wesley's visit to Marienborn, even though they were not to blossom for a long time. There was suspicion or misunderstanding on both sides. The Brethren, conscious of their great traditions, seem to have regarded the Wesleys as novices in religious matters, and, for his part, Wesley seemed particularly anxious about their secretiveness. In a letter to Peter Böhler, dated 18th February 1775, Wesley wrote:

> I never did speak but when I believed it was my duty to do so. And if they would calmly consider what I have spoken from 10th March 1736, and were open to conviction, they might be Christians as are hardly in the world besides;[26]

[24] *Letters*, II.175ff. [25] *Journal*, II.58. [26] *Letters*, VI.140.

and he had, apparently not long after the event, complained to Böhler of Spangenberg's want of straightforwardness at that time. Yet there is no indication in his *Journal* or *Diary* of such dissatisfaction; and it must not be forgotten that the letter quoted above was written after nearly forty years of misunderstandings and recriminations. In any case, what differences there were were differences of method and not diversities of theological opinion.

The charge of dissimulation and secretiveness is so often made by Wesley as to deserve close examination. Moravian historians have been commendably candid about Zinzendorf's character, and especially about his misrepresentations, but there is no evidence that this weakness was infectious. Overstatement is a common failing of religious propagandists; understatement is much less common, and it was probably the refusal of the Brethren to indulge in theological controversy which aroused the ire and suspicion of their critics. In other words, they were blamed for their virtues. The one feature on which the Moravians could justly pride themselves was that they consistently refrained from any attempt to make proselytes, and indeed placed difficulties in the way of those who wished to join them as members. A statement by Spangenberg, their statesman and theologian, about their attitude to other Communions on the mission field is typical:

> (1) We never enter into controversy with any other denomination, nor do we endeavour to draw their members over to us.
>
> (2) Much less do we attempt to win over to our Church any of the heathen who are already in connexion with those of any other Church.[27]

It is conceivable that the reluctance of the Brethren to do anything which might look like proselytizing gave to observers the appearance of hiding their light under a bushel.

There was, at any rate, no hint of any forthcoming cleavage for some time after John's return from Herrnhut. Though he spent a good deal of time in preaching to the various Religious Societies, in London and elsewhere, he remained closely attached to the Society at Fetter Lane. On 1st January 1739, for example, a Love-feast there was attended by over sixty people, including the Wesley brothers, Westley Hall, Ingham, Whitefield, Hutchins, and Kinchin.[28] Tyerman uses the phrase 'and about sixty

[27] Benham, op. cit., p. 576. [28] *Journal*, II.121-2.

Moravians',[29] but this is going beyond the evidence, for Wesley refers only to 'about sixty of our brethren'. There are numerous references in John Wesley's *Diary* to his friendship with individual Moravians, with whom he appears to have been on the most intimate terms—Bell, the Misses Hopson, Hutton, Okely—and in all this there is no evidence of any dissension, though there is an early reference to enthusiasm which is somewhat ominous, in view of later developments.

The Love-feast of 1st January 1739 was the high-water mark of Methodist and Moravian fellowship, for though it was, as might be expected (for the Love-feast was a Moravian revival) Moravian in style and procedure, the powerful personality of John Wesley asserted itself. Indeed, there were already indications that the Brethren were beginning to be restive about Wesley's autocratic methods, and, as will be seen, they afterwards ascribed the breach to his desire to rule. There was at this time nothing denominational about the Fetter Lane Society. It was neither Moravian nor Methodist, though the influence of both points of view was strong. It was one of the many Religious Societies attached to the Church of England, using the Book of Common Prayer, and taking the Sacrament of Holy Communion in the Parish Churches. It is noteworthy that at the New Year Love-feast just mentioned seven clergymen of the Church of England were present. The establishment of a Moravian congregation was yet to come. John Wesley at this time was away a good deal in Bristol, and perhaps his absence from Fetter Lane, where James Hutton, already committed to Moravianism, conducted the meetings while the Wesleys were away, allowed dissension to arise. On 11th June 1739, for instance, John Wesley received a pressing letter from a Mr Edmonds, asking him to go to Fetter Lane, where the members were in great confusion for want of his presence and advice.[30] There is no indication of the cause of this confusion (which Edmonds afterwards denied), but there are other hints of differences of opinion. On 16th June 1739 Wesley records:

We acknowledged our having grieved Him by our divisions: 'one saying, *I am of Paul*; another, *I am of Apollos*'[31]—

[29] op. cit., I.229. [30] *Journal*, II.216. [31] ibid., 222-5.

Our divisions were healed; misunderstandings vanished away; and all our hearts were sweetly drawn together and united as at the first.

So too on 9th September:

I went to our Society at Fetter Lane, and exhorted them to love one another. The want of love was a general complaint. We laid it before the Lord. . . . Evil surmisings vanished away. The flame kindled again as at the first, and our hearts were knit together.[32]

In spite of these happy reconciliations, the need for them indicates some underlying difficulty. What this was will become clear in the next chapter.

[32] *Journal*, II.273.

CHAPTER FIVE

DISRUPTION

IF THE story of Methodist and Moravian fellowship is brief but happy, the history of its disruption is long and distressing. No attempt will be made in this chapter to give a complete account of the arguments and counter-arguments, the animosities and suspicions which caused to diverge two Christian groups which had so much in common in faith and practice; but as the development of both Communions was influenced by the separation, an outline of those circumstances cannot be omitted. As has already been indicated, there are some writers who contend that the differences were fundamental, and that any continued union was impossible. But this is by no means proved. Whatever differences had already shown themselves—for example, in the use of the Liturgy, and in the refusal of the Marienborn Brethren to administer the Sacraments of the Lord's Supper to John Wesley—can hardly be called fundamental. On the former count, it is necessary to point out that there are wide divergences of practice within the Methodist Church today, some individual churches using the full Prayer Book service of Morning Prayer and others adopting a 'Mission type of service; some observing Holy Communion with a liturgical form almost identical with that of the Church of England and others adopting a 'Free' and almost extemporary order; while in general the Moravians today are more liturgical than the Methodists. Differences there were in theological opinion, indeed, but it is hard to believe that these were of sufficient magnitude to make a permanent break, or that they would have gained such prominence but for two factors, (i) Molther's doctrine of 'stillness', and (ii) the conflicting personalities of Wesley and Zinzendorf, factors which were transitional. There is not much in Spangenberg's *Idea Fidei Fratrum*, an authoritative conspectus of Moravian doctrine, published (in an English edition) in 1784, which would offend the Methodists of that day, or which could be regarded as establishing, or built upon, fundamental differences. On the second count, the refusal of Holy Communion to Wesley, there is no recorded evidence that he ever complained of his exclusion or regarded it as unjustifiable.

Other possibilities of conflict were, however, emerging. The friction—or rivalry—between Zinzendorf and Wesley was not merely a matter of personal pride or prerogative: it was reinforced by, perhaps even founded on, suspicion; on the one hand, by Wesley's suspicion of Moravian Antinomianism, and on the other by Zinzendorf's suspicion of what he deemed to be Wesley's spiritual pride and legalism. Both placed a high value on the primitive discipline of the Church, and the Brethren, as will be seen, adopted some of its distinctive features; but Wesley, though at first much attracted by Moravian loyalty to tradition, was to show that, when he thought it necessary, he could break with the past. A further cause, if not of dispute, yet of coolness was to arise in the Moravian dislike of the Methodist 'scenes', the emotional excesses in which many of the converts indulged. Doctrinal divergences followed. Wesley's characteristic doctrine of Perfect Love (or Christian Perfection), the one doctrine which may be regarded as indigenous to Methodism and which differentiated Methodists from other evangelical Christians in the eighteenth century, was already being shaped; and there were signs that Zinzendorf, who abominated anything which might seem to emphasize human strength as against the power of God in Christ, looked upon this with horror.

To what extent were these differences inherent, and how far were they accentuated by temporary circumstances? Suspicion, however well justified, is not of itself sufficient reason for a permanent breach. Both quietism and 'the scenes' tended to diminish and were in large part disowned by those who had approved of them or tolerated them; and the diversity of views on Christian Perfection was not as marked as might have appeared from the famous conversation between Wesley and Zinzendorf in Gray's Inn Walks on 3rd September 1741. Perhaps Wesley was not far wrong in saying that the difference was largely one of words.[1]

It is evident, in any case, that the barriers, whatever they were, were not regarded by John Wesley as insuperable. His frequent expressions of esteem and affection, of which there are many instances, need not in themselves indicate a desire for reunion,

[1] '*Omnino lis est de verbis*', *Journal*, II.489.

but they are reinforced by definite statements of that desire. In May 1742 John Cennick, once a supporter of Wesley and afterwards a Moravian, but at the time a Calvinist, wrote in a letter to Whitefield's wife: 'I have had it much impressed upon my mind, that it would be right in the sight of God, that all our preachers, all Mr Wesley's, and all the Moravian Brethren should meet together. Who knows but we might unite?'[2] John Wesley was apparently of the same mind, for he travelled to such a conference from Newcastle, and summoned his brother from Cornwall and John Nelson from Yorkshire.[3] The conference did not take place. Wesley, however, still envisaged the possibility of a *rapprochement*. In a letter to Benjamin Ingham on 8th September 1746, he wrote:

I am in great earnest when I declare once more, that I have a deep abiding conviction by how many degrees the good which is among them overbalances the evil, and that I cannot speak of them but with tender affection, were it only for the benefits I have received from them; and that at this hour I desire union with them (were those stumbling-blocks once put away which have hitherto made that desire ineffectual) above all things under heaven.[4]

The importance of this must not be exaggerated, for Wesley qualified his assurance (already modified by the parenthesis) by a footnote in which he limited it to 'the simple and artless part of their congregation'; but it is clear that he still cherished a desire for a closer fellowship. It must be admitted that he was not always so friendly, and he appears to have allowed his judgement to be unduly influenced by contemporary events. In November 1750, for instance, in a letter to the Rev. George Stonehouse,[5] he severely criticized the Moravians, their doctrine, their preaching and their practice; and this attack is so different from his sturdy defence of them in his letter to the Rev. Thomas Church in February 1745, as to suggest some specific and immediate cause. Conversely, whenever he met Peter Böhler, he seems to have become more warmly disposed toward the Brethren. In his *Journal* for 6th April 1741 he wrote (only a few months after the disruption):

[2] Tyerman, *Life and Times of the Rev. John Wesley*, I.419.
[3] Charles Wesley, *Journal*, I.334.
[4] *Letters*, II.83. [5] ibid., III.52.

I had a long conversation with Peter Böhler. I marvel how I refrain from joining these men. I scarce ever see any of them but my heart burns within me. I long to be with them, and yet I am kept from them.[6]

And in February 1775, only two months before Böhler's death, he wrote to him thus:

By the grace of God I shall go on, following peace with all men, and loving your Brethren beyond any body of men upon earth except the Methodists.[7]

Indeed, it is probable that had Böhler been in England in July 1740, and especially if Spangenberg's wisdom could have replaced Zinzendorf's impulsiveness, the misunderstanding with the Moravians might have been easily dissipated.

It is probable therefore that the most lasting cause of the rift between the Methodists and the Moravians lay in the personalities of the two leaders, John Wesley and Zinzendorf. Each was too dominating—which need not mean 'domineering'—to tolerate a rival. As Sir Robert Walpole said in a different connexion: 'The firm is Walpole and Townshend, not Townshend and Walpole.' In fact each *did* accuse the other of being 'domineering'. More than once Wesley blamed the Count for his overweening power, and the Brethren for pandering to it, as in the projected letter of September 1738, and the Moravians in their turn suspected Wesley of unlimited ambition. James Hutton, for instance, writing to Zinzendorf on 14th March 1740 (before the breach), said: 'John Wesley, being resolved to do all things himself . . . is at enmity against the Brethren';[8] a Committee of the Synod held at Herrnhaag in 1747 said much the same thing: 'Had Molther let J. Wesley be the head, and had he done all things under him, as his servant, he might have done with him what he pleased';[9] and Benjamin La Trobe, in a letter to Loretz, in 1785, reveals that age had not softened the old warrior: 'As John is accustomed to be Pope (as his brother says) the old man will, without a particular work of God on his heart making him humble, hardly submit to it.'[10] Charles Wesley had asked his brother in March, 1741: 'Are you not afraid lest they [the Brethren] should eclipse your own glory or lessen your own praise?'[11]

[6] *Journal*, II.441-2.
[7] *Letters*, VI.141.
[8] Benham, *Memoirs of James Hutton*, p. 47.
[9] See p. 132, *infra*.
[10] See p. 160, *infra*.
[11] See p. 111, *infra*.

This opinion of John Wesley's desire for precedence, which is probably based in the main on the reports of James Hutton, went beyond the borders of Moravianism. Lavington, Bishop of Exeter, who was no friend of the Brethren, in his scurrilous pamphlet, *The Moravians Compared and Detected*, wrote: 'Mr John Wesley went among them, but afterwards from contentions who should be the greatest made very free with them.'[12]

But could autocracy be avoided? The necessities of the infant Communions demanded strong leadership. Indecision and compromise would have opened the way to revolt and separatism. Indeed, both Zinzendorf and Wesley, in spite of their strength, had to face many defections, Wesley more than the Count. It is not surprising that, after the death of the Methodist leader in 1791, the separatist tendencies which he with such difficulty had restrained now burst the bonds which had kept his followers within the limits of official Methodism. Moreover, unlike though Wesley and Zinzendorf were, they were both born to rule and not to follow. Both were of noble descent, both possessed strong and robust personality, both were inspired by a flaming ideal, and both no doubt, were encouraged, perhaps inflated, by the loyalty and even the flattery of their supporters. But in many ways their vivid personalities were strikingly different. One responded to an inner urge, the other to a distant ideal; Zinzendorf to the emotional impulse within him, Wesley to the vision of perfect holiness. To the Moravian leader, creeds mattered little—what was essential was a right relationship with God through Jesus Christ; the Methodist perceived the risk of mere subjectivity and demanded the safeguards of objective forms of worship and of ecclesiastical ordinances. Moreover, Zinzendorf, sure of the purity of his own motives, exercised a reserve which might have given the impression of [illegible], Wesley's clear-cut mind demanded positive statement and strict literal truth. It has been suggested that Wesley was too cool and calculating to understand the mental operations of the poet Zinzendorf, but this is too sharp a distinction. There was a good deal of the poet about the Methodist leader, and Zinzendorf was not devoid of practical wisdom.

Wesley was certainly straightforward, but there were times when he seemed to use derogatory terms too vaguely. His

[12] 1754.

frequent charge of 'Antinomianism', for example, though it contained some truth, was an exaggeration; and it is difficult to avoid the conclusion that his arguments were sometimes sophistical. In his letter of June 1746 to the Rev. Thomas Church, he wrote:

As to Mr Molther, I must observe once more that I do believe there was a particular providence in his sickness. But I do not believe (nor did I design to insinuate) that it was a judgement for opposing me.[13]

But surely there *is* that implication in his entry in his *Journal* for 23rd April 1740: 'Mr Molther was taken ill this day. I believe it was the hand of God that was upon him.'[14]

Both Wesley and Zinzendorf had faults, but they also shared a passionate love for God and an extraordinary devotion to His service. Wesley's long life as preacher and teacher has no parallel in Church history, and Zinzendorf's generosity and enthusiasm knew no limits. Moreover, in speaking of both leaders as autocrats, we ought not to forget that they lived in an undemocratic age. In particular, more than once the Brethren were saved from disaster by Zinzendorf's generosity.

This brief survey of the causes of the dispute between the Wesleys and the Moravians has anticipated the story of the event, but will serve as a background to it, and, to some extent, as an explanation of it.

John Wesley's first references to dissensions have already been mentioned, but until November 1739 there is no hint that these were likely to last. Before that date, if Wesley's *Journal* is a reliable record—it must be remembered that much of it was written some time after the incidents recorded—the differences of opinion were settled and the divisions healed. But the entry for 1st November shows that a Mr Molther was preaching, with considerable success, the doctrine of 'stillness'.[15] It is possible that this doctrine had made itself known even before Molther's arrival in London. Molther reached London on 18th October 1739; more than a month earlier, on 12th September, Wesley had urged the Society at Fetter Lane 'to keep close to the Church and to all the ordinances of God'.[16]

In essence, 'stillness' was a reaction against what Philip Henry

[13] *Letters*, II.249. [14] op. cit., II.343.
[15] ibid., II.312. [16] ibid., p. 274.

Molther, an Alsatian who had been much influenced by Zinzendorf, regarded as an undue emphasis on the 'ordinances', and therefore as being contrary to the Lutheran doctrine of Justification by Faith alone, though it is probable that it was encouraged to some extent by his opposition to the hysterical behaviour of some of those who took part in Wesley's services. But Molther proceeded to assert, and for a time was supported by Zinzendorf and even Spangenberg in asserting, that those who believed themselves 'converted' should abstain from what Wesley called 'the means of grace'—worship, Bible-reading, corporate prayer and especially the Lord's Supper—until all their doubts were removed; and that they should not attempt to do good, for no good could proceed from those who had not the Spirit of God, and they would thus be substituting works for faith. Wesley held, on the contrary, that there were degrees of faith, and that the ordinances were 'converting ordinances', tending to remove doubts, to establish true faith, and to build up the Christian life; and that to neglect good works (especially 'works of outward mercy') was to shirk a Christian duty and to disobey biblical injunctions. Molther even went so far as to say that in certain circumstances it might be allowable to 'use guile' and to draw attention to the truth by going beyond the truth.

On 7th November there was a long discussion (after an hour's silence) on the Lord's Supper, which many, said Wesley, 'warmly affirmed none ought to receive till he had "the full assurance of faith" '.[17] This is interesting, for Ingham later maintained that Molther and his supporters had been misrepresented. In the letter sent to Ingham on 8th September 1746 Wesley answers this defence point by point. In particular he quotes from Ingham's own letter:

> 'First, as to *stillness*: The thing meant hereby is that man cannot attain to salvation by his own wisdom, strength, righteousness, goodness, merits, or works; that therefore, when he applies to God for it, he is to cast away all dependence upon everything of his own, and, trusting only to the mercy of God through the merits of Christ, in true poverty of spirit to resign himself up to the will of God, and then quietly wait for his salvation';[18]

and says in reply:

[17] op. cit., II.314. [18] *Letters*, II.80.

I have nothing to object to in this *stillness*. I never did oppose *this* in word or deed. But this is not 'the thing meant thereby', either by Molther, or the Moravians, or the English Brethren, at the time that I (and *you* at Mr Bowers's) opposed them.

He then quotes another sentence from Ingham's letter:

'That the Brethren teach that people who are seeking after salvation are all the while to sit still and do nothing—that they are not to read, hear, or pray—is altogether false.'

To this Wesley replies:

Whatever *the Brethren* do now, they did teach thus, and that explicitly, in the years 1739 and 1740. In particular, Mr Brown, Mr Bell, Mr Bray, and Mr Simpson, then with the Moravians. Many of their words I heard with my own ears: many more I received from those who did so.[19]

And then he refers to his interview with Molther on 31st December 1739, at which, he asserts, Molther maintained that the way to attain faith was 'to be still', that is (amongst other things) 'not to communicate'.

Though there was something of truth in Molther's general position (for there is a vague ethicalism which seeks to achieve salvation by philanthropy, and, worse, a fussiness in performing Church duties which only hides spiritual poverty), he spoilt his case by exaggerating it. How far John Wesley was whittling down Luther's doctrine of Justification by Faith is a matter of debate. It is arguable that Wesley was truer to the spirit of Luther's teaching than were the Moravians. 'They follow Luther for better, for worse',[20] Wesley himself wrote, though this charge was based on the utterances of unrepresentative Moravians, and sometimes on the words of those, like Bray, who were not Moravians at all. One of his main accusations against the Brethren was that they were 'Antinomian'. If this was true, they were certainly not in the true Lutheran tradition; but Zinzendorf and the other Moravian leaders stoutly denied that they were Antinomian, and, indeed, accused Wesley of being too hide-bound and legalistic. Certainly, John Wesley could not be accused of following Luther 'for better, for worse'. It is ironical that the John Wesley who had

[19] *Journal*, II.328-31. [20] ibid., p. 467.

been so profoundly impressed by the reading of Luther's *Preface to the Epistle to the Romans* on 24th May 1738, should react so strongly against the same writer's *Comment on the Epistle to the Galatians*, which had so deeply moved his brother. 'He is deeply tinctured', he wrote, 'with mysticism throughout, and hence often dangerously wrong.'[21] It is plain from this that if Wesley misunderstood Luther, the Moravians could hardly be blamed. In any case, he could not justly complain if his misunderstanding arose from his own limited knowledge, for he admits that his previous esteem for this book was based on 'a few excellent sentences found in it'. He now adds: 'I thought it my bounden duty openly to warn the congregation against that dangerous treatise, and to retract whatever recommendation I might ignorantly have given of it.'

There is no need, nor indeed would there be space in this essay, to give a full account of the growth of the doctrine of stillness in the Societies with which the Wesleys were in touch. Both brothers make frequent references to it in their *Journals*. On 1st November 1739, for example, John speaks of a woman who had been advised by Molther to be ' "still", ceasing from outward works',[22] and of Bray, in whose house Charles Wesley had undergone his Whitsuntide experience, and who now condemned 'the folly of people who keep running about to church and sacrament, as I', he said, 'did till very lately'.[23] It was not Molther alone who preached this doctrine, for Spangenberg denied that any one could have any faith as long as he was liable to any doubt or fear, i.e. that there were any degrees of faith, or that one ought to participate in the Lord's Supper or any other ordinance of God until his faith was completely established.

Wesley did not let the matter go by default, and both he and his brother sought in public and in private to check the growth of what they believed to be a dangerous heresy. His *Diary* for 10th November 1739 records discussions with Hutton, Spangenberg, Molther, and Bray, and five days later he 'exhorted four or five thousand people at Bristol neither to neglect nor rest in the means of grace'.[24] He was less successful in London, and he records several unpleasing accounts of the divisions which were developing in his absence.[25] It was probably at this time that the

[21] *Journal*, II.467-8, and pp. 65-6, *supra*.
[22] ibid., p. 312.
[23] ibid., p. 314.
[24] ibid., II.316, 320.
[25] ibid., p. 328.

United Societies were formed. According to Whitehead,[26] who seems to have had access to an unpublished *Journal* of John Wesley (the *Diary* is silent from 10th November 1739 to 1st June 1740), John took his first service at the Foundery, Moorfields, on 11th November 1739: 'I preached . . . at five in the evening to seven or eight thousand, in the place which had been the King's Foundery for cannon.'[27] The first reference to the new Society is found in the *Diary* for 30th October, and relates to a meeting held at the newly erected room in the Horse-fair, Bristol; and the 'Rules of the Society of the People called Methodists' begin thus:

In the latter end of the year 1739, eight or ten persons came to me in London, who appeared to be deeply convinced of sin, and earnestly groaning for redemption. They desired (as did two or three more the next day) that I would spend some time with them in prayer and advise them how to flee from the wrath to come. . . . I appointed a day when they might all come together. This was the rise of the United Society.

This first meeting took place apparently on 23rd December, for on the following day, Wesley recorded:

After spending part of the night at Fetter Lane, I went to a smaller company, where also we exhorted one another with hymns and spiritual songs, and poured out our hearts to God in prayer.[28]

In view of the fact that the Bristol Society was formed as early as 30th October 1739, only a few days after Molther's arrival in England, it seems clear that other factors than stillness were threatening to sever Wesley from the Moravians; and the creation of separate Societies by Molther and by Wesley, within a few days of each other, in December of the same year seems to indicate that disruption, from whatever cause, was by now inevitable.

On the last day of 1739 Wesley had 'a long and particular conversation' with Molther himself, and he records in his *Journal* for that day what he deems to be the essential difference between them.[29] In brief (summarizing what is already a summary), Molther held:

(1) that there are no degrees of faith less than full assurance; and

[26] *The Life of the Rev. John Wesley* (1793), II.125.
[27] *Journal*, II.319 n. [28] ibid., II.328. [29] ibid.

(2) that the joy attending 'the gift of God which many received since Peter Böhler came to England' was merely a matter of animal spirits.

Wesley, on the contrary, believed:

(1) that there are degrees of faith, which a man may have before he has the full assurance of faith;

(2) that the 'gift of God' referred to above was 'justifying faith', and

(3) that the joy and love attending was 'joy in the Holy Ghost' and 'the love of God shed abroad in their hearts'.

Arising from these beliefs, Molther maintained that the way to faith was not to use the means of grace—worship, fasting, private prayer, Scripture-reading, partaking of the Lord's Supper—for to do so was to trust in them; and not to do good, spiritual or temporal, for only those who have complete faith can transmit it; while Wesley held that one should use all these means of grace, and do all the good he could. Finally, if Wesley's account of the interview is correct, Molther held that 'guile', in exaggeration and even in deception, was justified in order to reach the truth, while Wesley held that guile must not be used 'on any account whatsoever'.

There seems little doubt that Molther overstated his case, and that the responsible leaders of the Moravians did not go all the way with him. Zinzendorf, in particular, with his dream of an *ecclesiola in ecclesia* ever before him, would not have approved of Molther's action in gathering together a group of his followers who proposed to found a new Church for themselves. Recent Moravian historians make no attempt to justify Molther in this matter;[30] but a good many of the Fetter Lane congregation were influenced by him—Bray, Hutton, Gambold, Westley Hall, Simpson, Stonehouse, and, for a time, Charles Wesley himself, though this was not for long, and took place after the disruption; and the responsible Moravian leaders, even 'the sober Spangenberg', seem to have been at fault in not disowning Molther's

[30] e.g. G. A. Wauer, *The Beginnings of the Brethren's Church in England*, pp. 74-7; J. E. Hutton, *History of the Moravian Church*, p. 301. J. Taylor Hamilton, *A History of the Moravian Church*, says: 'Molther appears to have been inclined to quietism'—a masterpiece of understatement.

extreme statements, probably because they had their hands full at the time with difficult Church affairs in Germany.

It is clear, however, that Molther and his supporters were moving away from the general doctrinal standards of the Brethren. Though, by their utterances, or by their silence, some of their responsible leaders gave Molther their support—probably from loyalty to one who in other respects did admirable work—this teaching appears to have dropped into obscurity very soon after the breach at Fetter Lane. At any rate, there is no suggestion that the Brethren continued to neglect the means of grace in their general work, though pockets here and there still stoutly defended the offending doctrine—and the authoritative summary of doctrine expounded later in the century by Spangenberg and La Trobe contained no mention of it.

At first Charles Wesley was as strongly opposed to Molther's teaching as his brother. On 4th April, for instance, he wrote in his *Journal*:

> I talked with poor perverted Mr Simpson. The still ones have carried their point. He said some were prejudiced against the Moravian brethren; and particularly against Molther; but that he had received great benefit from them. . . . I asked whether he was *still in* the means of grace or *out* of them. 'Means of grace?' he answered. 'There are none. Neither is there any good to be got by those you call such, or any obligation on us to use them. Sometimes I go to church and sacrament for example sake; but it is a thing of mere indifference. Most of us have cast them off. You must not speak a word in recommendation of them: that is setting people upon working.'[31]

A few days later, he wrote: 'Simpson draws away all he can, bidding them go to Molther, or they cannot come to Christ.'

Simpson was by no means the only one convinced by Molther. James Hutton said of him (Molther) 'that he had drawn men away from a false foundation, and had led them to the only true foundation, Christ'.[32] 'No soul', said another, 'can be washed in the blood of Christ unless it first be brought to one in whom Christ is fully formed. *But there are only two such men in London, Bell and Molther.*' Bray went so far as to say that it was impossible for anyone to be a true Christian outside the Moravian Church. As Bray was never a Moravian, this was a handsome but somewhat mystifying tribute.

[31] op. cit., I.205-6. [32] Benham, op. cit., pp. 205-6.

According to Simpson, it was *Charles* Wesley's adherence to the ordinances which was primarily responsible for the confusion into which the Fetter Lane Society had been plunged. 'Believers', he claimed, 'are not subject to ordinances; and unbelievers have nothing to do with them. They ought to be still, otherwise they will be unbelievers all the days of their life'[33]—a dilemma which Simpson apparently had no difficulty in resolving, for he left the Moravians in 1750! Charles Wesley's account of these disturbances shows that though later he seemed attracted by the doctrine of stillness, he was at this time its doughty opponent. On 22nd April 1740 he wrote:

> I met Molther: . . . he expressly denies that grace, or the Spirit, is transmitted through the means, particularly through the sacrament. This, he insists, is no command; is for believers only, that is, for such as *are* sanctified, have Christ fully formed in their hearts. Faith, he teaches, is inconsistent with any following doubt, or selfish thought. Forgiveness, and the witness of the Spirit, the indwelling, the seal, are *always* given *together*. Faith, in *this* sense, is a pre-requisite of baptism. That is, the candidate must have received the Holy Ghost, must have Christ living in him, must be justified, and sanctified, must be born of God.[34]

It is difficult, in view of this claim to entire sanctification, to understand the fierce opposition of the Moravians to John Wesley's doctrine of Christian Perfection.

Molther's contention that justification and assurance always come together is markedly different from the belief of other Moravians. It will be recalled[35] that Zinzendorf had maintained that the sense of assurance did not always coincide with the moment of justification; Molther safeguarded himself against the charge of inconsistency by claiming that this coincidence was found only in 'the true believer', and that the joy and love which came to those who had not 'true faith' (i.e. faith without any element of doubt at the time or subsequently) were merely the expression of animal spirits.

At this time Molther was taken ill: John Wesley believed 'it was the hand of God that was upon him'. It could hardly have been a serious illness, for two days later the brothers spent two hours in conversation with him, in which he explicitly asserted:

[33] *Journal*, II.343. [34] Charles Wesley, *Journal*, I.221. [35] See p. 60, *supra*.

(1) that there are no degrees of faith, for he who has any doubt or fear has no faith at all;

(2) that those who have no faith must be 'still' until they have it; i.e. they must not use the means of grace in order to procure it;

(3) that those who have 'a clean heart' need not use the ordinances;

(4) that those who have not a clean heart ought not to use them, partly because they have no right to, and partly because they are ineffectual, the only means of grace being Christ Himself.[36]

Here is Charles Wesley's account of the same interview:

I had a conference with Molther and our still brethren, but could come to no agreement. They contend for the impossibility of doubting after justification, and an absolute liberty from the means of grace, as we falsely call them, when they are neither means nor commands. . . . I talked in the evening with James Hutton. I asked, 'Have you the witness in yourself?' 'No.' 'How then can you have faith?' 'I have it not in the full proper sense; but I am in no fear. I have the full assurance of hope; and know my Saviour will give it me.'

This [says Charles Wesley] is giving up the point. Here is a lower faith, where the abiding, indwelling Spirit is *not yet*. And I see no necessity of denying the imperfect faith, in order to gain the perfect.

He adds:

I sent a friend in Bristol the following account: . . . 'Many here insist that a part of their Christian calling is liberty *from* obeying, not liberty *to* obey.' The unjustified, say they, are *to be still*: that is, not to search the Scriptures, not to pray, not to communicate, not to do good, not to endeavour, not to desire; for it is impossible to use means without trusting in them.[37]

John Wesley, who confessed himself 'utterly at a loss what course to take', records a similar instance of this 'lower faith', but this time from Stonehouse's servant and not from a theologian:

I turned and asked his servant, 'Esther, have you a clean heart?' She said, 'No; my heart is desperately wicked; but I have no doubt or fear. I know my Saviour loves me, and I love Him; I feel it every moment.' I then plainly told the master, 'Here is an end of your reasoning. This is the state the existence of which you deny.'[38]

There was little comfort to be gained, however, from the recognition of inconsistency; nor is it enough to assume that stillness

[36] *Journal*, II.344. [37] Charles Wesley, *Journal*, I.222-3.
[38] *Journal*, II.345.

was merely 'an example of fanatical misinterpretation of a few Scripture texts, promulgated among simple-minded people by a fervent enthusiast who came to them, endorsed by Zinzendorf's great name and all the associations of Halle and Herrnhut'.[39] By no means all those who held this doctrine were 'simple-minded people'. Molther himself was a man of great power. In a letter to Zinzendorf dated 14th March 1740, James Hutton, a man whose friendship, then and thirty years later, the Wesleys valued highly, wrote warmly of his growing influence;[40] Bray had been instrumental in Charles Wesley's conversion; Simpson and Stonehouse were both in Holy Orders, and the former had been a member of the Holy Club at Oxford. Perhaps Molther's ablest supporter was John Gambold. He too had been a member of the Oxford fellowship and had been appointed Rector of Stanton Harcourt; and afterwards became the first Bishop of the Brethren in England, being responsible for the compilation of the *Moravian Hymn-book* of 1754. His letter to Charles Wesley, quoted by John Wesley in his *Journal*, shows him to have been a man of considerable mental gifts,[41] and there are other references to him which indicate that the brothers prized his friendship, and deplored the separation from him which was so soon to take place. On 2nd July 1740 John Wesley wrote:

> I met Mr Gambold again, who honestly told me he was ashamed of my company, and therefore must be excused from going to the Society with me.[42]

On this, Wesley makes no comment other than: 'This is plain dealing at least!' Nearly a quarter of a century later, on 5th May 1763, he wrote:

> I spent some time with my old friend, John Gambold. Who but Count Zinzendorf could have separated such friends as we were? Shall we never unite again?

and a month later:

> I spent an agreeable hour, and not unprofitably, in conversation with my old friend, John Gambold. Oh, how gladly could I join heart and hand again.[43]

[39] N. Curnock, *Journal*, II.337. [40] Benham, op. cit., p. 46.
[41] *Journal*, I.462-3. [42] ibid., II.472. [43] ibid., V.40-2, and p. 254-5, *infra*.

It is difficult to believe that a friendship so warm and intimate as this could have been broken irreparably by a mere difference of interpretation, and it is probable, therefore that other causes contributed, not only to this severance, but to the break-up of the Fetter Lane fellowship.

Some others of the supporters of Molther were not of the same quality, though they could hardly be described as 'simple-minded'. Westley Hall, for example, who had married Wesley's sister Martha after jilting another sister, Kezia, was notoriously unstable and became an adulterer; while Richard Viney, at first warmly attracted by the Brethren, became later their severe critic, and afterwards caused dissension in the Methodist Society at Birstall.

The rift became wider. Charles Wesley sought to check it by publishing his hymn of twenty-three stanzas on 'The Means of Grace', and by circulating it as 'an antidote to stillness'. If any hymn could have availed at this juncture, this one would have been effective, for some of its verses could have been sung by either party! Could any follower of Molther, for instance, have quarrelled with the following?

Here, in Thine own appointed ways,
I wait to learn Thy will:
Silent I stand before Thy face,
And hear Thee say, 'Be still!'

'Be still!, and know that I am God!'
'Tis all I live to know;
To feel the virtue of Thy blood,
And spread its praise below.

Fruitless, till Thou Thyself impart,
Must all my efforts prove;
They cannot change a sinful heart,
They cannot purchase love.

I do the thing Thy laws enjoin,
And then the strife give o'er;
To Thee I then the whole resign;
I trust in means no more.[44]

[44] *A Collection of Hymns, etc.* (1780), No. 91.

In the light of after events, it is clear that Charles Wesley's reference to 'Thine own appointed ways' and 'The things Thy laws enjoin' are a defence of the ordinances; but a simple-minded person might well be forgiven if he construed some parts of the hymn—the last line, for example—as a defence of stillness.

A hymn published later makes his position more definite:

Place no longer let us give
To the old Tempter's will;
Never more our duty leave,
While Satan cries, 'Be still!'

Stand we in the ancient way,
And here with God ourselves acqaint;
Pray we, every moment pray,
And never, never faint;[45]

while two hymns appended to a tract entitled *A Short View of the Difference between the Moravian Brethren lately in England and the Rev. Mr John and Charles Wesley*, published in 1745, show that his leanings toward stillness were only temporary.

Whom still we love with grief and pain,
And weep for their return in vain,
In vain, till Thou the power bestow,
The double power of quickening grace.
And make the happy sinners know
Their Tempter, with his angel face;
Who leads them captive at his will,
Captive—but happy sinners still—;

a lament for those who had lapsed into stillness.

I would be truly still,
Nor set a time to Thee,
But act according to Thy will,
And speak, and think, and be.

I would with Thee be one;
And till the grace is given,
Incessant pray, Thy will be done,
In earth as 'tis in heaven.

[45] *A Collection of Hymns, etc.* (1780), No. 295.

On 5th June 1740 John Wesley, urged to return from Bristol by the Countess of Huntingdon, who was anxious about the spread of stillness in the Fetter Lane Society, reached London, 'where, finding a general temptation prevail of leaving off good works in order to an increase of faith', he 'began, on *Friday* the 6th to expound the Epistle of St James, the great antidote to this poison'.[46] Zinzendorf, as a true Lutheran in this matter, had little regard for this 'epistle of straw', and Charles Wesley has an interesting entry in his *Journal*, under the date 6th September 1741, in which he refers to his brother's conversation on 3rd September in Gray's Inn Walk with 'the apostle of the Moravians':

If thou art he; but, O, how fallen! Who would believe it of Count Zinzendorf, that he should utterly deny all Christian holiness? I never could, but for a saying of his, which I heard with my own ears. Speaking of St James's Epistle, he said: 'If it was thrown out of the Canon, *ego non restituerem*.'[47]

And six years later, on 4th December 1747, he writes:

I passed an hour at Mr Millar's, the Lutheran minister, who favoured me with a sight of Zinzendorf's famous declaration against my brother and me, and likewise his translation of the New Testament. We looked for St James's Epistle, but he was not to be found, the Count having thrust him out of the Canon by his own authority.[48]

On 11th June, John went to Islington with Ingham, who 'bore at this time a noble testimony for the ordinances of God and the reality of weak faith', to meet Molther, who was too weak to be seen, and in the evening spoke to 'the poor, confused, shattered society' at Fetter Lane, explaining where they had erred from the faith'.[49] Charles Wesley gives a graphic account of this meeting:

I returned to be exercised by our *still* brethren's contradiction. My brother proposed new-modelling the bands, and setting by themselves those few who were still for the ordinances. Great clamour was raised by this proposal. The noisy *still*-ones knew that they had carried their point, by wearying out the sincere ones, scattered among them, one or two in a band of disputers, who had harassed and sawn them asunder;

[46] *Journal*, II.349. [47] Charles Wesley, *Journal*, I.297.

[48] ibid., II.465. Zinzendorf had 'publicly called the two Wesleys false teachers and deceivers of souls'; Benham, op. cit., p. 112.

[49] *Journal*, II.350-1.

so that a remnant is scarcely left. . . . We gathered up our wreck . . . *raros nantes in gurgite vasto*, for nine out of ten were swallowed up in the dead sea of stillness. Oh why was not this done six months ago?'[50]

The leaven, however, was still working. Jane Davis, a woman from Deptford, who a week earlier had spoken 'great words and true', now forbade Joseph Humphreys to preach, and ordered him to cease doing good, and to be still.[51] Humphreys is of importance as being the first lay preacher (not the first *Methodist* lay preacher) to assist Wesley, and as being one of the organizers of the Welsh Calvinistic Methodism. Finally, seeing that plain speaking was urgently needed, Wesley 'began to execute what he had long designed' (the 'long' is significant)—'to strike at the root of the grand delusion'; and, on Sunday 22nd June at 6.30 in the morning, preached to the Society in the Foundery band-room on 'Stand ye in the way, ask for the old paths' (Jer. 6^{16})[52]—one of a series of expositions in which he attempted to prove.

(1) that there are degrees of faith,

(2) that belief is not enough by itself,

(3) that the ordinances—prayer, searching the Scriptures, 'eating bread and drinking wine in remembrance of Him' are Christ's own commands,

(4) that sin may remain even after belief,

(5) that God's ordinances are 'means of grace',

(6) that the Lord's Supper is sometimes a 'converting ordinance', no previous preparation being 'indispensably necessary, but a desire to receive whatsoever He pleases to give', and

(7) that believers ought to maintain good works, not merely praying, communicating, and searching the Scriptures, but 'feeding the hungry, clothing the naked, assisting the stranger, and visiting or relieving those that are sick or in Prison'.

This final exposition, on the Christian obligation of good works, on what would now be called 'the social gospel', was as fuel to the flames; for at Fetter Lane in the evening of that day—Sunday 29th June (John Wesley does not appear to have been present)—the gist of the sermon was reported by Simpson, who told a group of those present that Wesley had been 'preaching up the works

[50] Charles Wesley, *Journal*, I.239. [51] *Journal*, II.352. [52] ibid., 354-62.

of the law', which, said Viney, 'we believers are no more bound to obey than the subjects of the King of England are bound to obey the laws of the King of France'—an unconvincing analogy.[53]

The crisis could not now be long delayed. Wesley sought, at Fetter Lane and elsewhere, to 'explain' (his own word), but to no effect. On 16th July he borrowed a copy of a book entitled *The Mystic Divinity of Dionysius*, which contained the following extract:

> The Scriptures are good, prayer is good, communicating is good; but to one who is not born of God, none of these is good, but all very evil. For him to read the Scriptures, or to pray, or to communicate, or to do any outward work, is deadly poison. First, let him be born of God. Till then, let him not do any of these things. For if he does, he destroys himself.[54]

It is difficult to understand why, at this crucial stage in the relationship between Wesley and Fetter Lane, he should have produced this book, which seems to have been shown him by a woman follower, but which had no claim to be considered as an authoritative statement of Moravian doctrine. Probably he felt it was better to force the issue, and to discover if extracts like these truly represented the opinions of members of the Society. Certainly, Richard Bell, 'honest Bell', as Charles Wesley calls him, declared his entire agreement with it, though Bray, who had at other times spoken in extravagant praise of the Moravians,[55] seemed unwilling to commit himself. One member, Bowes or Bowers, declared that he had not found Christ until he 'left off' the ordinances; and the debate seems to have become purely personal, revolving round the respective merits of Wesley and 'the Germans'. The refusal to allow Wesley to preach in the Fetter Lane *Chapel*, which was 'taken for the Germans', probably confirmed him in his resolution to sever his connexion with the Society. The next day, 18th July, after a consultation at which Lady Huntingdon and Benjamin Ingham were present, he realized that 'the thing was now come to a crisis', and records that they 'were therefore unanimously agreed what to do'.[56]

Two days later, the matter came to a head. John Wesley went with a Mr Seward to Fetter Lane, where, contrary to his usual practice of extempore speech, he read a paper. After accusing

[53] *Journal*, II.362. [54] ibid., p. 365. [55] See p. 90, *supra*. [56] *Journal*, II.369.

those present of false teaching, namely of denying the possibility of weak faith, and of condemning the use of ordinances or 'means of grace' unless the heart is completely free from doubt or fear, he declared:

I believe these assertions to be flatly contrary to the word of God. I have warned you hereof again and again, and besought you to turn back to the Law and the Testimony. I have borne with you long, hoping you would turn. But as I find you more and more confirmed in the error of your ways, nothing now remains but that I should give you up to God. You that are of the same judgement, follow me.[57]

'I then', Wesley adds, 'without saying more, withdrew, as did eighteen or nineteen of the Society.'

Oddly enough Charles Wesley gives no account of these historic proceedings. This is surprising, in view of his severe strictures against stillness a month earlier. Perhaps the leaven of Quietism, which within the next few months was for a time to threaten his loyalty to his brother, was beginning to work; perhaps the motives which had prompted his own resistance—his determined adherence to the National Church, an adherence from which he never wavered all his life, were somewhat different from those of his brother, with whom the issue was one of doctrine rather than of ecclesiastical practice; perhaps, even at this early date, he had begun to share the Moravian dislike of John's autocratic methods. Whatever the reason, his silence is remarkable. So, too, was the rapidity of the growth of stillness, in view of its subsequent refutation by the Moravians themselves.

It is necessary, of course, to give the Moravian account of this dispute. It is much less full than that given by the Wesleys; indeed, the reticence of Moravian leaders at the time (and of Moravian historians since) had probably a special significance. It is similar to the reluctance of the principal Brethren to resume close relations with the Methodists later in the century, and some attempt will be made on another page to explain this attitude.[58] In the life of Spangenberg written by C. T. Ledderhose, a German pastor, the name of John Wesley is mentioned only once,[59] and there is complete silence about the association at Fetter Lane and about the disruption; while Cranz, in his *The Ancient and Modern History of the Brethren* (1780), an almost contemporary record,

[57] *Journal*, II.370. [58] See p. 168, *infra*. [59] Page 46.

makes light of the whole affair: 'As Wesley disagreed', he says, 'with Molther in point of doctrine, and did not choose to submit to certain regulations made among the Brethren with a view to prevent all offence and scandal, he separated and established Societies of his own.'[60]

Here is Molther's own account:

At that time, brother Peter Böhler having left England in June, the Society in Fetter Lane had been under the care of John and Charles Wesley. The good people, not knowing rightly what they wanted, had adopted many most extraordinary usages. The very first time I entered this meeting, I was alarmed and almost terror-stricken at hearing their sighing and groaning, their whining and howling, which strange proceeding they called the demonstration of the spirit and of power. In the midst of it all, it was quite apparent, from conversation with individuals, that most of them, from the very depths of their hearts, were yearning for the salvation of their souls.

When I had been in London about four weeks, at the repeated solicitations of its members, I was prevailed upon to conduct some of their Society meetings.

In 1740, John Wesley attacked the Society, with the view of confounding it. But as most of the members loved the doctrines of our Saviour and the Atonement in His blood, his efforts remained fruitless; and perceiving his object to be foiled, he separated from the Society, exclaiming: 'Whoever belongs to the Lord, come with me!' A few followed him, the others remained with the Brethren.[61]

Hutton's account is similarly very general, and the specific points at issue are not enumerated or discussed:

John Wesley, displeased at not being thought of so much as formerly, and offended, as he said, with the easy way of salvation as taught by the Brethren, publicly spoke against our doctrine in his sermons, and his friends did the same. In June 1740 he formed his 'Foundry Society', in opposition to the one which met at Fetter Lane, and which had become a Moravian Society. [This is an interesting claim, which may explain Wesley's restiveness.] Many of our usual hearers consequently left us, especially the females. We asked his forgiveness if in anything we had aggrieved him, but he continued full of wrath, accusing the Brethren, that in following Luther without discrimination, they, by dwelling exclusively on the doctrine of faith, neglected the law and zeal for sanctification. In short, he became our declared opponent, and

[60] Page 226. [61] Benham, op. cit., p. 53.

the two societies of the Brethren and the Methodists thenceforward were separated and became independent upon each other.[62]

In another account, Hutton admits that Wesley's annoyance was due in part 'to our imprudent behaviour toward him'.[63]

From these accounts, it will be noticed:

(1) that neither writer attempts to *debate* the question of stillness. Molther speaks of 'the free grace in the blood of Jesus', and Hutton of 'the easy way of salvation as taught by the Brethren'. Probably, as these reports were intended only for Moravian reading, no explanation or defence was necessary;

(2) that only a minority of the Fetter Lane congregation remained loyal to Wesley. Molther speaks of 'a few', Hutton of 'many specially the females'. The actual number, according to Wesley, who was not likely to understate, was eighteen or nineteen. It is probable that a good many of Wesley's supporters had already ceased to attend Fetter Lane, because of the continued dissensions, and had made their home at the Foundery, and that the Fetter Lane congregation was by this time, as Hutton claims, actually a Moravian Society;

(3) that John Wesley had considerable influence over women. Hutton had referred to this in a letter to Zinzendorf in March 1740, before the breach: 'J.W. and C.W., both of them, are dangerous snares to many young women; several are in love with them. I wish they were married to some good sisters, but I would not give them one of my sisters if I had many.'[64]

(4) that the dispute was not merely a matter of difference of doctrinal view or interpretation. Molther's reference to 'sighing and groaning' and Hutton's suggestion that John Wesley resented the challenge to his authority make it clear that the arguments about stillness were not much more than an incident, or were perhaps the spark which kindled inflammable material.

A letter sent by John Wesley to James Hutton three months earlier [illegible] reveals some tension. A certain Edward Nowers, who had withdrawn from the Moravians at Herrnhaag, had been 'adopted' by Wesley, 'speaking against the Brethren'. In this

[62] Benham, op. cit., p. 53. [63] *Rylands Eng. MSS*, 1076.
[64] Benham, op. cit., p. 47.

letter, Wesley speaks warmly of Nowers' Christian character, and anticipates some of his own later criticisms of the Brethren:

> The chief thing wherein I think them wrong is in mixing human wisdom with divine, in adding worldly to Christian prudence. And hence cannot but proceed closeness, darkness, reserve, diffusing itself through the whole behaviour. . . .[65]

There is a hint too of an attempt to limit John Wesley's power at Fetter Lane in a much earlier letter from Hutton, sent in November 1738.[66] To this letter, which informed Wesley that at a general meeting of the bands at Fetter Lane it had been decided that two monitors should be appointed 'to tell every one what faults are observed in him', and that lots should be cast for the choice of a president of the meetings, who would only 'see to the execution of what shall be determined by the whole Society,' Wesley replied:

> Every man in my band is my monitor, and I his; else I know of no use of our being in band. . . . What is proposed as to casting lots concerning a president seems liable to no exception. But you seem to design him nothing to do!

Writing the next day, he expresses his doubts about 'pastors appointed by the congregation', and adds:

> I believe you don't think I am (whatever I was) bigoted either to the Ancient Church or the Church of England. But have a care of bending the bow too much the other way. The National Church, to which we belong, may doubtless claim some, though not an implicit, obedience from us—

advice which, in the whirligig of time, the Brethren were to give to Wesley nearly half a century later!

On the disputed question of stillness, each side could make a good case. If Molther's and Hutton's description of their teaching as concerned with 'the free grace of the blood of Jesus' and 'the easy way of salvation as taught by the Brethren' is at all complete, there was not much with which the Wesleys could quarrel.

> *Strange all this difference should be*
> *'Twixt Tweedledum and Tweedledee!*

[65] *Letters*, I.342. [66] ibid., I.272, 274.

For Wesley himself believed in the restfulness of spirit, the open mind and inward ear, the waiting upon God, which are encouraged by silence. Moreover, even before his Aldersgate Street experience, the elder brother had begun to doubt the efficacy of ritualistic practices and even of the ethical aspects of religion. In his account of his conversion, he wrote of his regular fasting, his self-denial, his careful use, both in public and in private, of 'all the means of grace at all opportunities', and his pursuit of inward holiness.[67] He went on:

In this refined way of trusting to my own works and my own righteousness, . . . I dragged on heavily, finding no comfort or help therein till the time of my leaving England. On shipboard, however, I was again active in outward works; where it pleased God of His free mercy to give me twenty-six of the Moravian brethren for companions, who endeavoured to show me 'a more excellent way'. But I understood it not at first.

The Wesleys were not the only ones to feel some anxiety about Molther's teaching. The Countess of Huntingdon was disturbed about it, and her biography records:

At a meeting held at Lady Huntingdon's house it was unanimously agreed by Mr Ingham, Mr Stonehouse, and others that she should write an account of the proceedings (of the *still* Moravians) to M Wesley, and urge his presence in London as speedily as possible.[68]

The reference to Ingham and Stonehouse is of particular interest. Ingham was afterwards very friendly to the Brethren, though his letter to John Wesley, quoted above, shows that his conception of stillness differed considerably from that held by Molther; while Stonehouse seemed definitely influenced by Moravian teaching. According to Wesley's *Journal*, he had determined to sell his living, on the ground that no honest man could either officiate as a minister in the Church of England or join in its prayers, for, he said, 'they are all full of horrid lies'.[69] It was probably the exaggerated formulation of the doctrine of stillness which aroused Wesley's opposition, just as it was Molther's anxiety about Wesley's personal pride, and the excesses of some of his followers, which made him overstate his case. James Hutton, at first a close and intimate friend of the Wesleys, under

[67] *Journal*, I.469-70. [68] 1840, I.36. [69] *Journal*, II.349-50.

H

whose preaching he had himself been converted, and with whom he was to resume friendly relations late in the century, wrote severely about Wesley's pride in his letter to Zinzendorf on 14th March 1740:

John Wesley, being resolved to do all things himself, and having told many souls that they were justified, who have since discovered otherwise; and having mixed the works of the law with the Gospel as *means* of grace, is at enmity against the Brethren. . . . But he will have the glory of doing all things. I fear by and by he will be an open enemy of Christ and His Church.[70]

How far Hutton's assertion that both the Wesleys were 'dangerous snares to many young women' had any basis in fact it is difficult to discover; certain it is that they had a considerable female following. Of the seventy-two members who met at the Foundery on 23rd July 1740, two-thirds were women, as were many of those who were guilty of the extravagant manifestations which had so startled Molther on his arrival in England. In a list of nine Methodists who died in the joy of the faith, all were women.[71]

From Wesley's point of view, there were causes of dissension a good deal more potent than Quietism. The letter which he began in September 1738, but did not send, makes detailed criticisms which he amplified later. It is probable that those tendencies toward Universalism and Antinomianism which he afterwards censured so severely were already giving him some concern. But his immediate anxiety was about this special kind of Quietism, which he particularly disliked, and which threatened to corrupt his own little Society. It is possible that a more tactful approach by the Moravians might have secured, if not his support, at least his acquiescence—this is hinted at more than once by their own contemporary writers—but, as often happens, the extremeness of their advocacy encouraged him in extreme opposition.

And so an association which had promised so well for the two parties and for the Kingdom of God came to an end. Charles Wesley showed little regret at the time—'Oh, why was not this done six months ago?'[72]—though in later life he sought to bridge the gulf. Methodist writers on the whole have regarded the

[70] Benham, op. cit., p. 47. [71] e.g. *Journal*, II.413; 347, 377, 415, 457.
[72] Charles Wesley, *Journal*, I.239.

disruption as tragic, if only for the ill-feeling engendered, though they have found some consolation in the fact that henceforward Moravian and Methodist were able to pursue their evangelical aims in their own fashion. But this is perilously like 'sour grapes', for, as was to be seen, the evangelistic methods of the two Communions were not very different—Cennick's and John Wesley's remarkably alike—and each could have strengthened the other's hand. In any case, Wesley's separation from friends with whom he had been intimate—Hutton, Ingham, the Delamottes and especially Gambold—not only caused him heartache but seriously weakened his forces.

More than this was involved in the disruption; it was followed by rivalry and controversy, in which both sides said and did things which were unworthy of their Christian professions; and the two groups spent much time in establishing their own positions which might have been given with profit to the task of combating the evils of one of the most depraved ages of English history.

John Wesley did not give up without a struggle, and in a letter to Hutton on 14th November 1741, protested against his ill-treatment at the hands of the Brethren:

> I am afraid [he said] that the Moravian teachers who have been lately in London (I mean Mr Spangenberg, Molther, and the rest) have, with regard to my brother and me (I speak plainly), acted contrary to justice, mercy, and truth.[73]

In the first place, he accused the Count of 'poaching' at Fetter Lane, suggesting that if he, by analogy, preached at Herrnhut contrary to the judgement of Zinzendorf, he would be justly regarded as 'a robber on the highway'. They were unmerciful because they had allured his friends—Gambold, Hutchins, Kinchin, and Hall—from his fellowship. 'What use', he asked 'are these of to you now you have them?'—a question to which Gambold's great work for Moravianism later was a partial answer. And again he makes the charge of dissimulation, of reserve, darkness, and evasion 'so much', he says, 'that in very deed I know not now where to have you or how to understand what you say'. Wesley is not very convincing in this letter. After all, he had no monopoly in deciding what should be taught at Fetter Lane. Nor

[73] *Letters*, I.363-4.

is his analogy with his visit to Herrnhut a sound one. After all, Herrnhut was specifically a Moravian settlement; Fetter Lane was not necessarily a Methodist stronghold.

For a time after the separation, each society pursued its own course, the Moravians at Fetter Lane (where, in October 1742, they were constituted a 'Church' or 'Congregation, of the Unitas Fratrum' by Spangenberg, acting for Zinzendorf), and Wesley's followers at the Foundery. William Holland, who had been an instrument in Charles Wesley's conversion,[74] and perhaps in John's also, became the first Elder, and Hutton the Warden, of the Moravian Society. One coming event which cast a shadow happened on 16th December, when the first hint of a cleavage between Wesley and John Cennick became evident. Cennick, one of the most controversial figures in Methodist and Moravian history, had met John Wesley at Oxford, and soon became a Methodist preacher. Wesley authorized him to visit the sick, and to preach the Gospel, and gave him occasional employment in his charity school for the children of colliers at Kingswood, near Bristol. His early preaching had been accompanied by the sensational scenes to which Molther had taken such exception; but before long Cennick distrusted these manifestations, and, long before John Wesley's breach with Fetter Lane, Cennick had found himself out of touch with the methods and teaching of the two brothers. His objections were not merely on the question of the 'scenes': he objected to Wesley's doctrine of Christian Perfection, and later was himself attracted to predestinarianism. Indeed, it is one of the mysteries of religious history that a man who was so obviously sincere should, though a Calvinist, ally himself with the Moravians, with their tendencies toward Universalism. In *An Account of the Most remarkable Occurrences in the Awakening at Bristol and Kingswood till the Brethren's labours began there in 1746*, Cennick gives a hint of dissidence:

It was 17th April that people began to fall into fits under the discourses, especially as Mr Wesley began to preach perfection and to speak terribly out of the law. . . .

Some were offended and entirely left the Societies when they saw Mr Wesley encourage it. I often doubted if it was not the enemy when I saw it, and disputed with Mr Wesley for calling it the work of God; but he was strengthened in his opinion after he had wrote about it to

[74] See p. 64, *supra*.

Mr Erskine in Scotland (who at that time had made a great stir among the religious Scots) and had received a favourable answer. And frequently, when more were agitated in the meetings, he prayed, Lord, where are Thy tokens and signs? . . . and several more were seized and screamed out.

This is how he records his own revolt against 'scenes':

One day I walked by myself into the wood, and wept before the Saviour, and got again a sensible feeling of His presence and determined thenceforward to preach nothing but Him and His righteousness. And so all fits and crying out ceased wherever I came, and a blessing attended my labours. Only this opened a way for Mr Wesley and me to jar and dispute often, because, firstly, I could not believe or preach Perfection, and, secondly, I resolved to mention only the righteousness of Christ and the final perseverence of souls truly converted.

Later, speaking of the events of 1740, he writes:

In all this time Mr Wesley and I disputed often, and chiefly it was because they said if we have no other righteousness than the righteousness of Christ imputed to us we can't be saved. Also, that a soul justified—and having the assurance of forgiveness—can finally and eternally perish. Also that a man can become so perfect in this world that he shall not only not commit sin but he shall be without sin and be inherently holy as God. . . . We argued hotly, and sometimes both were to blame.[75]

As Cennick was not at this time a Moravian, this account may seem hardly relevant to the story of Wesley's separation from the Brethren, but in view of the later influence of Cennick, especially in the Moravian work in Ireland, it has a direct connexion with Wesley's subsequent attitude.

Wesley's first reference to this dissension is in his *Journal* for 16th December 1740:

The next evening Mr Cennick came back from a little journey into Wiltshire. I was greatly surprised when I went to receive him, as usual, with open arms, to observe him quite cold; so that a stranger would have judged he had scarce ever seen me before.[76]

A day or two later, he wrote:

[75] *W.H.S. Proceedings*, VI.101. [76] *Journal*, II.407-9.

I pressed him to explain his behaviour. He told me many stories which he had heard of me; yet it seemed to me something was still behind. . . . (He) now told me plainly he could not agree with me, because I did not preach the truth, in particular with regard to Election.

This was a new cause of dispute. Cennick's account, quoted above, reveals his disquiet at the convulsions of Wesley's followers (convulsions which he admits had attended his own preaching) and his disagreement with Wesley's doctrine of Perfection. He appears not to have been offended by 'stillness', but now showed definite leanings toward Calvinism. There is, of course, a link between Quietism and Calvinism. Both are a revolt against any undue emphasis on the importance and power of man; both can be related, though perhaps tenuously, to the doctrine of Justification by Faith alone. Indeed, as Wesley tells us, this attitude was behind the objection of Cennick and his followers at the crucial meeting at Bristol on 22nd February 1741: 'Mr Cennick . . . replied . . . that I did preach up man's faithfulness, and not the faithfulness of God.'[77]

At the Love-feast held the same evening, Wesley told the Society of the various separations in London, and accused Cennick of precipitating another conflict by his false teaching. A painful scene ensued. Wesley charged Cennick with 'stealing the hearts of the people, and, by private conversations, separating very friends',[78] and supported his charge by reading a letter which Cennick admitted having sent to Whitefield, and in which he said:

With Universal Redemption brother Charles pleases the world. I believe no atheist can more preach against Predestination than they; and all who believe Election are counted enemies to God, and called so.

The suggestion here that Charles had the greater initiative of the two brothers matches an earlier reference (23rd April 1740) in which Simpson alleged that 'all the confusion was owing to my brother, who would preach up the ordinances'.[79] If, as is implied, John relied so much on the younger brother (a picture not always given by recent writers), the discovery at this time that Charles was flirting with stillness must have come as a bitter blow. His *Journal* entry is brief and poignant:

[77] *Journal*, II.227. [78] ibid., II.427ff. [79] ibid., p. 343.

I began expounding where my brother had left off, viz. at the fourth chapter of the first Epistle of St John. He had not preached the morning before; nor intended to do it any more. 'The Philistines are upon thee, Samson.' But the Lord is not 'departed from thee'. He shall strengthen thee yet again, and thou shalt be 'avenged of them for the loss of thine eyes'.[80]

Peter Böhler seems never to have been committed to the doctrine of stillness, but two other friends of the younger Wesley certainly were, John Gambold and Westley Hall. A week later they called upon the Wesleys and urged that the only possible way to attain 'living, saving faith' was by 'silent prayer and quiet waiting upon God'.[81] Charles was certainly attracted by the Moravians at this time, and by Böhler in particular, and contemplated the possibility of going to Germany with him; but, he added:

I do not depart by reason of any alteration of my judgement (much less affection), but merely through weakness both of soul and body.[82]

Charles's threatened defection came to nothing, perhaps through the remonstrances of the Countess of Huntingdon, more probably through the gathering controversy with George Whitefield, a controversy in which he stoutly supported his brother.[83]

Meanwhile, trouble was still brewing in Bristol, and on 28th February 1741 John Wesley forced the issue by reading a paper, in which he sternly reproved those members of the band society in Kingswood who had 'made it their practice to scoff at the preaching of Mr John and Charles Wesley'; and then 'by the consent and approbation of the band-society', he declared them to be no longer members.[84] Cennick and two of his supporters, though shocked at first, soon recovered, and declared that they had heard both the brothers preach Popery, but would not admit that they themselves had been at fault. A week later, however, the trouble came to a head, and John Wesley plainly accused his critics of disloyalty, giving them the choice of quitting one society or the other. 'Then', he adds, 'after a short time spent in prayer Mr

80 *Journal*, II.418. 81 ibid., II.419.

82 Frank Baker, *Charles Wesley as revealed by his Letters* (1948), 41.

83 In a letter to John Wesley on 24th October 1741, Lady Huntingdon speaks of Charles having declared war on stillness, and of herself as being 'the instrument in God's hand that had delivered him from it'. *Life and Times of the Countess of Huntingdon*, I.41.

84 *Journal*, II.430.

Cennick went out, and about half of those who were present with him'.[85] Apparently, fifty-two left the Society and over ninety remained, a much higher proportion than in the final scene at Fetter Lane. John Wesley closes 'this melancholy subject' with a letter which he had received from his brother Charles, and in which Cennick is accused of disloyalty and desertion. It adds nothing to the subject, but merely repeats a charge, not a very fruitful way of healing a wound or preventing an injury. Moreover, there is a somewhat patronizing tone in some of the phraseology, as, for instance, when Charles speaks of his brother 'having humbled himself' by giving Cennick 'the right hand of fellowship', and of himself as having been 'condescendingly loving'.[86]

Strangely enough, Moravian historians do not mention this disruption, except to say that Cennick was dismissed by John Wesley on account of doctrinal differences on Election and Christian Perfection.[87] In view, however, of the importance of Cennick in Moravian history, neither his Methodist origins nor the facts of his quarrel with Wesley should be ignored.

Cennick's own account of these proceedings lets some light into the matter. He shows, for example, the danger which an idea may gather when adopted by the irresponsible: 'The persons *who said they were perfect* were chiefly Mr Nowers,[88] who often preached, 'I am the sinless perfect man'[89]—a claim which John Wesley certainly never made. Of his discussions with the Wesley brothers, he says:

> I assured them I knew no Calvinist in the world, nor believed reprobation, or in the least doubted of universal redemption; only I told them I should be glad to find a doctrine whereby the election and universal redemption should be made to agree. . . . The Perfectionists strove all this while daily with Mr Wesley against me, and at last before Christmas he forbade me to preach in the school any more, and without any noise I yielded and never did.

According to Cennick, Wesley agreed to discuss the matter of his expulsion (this agrees with Wesley's record); but, he adds: 'He publicly put me out by name. . . . Twelve men and twelve women followed me'.[90]

[85] *Journal*, II.433.
[86] ibid., p. 434.
[87] J. E. Hutton, op. cit., p. 319.
[88] See p. 101, *supra*.
[89] '*An Account of the most remarkable Occurrences in the Awakening at Bristol and Kingswood*' (*Wesley Historical Society Proceedings*, VI.101).
[90] *Journal*, II.431.

Apparently, about thirty others joined later. It is pleasing to note that, in spite of the separation, friendly intercourse continued. Wesley read Cennick's hymns, and helped him to prepare them for the Press.

It seems that Cennick had already become friendly with the Moravians.

> At the end of this year [he writes] I got acquainted with Br Telschig (Töltschig), who often came when I preached, and whom I loved dearly; but because he saw that Mr Wesley was about to break off from the Brethren in London, and knew he and I preached not directly the same, he would not speak much with me; only told me he loved me and wished I had more experience.

an honourable reluctance to proselytize which is typically Moravian.

Charles Wesley overcame the attractions of stillness very soon, for John records on 12th February 1741:

> My brother returned from Oxford, and preached on the true way of waiting for God; thereby dispelling at once the fears of some, and the vain hopes of others, who had confidently affirmed that Mr Charles Wesley was *still* already, and would come to London no more;[91]

but there are indications that his admiration for the Brethren persisted.

On 10th March, for instance, he wrote to his brother:

> I fear all is not right in your own breast, otherwise you would not think so hardly of them. Is there not envy, self-love, emulation, jealousy? Are you not afraid lest they should eclipse your own glory or lessen your own praise? Do you not give too much credit to all that you only hear of them? I am sure they are a true people of God. There is life and power amongst them.

There is probably some point in the suggestion that John Wesley was very ready to believe all he heard against the Brethren, whatever the source.

It was probably because of this predilection that John wrote to Charles on 21st April, a long letter, which the younger brother endorsed 'when I inclined to the Germans',[92] and in which he repeated his charges of Moravian 'closeness', self-indulgence, and neglect of good works, except to their own people; and adds:

[91] *Journal*, II.424. [92] *Letters*, I.352ff.

O my brother, my soul is grieved for you; the poison is in you; fair words have stolen away your heart. . . . So the matter is come to a fair issue. Five of us did still stand together a few months since: but two are gone to the right (poor Hutchings and Cennick); and two more to the left (Mr Hall and you). Lord, if it be Thy gospel which I preach, arise and maintain Thine own cause!

It is difficult to resist the conclusion that the vigour of this attack arose in the main from Wesley's fear of losing a supporter. His attitude to Stonehouse and Okely was to be very similar.[93] Most of his charges are very vague. It is difficult, moreover, to reconcile his charge of 'darkness and closeness' of behaviour with his continued good relations with some of their leaders. Apart from the conference with Böhler on 6th April, he had a further conversation, 'for several hours', with Böhler and Spangenberg on 2nd May,[94] others of his own supporters being present; and though there was considerable difference between them on the matter under discussion (Perfection), the disputants gave no sign of suspecting guile in their opponents. On 6th May a further meeting was held of all the bands, both men and women, to ask for God's will concerning reunion with the Fetter Lane Society; but it was clear that the time was not opportune.[95]

Some element of asperity seems, however, to have entered into the discussions, for Wesley's old friend, Gambold, declined to go to the Society with him.[96] With Ingham, nevertheless, he came to a partial agreement—on the necessity of good works by the justified—though they disagreed on Wesley's contention that the 'unjustified' should wait for faith in doing good. It is not difficult to understand why the Brethren should see in this insistence a substitution of works for faith.

There were approaches too from the Moravian side. The day before Wesley's long conversation with Böhler and Spangenberg, the former, always a peace-maker, had arranged a little Love-feast 'for those ten who joined together on this day three years' (i.e. at the formation of the Fetter Lane Society) ' "to confess our faults one to another" '. Seven of the ten, including the elder Wesley, were present, and John seems to have been stirred by happy memories. 'Surely the time will return', he says, 'when there shall be again "Union of mind, as in us all one soul".'[97]

[93] See pp. 189 and 140, *infra*. [94] *Journal*, II.451.
[95] ibid., II.453. [96] ibid., p. 472. [97] ibid., pp. 450-1.

On 3rd September 1741 came the remarkable conversation in Gray's Inn Walks between Wesley and Zinzendorf.[98] Wesley gives the bulk of it (which was in Latin) in his *Journal*, but does not translate it—'to spare the dead', he explains, for the edition in which this sentence appears was published after Zinzendorf's death in 1760. This restraint is puzzling, in view of his severe strictures on Zinzendorf some years later. The Count began the conversation by asking Wesley why he had changed his Church (*religionem*), and justified this assumption by referring to a letter which Wesley had written to him a year earlier.[99] In this letter, which is written in a distinctly didactic and indeed censorious tone, Wesley had repeated some of the charges made both before and after that time. He criticized Moravian doctrine, which, he said, conferred liberty to disobey God's commandments, to adapt themselves to the world's standards, and to avoid persecution by guile and dissimulation; he maintained again that there are degrees of faith; he condemned their neglect of the ordinances, and quoted some of their members who openly censured public prayer and sacrament; he accused them of pride, arrogance and self-satisfaction, and of despising other communions; he declared that they were disloyal to ancient tradition and that they followed the mystics; and maintained that they undervalued good works, and neglected opportunities of doing good.

In this letter Wesley revealed his strength and his weakness. He was right, or at any rate he was in accord with current theological opinion, and of the Moravians at a later date, in his protest against stillness; but in his other charges, as in his letter of September 1738,[100] he overstated his case, perhaps to convince himself, 'battering himself into a passion'. He was too narrow, for example, in his condemnation of the Brethren for 'conforming to the world'; he quoted, as evidence, the testimony of individuals, not necessarily Moravians (Bray, for instance); and his criticism of Moravian discipline was far removed from his praise in his letter to the Moravian Church which forms the Preface to Part IV of his *Journal*, and from his similar commendation in his letter to the Rev. Thomas Church.

Zinzendorf, in this conversation, retorted in much the same tone, accusing Wesley of being uncompromising, and of rebuffing the Brethren when, after offending him, they had begged his

[98] *Journal*, II.487-90. [99] *Letters*, I.345ff. [100] ibid., p. 257.

pardon. From this altercation, the two disputants proceeded to argue about Perfection, Wesley claiming that Christians may achieve perfection in this life, the Count denying this, and maintaining that there is no perfection except in Christ (a statement capable of two interpretations), that justification and complete sanctification take place at the same moment, that after that time there can be no growth in holiness, and ending with the astonishing statement:

We spurn all self-denial; we trample it under foot. Being believers, we do what we will, and nothing more. We ridicule all mortification. No purification precedes perfect love—

which is not easily reconciled with our Lord's words: 'If any man would come after me, let him deny himself, and take up his cross, and follow me' (Matt. 16^{24}).

It is useful to pause a little here, for Wesley's doctrine of Christian Perfection was as much a stumbling-block to the Moravians as stillness was to the Methodists. 'I recognize no inherent perfection in this life', said Zinzendorf. 'This is the error of errors—Christ is our sole perfection. Whoever seeks perfection denies Christ.' According to a letter written by Wesley on 26th December 1769 to Joseph Benson, the Headmaster of Lady Huntingdon's school at Trevecca, the Count declared that he would suffer no one in *his* Society who even *thought* of Perfection. Wesley comments: 'However, I trust you shall not only think of it but enjoy it.'[101]

John Roche, a Dublin clergyman, in 1751 attacked both Moravians and Methodists in *Moravian Heresy*. After criticizing 'the extravagant notions in which the Methodists and Moravians principally agree', by which he meant the doctrine of Assurance, he defined the point at which they diverged:

The Methodists hold [he said] that notwithstanding the gift [of the Holy Ghost] be instantaneous and saving, yet that it admits of perfection; and that those degrees are constituted by a faithful observation of, and obedience to, external means; which comprehend all the appointed ordinances of Christ, and every specie [*sic*] and degree of good works. They also hold that a perseverance is necessary to constitute such degree of perfection. And further they hold, that the pardon so brought by the gift is not so certain and absolute as that a

[101] *Letters*, V.166.

wilful neglect of, or breach in, the above duties will not annul this pardon, and render it ineffectual to the creature.

The Moravians hold the direct contrary: they teach that this gift cannot admit of any degrees of perfection or change whatsoever from the instant they receive it till death. That all the good acts we do cannot give us more strength of grace than we have nor make us more holy than we *are* the instant that we receive this gift. And also that no evil act, the most shocking and cruel, can abate its force or impede its efficacy. Likewise that the pardon it brings is absolute, certain and unchangeable, let the conduct of him that receives it be what it may: because (say they) *Christ changes not*.

This is no doubt a travesty of Moravian teaching, and Roche was a hostile critic, but it is significant as indicating the views held about Moravian theology ten years after Zinzendorf's own statement. Wesley felt it was not sufficient to recognize the imputed righteousness of Christ, and at the same time 'to forget that a righteous Master demands righteousness in His servants'.

Zinzendorf's language in the Gray's Inn conversation was undoubtedly extravagant. It widened the breach between Wesley and the Brethren. Henceforward the ways of Moravian and Methodist lay apart, and friendly discussion gave way to a discussion which was seldom fruitful and often acrimonious. Contemporary Moravian records emphasize the request for forgiveness, and imply that Wesley did not desire a reconciliation, for this would have continued an association which threatened to limit his powers.[102] This insistence upon his unwillingness to be pacified suggests that the offence given to him was of considerable magnitude. More probably, the Gray's Inn conversation revealed the extent of the difference between the two leaders if not between the Brethren and the Methodists, for on some points—the necessity of an agony of repentance and of instantaneous conversion—John Wesley had many supporters among the Moravians. Wesley was generally careful to differentiate between the beliefs of individuals among the Brethren and especially by those at Fetter Lane from the official doctrines of the Moravian Church. In his letter of 2nd February 1745 to the Rev. Thomas Church,[103] for instance, he says:

You commend them for loving one another; and yet charge them with biting and devouring one another. 'Them!' Whom? Not the

[102] *Letters*, II.81. [103] ibid., p. 185.

Moravians, but the English Brethren of Fetter Lane before their union with the Moravians;

while in the letter to the Moravian Church, 'more especially that part of it now or lately residing in England', which forms the Preface to the Part IV of his *Journal*, and with which the period of controversy may be said to have begun, he says: 'What unites my heart to you is the excellency (in many respects) of the doctrine taught among you.'[104]

How far Molther's opinions were his own, and how far they were shared by Moravian leaders, cannot easily be determined. Zinzendorf made little mention of stillness, Böhler even less, and Spangenberg's references to it were studiously vague, and may have proceeded from loyalty to his brother evangelist rather than from any convinced acceptance of his doctrinal views. On the other hand, it must be admitted that Wesley did not relish opposition, though he seemed to enjoy debating—on paper! Moreover, it must be remembered that if Molther differed from Böhler, Nitschmann from Gradin, the Wesley of one day was not necessarily identical with the Wesley of the day before. In a letter written to Samuel Wesley, John's elder brother, on 6th June 1738, James Hutton's mother records a wild speech in which he seemed to her son to 'despise the two sacraments.'[105] Mrs Hutton, however, could hardly be described as a judicial critic, for in the same letter she speaks of Wesley as 'not a quite right man', and declares that he 'was converted, or I know not what, or how, but made a Christian, on 25th May'—a rather haphazard description of an event which may have altered the course of history. Perhaps there was a little jealousy behind her attitude, for in a letter sent a fortnight later she described Wesley as 'my son's Pope'.[106]

SUMMARY

Out of the confused medley of suspicion and fear, of criticism and rebuttal, of argument and counter-argument recorded in the last two chapters, the following conclusions may be drawn:

(1) that for the first year of the fellowship at Fetter Lane peace and goodwill reigned;

(2) that there were underlying possibilities of friction which only awaited a suitable opportunity for their expression. These possibilities were to be found in

[104] *Journal*, II.309-11. [105] Benham, op. cit., p. 34. [106] ibid., p. 39.

(*a*) the growing influence of the Brethren;

(*b*) Wesley's suspicion of Zinzendorf's autocracy;

(*c*) his dislike of Moravian secretiveness, which seemed to him cowardly and dishonest;

(*d*) Moravian suspicion of Wesley's passion for power;

(3) that the doctrinal differences which arose would not have assumed great importance but for this background of suspicion and dislike. The foundation of these differences was a different emphasis on the doctrine of Justification by Faith, Wesley maintaining that the Christian life at all times needed support from the ordinances of the Christian Church, and especially from Holy Communion, and expression in 'good works', the Moravians fearing that this support and this expression might tend to take the place of the unique power of salvation in Christ Jesus;

(4) that the doctrines of stillness and perfection were the extreme outcome of this cleavage, which might have been reduced, if not bridged, by trust and goodwill; and

(5) that the preaching of Molther was only the occasion and not the cause of the separation in July 1740, and merely registered a cleavage which already existed.

CHAPTER SIX

MORAVIAN AND METHODIST AT VARIANCE

WHETHER or not Molther's views were the official views of the Moravian Church, henceforward the paths of Moravianism and Methodism lay apart—sometimes running parallel, sometimes, unhappily, crossing each other. The next few years saw what has been called 'The Battle of the Books', an attack on the Moravians in which John Wesley took some share, and a spirited defence and counter-attack by Zinzendorf. The controversy was not uniform in character: with some severe criticism was mingled no little appreciation. Spangenberg, for example, recognized 'the excellencies of Methodism, as well as its defects'[1] and Benham, who had access to the writings of James Hutton, admits that the establishment of the work of the Brethren in Yorkshire was following in the footsteps of the Methodists.[2] Here Ingham, who, though never officially accepted as a Moravian, had always been most friendly to the Brethren, had been remarkably successful, and had formed several societies, which, to the number of a thousand members, he had handed over to the Moravians in July 1742. This caused a definite separation between the Brethren and the Methodists in Yorkshire, though hostile critics still regarded them as one. It was probably conflicts of this kind which persuaded Wesley to write the 'Declaration to the Moravian Church, more especially that part of it now or lately residing in England', with which he prefaced Part IV of his *Journal*.[3] This declaration was written in June 1744, nearly three years after the famous conversation between Wesley and Zinzendorf in Gray's Inn Walk, and is studiously moderate and friendly in tone. It gives Wesley's reasons for publishing his own account of the dissensions and disruption, in order that Christians might be better able to judge (for most of those who had written about the Brethren had been prejudiced against them), and that the Moravians might look to themselves 'and fully discern how to

[1] Benham, *Memoirs of James Hutton*, p. 88 [2] ibid., p. 110.
[3] II.309-11

separate that which is precious from the vile'. He avows his reluctance to say anything which may be 'an obstacle to that union which I desire above all things under heaven'; he declares his admiration for the general purity of Moravian doctrine, their integrity of life, their philanthropic concern for their own numbers, and their healthy discipline; and he ends by inviting a reply.

In view of Zinzendorf's attack on the Wesleys as 'false teachers and deceivers of souls', on account of their doctrine of Christian Perfection, the restrained tone of this Declaration is magnanimous. It must be admitted, however, that the contents of the *Journal* (which, be it noted, was published) do not always maintain this high standard. In his letter of 8th August 1740, for example, Wesley severely criticized Moravian errors of doctrine and practice, and seemed more anxious to make a charge than to hear a defence.[4] It is true that he added some extracts from the reply which he received some weeks later, but in giving these (and omitting others) he returned to the attack, accusing the Brethren of lack of candour and of evasion, and adhering to his own conviction that the Sacrament of the Lord's Supper was 'a means of getting faith'. In this letter he amplified his frequently repeated charge of 'a close, dark, reserved conversation and behaviour', and made it clear that, in so far as the charge could be sustained this attitude arose from a reluctance to invite controversy or to give offence. 'You so studied', he wrote, ' "to become all things to all men" as to take the colour and shape of any that were near you. So that your practice was no proof of your judgement; but only an indication of your design *nulli laedere os*.' Wesley was not the only one to complain of this apparent 'guile and dissimulation', for Sir John Thorold, a much-respected 'gentleman of fortune', who had regularly attended the meetings at Hutton's house, had criticized the Brethren for 'not giving an open, conscientious confession of their faith' and 'disowning their tenets when driven to a pinch'.[5] Hutton had answered the former criticism by saying that 'the Brethren had, in the *Manual of Doctrine*, already published an open confession of their faith', and the latter by saying that it was 'simply untrue'. Hutton gave another cause of disagreement some years later in a reply which he made to a question by Zinzendorf.

[4] *Letters*, I.345, *Journal*, II.488; and see p. 113, *supra*

[5] Benham, op. cit., pp. 82-3.

'Why', asked Zinzendorf, 'was not a friendly relation established between us and Wesley?' 'Because', said Hutton, 'Wesley thinks he cannot rely upon your words.'[6] Both Methodists and Moravians had the same end in view—to combat the deadness of religion in the Church on the one hand and the prevailing spirit of scepticism outside the Church on the other; but this identity of aim did not save them from a controversy which was often bitter and always harmful. Wesley answered the charge of inconsistency by giving a brief account of his relations with the Moravians.[7] He told of his early admiration, especially of Peter Böhler, and of his growing doubts, as revealed in the undespatched letter of September 1738, now included (and perhaps amplified). He made it clear that, in spite of these doubts, his affection persisted, and indeed was at that time undiminished. He felt it his duty, however, to point out their 'three grand errors'—Universal Salvation, Antinomianism, and a kind of 'new-reformed Quietism'—and quoted, as evidence of this, Zinzendorf's *Seven Sermons on the Godhead of the Lamb* (1742) and *Sixteen Discourses*. He ended this section of his *Journal* by imploring the Brethren to 'separate the precious from the vile', purging themselves of Antinomianism, 'calling no man "Rabbi"' (a sore point, this!), 'renouncing all guile, and using great plainness of speech', and, finally, 'commending themselves to every man's conscience in the sight of God'.

There is little here that can be called acrimonious, though the questioning of his authority would hardly please Zinzendorf, and the frequent suggestions of 'craft, subtlety, cunning, dissimulation' must have been galling. The Brethren took exception to many passages in the *Journal*, and felt that Wesley had done them injustice. They did not however retaliate, but merely entered upon their minutes (12th July 1744):

> Mr Wesley has at length published his *Journal*, but he has not once mentioned the Brethren's asking his pardon. He has also mentioned his letter to the Church at Herrnhut,[8] but has not inserted their full answer. . . . He does not go on to our satisfaction at all, but as he does not belong to us, we have nothing to do with him.

Mrs Hutton, James Hutton's mother, at this time wrote a sharp letter to John Wesley, complaining of his contractions in his *Journal*, for 'praising the Brethren and then saying all he can

[6] Benham, op. cit., p. 113. [7] *Journal*, II.495-500. [8] ibid., II.495-500.

against them'. In his reply, Wesley answered certain specific charges which Mrs Hutton appears to have made against his followers—their belief in dreams and visions, their acceptance of 'fits' as certain marks of the Holy Spirit, their use of pew-rents—and then makes this striking statement (previously quoted):

I love Calvin a little, Luther more; the Moravians, Mr Law, and Mr Whitefield far more than either. I have many reasons likewise to esteem and love Mr Hutton. But I love truth more than all. Nor does it yet appear to me that he has dealt near so tenderly with me (since our opinions differed) as I have done with him.[9]

Mrs Hutton had always been hostile to John Wesley, but for his evangelistic zeal rather than for any difference of doctrine. In a letter to Wesley's elder brother on 6th June 1738, she said that on 28th May Wesley had surprised his hearers by saying 'that five days before he was not a Christian . . . and the way for them all to be Christians was to believe, and own that they were not now Christians'.[10] James Hutton was much surprised at this 'unexpected, injudicious speech', but only said: 'Have a care, Mr Wesley, how you despise the benefit of the two Sacraments.'[11] A strange turn of the wheel for Hutton, afterwards a spokesman of the Brethren, to champion the ordinances, and for Wesley to be accused of Antinomianism!

Wesley's preference in this letter for Law to Luther is somewhat surprising, in view of his revolt against Law's mysticism, and it is odd to find Law linked to the Moravians, from whom on the question of Justification by Faith he was so far removed.

Wesley answers the criticism that he had not mentioned the Brethren's request for pardon in a letter to Benjamin Ingham, who had taken up the cudgels on behalf of the Moravians:

'As to the English that really were to blame, they confessed their faults and asked Mr Wesley's pardon. And some of them, if I mistake not, did it with tears.' I really think you do mistake again. I remember no such thing. Fifty persons and more spoke bitter things concerning me. One or two asked my pardon for so doing, but in so slight and cursory a manner that I do not so much as know who were the men, neither the time or place where it was done—so far were they from doing it

[9] *Letters*, II.25.

[10] Benham, op. cit., p. 34.

[11] Here is Wesley's entry for that day: 'I was roughly attacked in a large company as an enthusiast, a seducer, and a setter-forth of new doctrines' (*Journal*, I.479).

with tears, or with any solemnity or earnestness at all. As for the rest, if they were ever convinced or ashamed at all, it is a secret to me to this day.[12]

The Wesleys include extracts from this part of the *Journal* in *A Short View of the Difference between the Moravian Brethren, lately in England, and the Rev. Mr John and Charles Wesley*, published in 1745, with a second edition three years later. After recounting the history of the dispute, the account summarizes, in ten propositions, the Moravian arguments, and then proceeds to controvert these propositions, one by one, as ambiguous, or contrary to the Scripture, to reason, or to experience, and ends:

All these we renounce, detest, and abhor. Whenever they publicly renounce them also, we shall wish them good luck in the name of the Lord, and rejoice to be their servants for Christ's sake.

Stillness seems to have unsettled many of the Wesley's societies, and this may account for the occasional bitterness of their comments. Charles Wesley, for instance, writes on 20th October 1743, of the Society at Nottingham:

They have been sifted like wheat by their two potent enemies, stillness and predestination. . . . One poor simple soul . . . confessed that the Germans had taken great pains to wean her of her bigotry to the Church and ordinances; they laughed at her reading the Scriptures; at her praying, and fasting, and mourning after Christ. When she quoted any Scripture-proof, they set it aside with, 'O, that you must not mind; that is all head-knowledge'.[13]

(It will be remembered, on the other hand, that Scriptural 'watchwords' were regularly used by the Brethren.)[14] He writes again, on 24th August 1744:

I joined my brother in stirring up the Society [at Oxford]. They did run well, till the Moravians turned them out of the way of God's ordinances;[15]

and again on 16th November 1745:

I brought back (with the extraordinary blessing of God) two wandering sheep from the Germans;[16]

[12] *Letters*, II.81. [13] Charles Wesley, *Journal*, I.337.
[14] See p. 31, *supra*. [15] Charles Wesley, *Journal*, I.380. [16] ibid., I.407.

and on 23rd December 1746:

I met my old friend, J.G. [Gambold] at my printers, and appointed to meet him tomorrow at Dr Newton's. I brought my brother with me. I found the Germans had quite estranged and stole away his heart; which nevertheless relented while we talked over the passages of our former friendship, but he hardened himself against the weakness of gratitude, nor could we prevail upon him to meet us again.[17]

The elder brother similarly says on 3rd January 1743:

I rode to Birstall, where John Nelson gave a melancholy account of many that *did* run well. I told him I was as willing they should be with the Germans as with us, if they did but grow in grace. He said: 'But that is not the case. They grow worse instead of better.'[18]

Nelson was particularly bitter in his criticism. He met some friends in London, and asked how John Wesley was. They replied:

We do not know; poor dear man, he is wandering in the dark; but we hope our Saviour will open his eyes, and let him see that he is a blind leader of the blind. . . . He is under the law, and does not know the privilege of the gospel himself, therefore he preaches law and works. . . . They told me that I had never heard the gospel in my life, except I had heard the Brethren that preached in Fetter Lane; for they were the men that were to come to lead them into true stillness [which was] to cease from your own works, such as fasting and prayer, reading the Bible, and running to Church and Sacrament; and wholly to rely in the blood and wounds of the Lamb.[19]

Nelson goes on:

They told me that most of the people who had followed him (Wesley) before I left London had forsaken him, and were become happy sinners now; and wished I would go and hear the Brethren, for Mr Wesley was only a John Baptist to go before and prepare them for the Brethren to build up.[20]

Nelson gives a hint of dissension in the Moravian camp when he relates how Peter Böhler came to see him:

[17] Charles Wesley, *Journal*, I. 408. [18] *Journal*, III.62.

[19] John Nelson, *Journal* (1795), pp. 22-3.

[20] John Nelson, *Diary*, quoted in *Early Methodist Preachers* (1865), I.31, 46, 48.

'His conversation was profitable to me, for he spoke as contrary to the Moravians who are in London as black is to white. . . . He said, to confess Jesus was to live to Him, and to honour Him with body, soul and substance.'

Apparently, complaint was made about Böhler to Töltschig, for afterwards Böhler's attitude showed a marked change.

At this time, Ingham seemed thoroughly at one with the Brethren, for, according to Nelson, he refused to receive the sturdy Yorkshireman into his church. Nelson retorted: 'I don't want to be one of you; for I am a member of the Church of England.' . . . 'He answered, "The Church of England is no Church: we are the Church." I said, "Well who do you mean?" He replied, "I and the Moravian Brethren".'

Nelson also records an incident in which 'one of their exhorters' claimed that there were several of the Moravian preachers who could write 'as good Scriptures as the Bible, and that the very power that the Apostles had did rest on the Moravian Preachers.'

No doubt many extravagant things were said by both sides. Nelson himself was hardly of a judicial cast of mind, and was so suspicious of the Moravians that he said he would rather die than live to see his children 'devoured by these bears out of the German wood'. Examples of actual conflict are strikingly few in number, and the paths of the rival communions generally ran in parallel lines. John Cennick, indeed, had made an attempt to unite them. On 6th May 1742, as has been mentioned, he had expressed the hope to Mrs Whitefield that the Calvinists, the Moravians, and the Methodists might meet together with a view to union. 'Who knows', he asked, 'but we might unite? Or if not, we might consent in principles as far as we can, and love one another. At least, I think all *our* preachers should meet, as the apostles did, often.'[21] Unhappily, the conference did not take place. John Wesley travelled from Newcastle, John Nelson from Yorkshire, and Charles Wesley from Land's End, but the Moravians were not present, though Spangenberg had indicated his intention to be present. It is probable that at this time, Zinzendorf still clung to the hope that the Moravian Church in England might be recognized as in communion with the Anglican Church, and that he feared the separatist tendencies of both Calvinists and Methodists. It is interesting to notice that John Wesley does not

[21] Page 81, *supra*.

mention this proposed conference, though he does speak of a wide-spread desire that his followers should unite with the followers of Whitefield.[22]

This was not, however, the last attempt at union. Two years later, on 8th December 1745, John Wesley wrote to the Synod at Marienborn, suggesting a conference in order to consider points of agreement and disagreement, and the possibility of union.[23] Howell Harris, the Welsh Calvinist, who had sympathies with both parties, in spite of a sharp rebuff by the Brethren of Fetter Lane in March 1746, earnestly wished for a reconciliation. In his *Diary* of 1764 and 1765 he wrote:

I had a spirit to love them as little children . . . all the six branches to meet . . . viz. Moravians, Wesleys, Whitefield, Clergy, Dependents, and the (Methodists).[24]

On 1st January 1753 Harris had written a long letter to John Wesley in which he said: 'I wish your ministry and that of the Moravians were united. It would be for the public good.' There is some evidence both of the good will of the Brethren towards Harris and of their suspicion of the Methodists in the *Minutes* of the English Provincial Synod of 1761, in which the opinion is expressed that they 'must hear Mr Harris with love and respect, through whom perhaps may come a leaven of truth and grace among the Methodists'.[25] In the same account, the Moravians go on to accuse the Wesleyan Methodists of having slandered them, and further of creating a schism within the Established Church. Of much greater importance were the negotiations of 1785-6, in which Charles Wesley, Coke, Loretz, and Benjamin La Trobe were concerned, and of which further mention is made later.[26] For the time being, the relationship was polite if not friendly. In 1744, for example, Wesley published extracts from Zinzendorf's *Berlin Addresses*.

In February 1745 and June 1746 Wesley published his remarkable letters to the Rev. Thomas Church, Vicar of Battersea, who had attacked him for his connexion with the Moravians in a pamphlet entitled *Remarks on the Reverend Mr John Wesley's last Journal*.[27] Wesley's first letter is a closely-reasoned argument, in

[22] *Journal*, III.84. [23] *Letters*, II.54, and p. 135, *infra*.

[24] Benham, *Memoirs of James Hutton*, pp. 189-91. *Cylchgrawn Cymdeithas Hanes Eglwys Methodistiaid Calvinaidd Cymru*, XXXI, No. 3.

[25] *Rylands Eng. MSS*, 1055. [26] See p. 157, *infra*. [27] *Letters*, II.175-276.

which (*a*) he defends himself against the charge of 'too much commending the Moravians' by quoting extracts from his *Journal*, and (*b*) he stoutly champions the Brethren against some of the allegations made against them. He gives a shortened version of the letter which he had begun in September 1738, and which he gives in a fuller form in his *Journal*[28]—his restraint in thus abbreviating it is some indication of his goodwill—and not only confutes some of the accusations made against the Moravians but goes far to convince himself. In his second letter, which is entitled *The Principles of a Methodist farther explained*, and which answers a second letter from Mr Church (who had accused Wesley 'of having to some extent given rise to the errors which he lays at the door of the Moravian Church'), he distinguishes between the Moravians and the English Brethren, and makes this striking *amende*:

> I think it incumbent upon me to say, that whereinsoever I have contributed, directly or indirectly, to the spreading of anything evil, which is or has been among the Moravians, I am sorry for it, and hereby ask pardon both of God and all the world.

In these most interesting letters, he points out:

(1) that the practice of the Moravians was better than their principle;

(2) that his regard for the Moravians had lessened even while he was in Georgia, but had increased again after his return, especially while he was in Herrnhut (a convincing refutation of the suggestion made by some writers that the refusal of the Sacrament to him at Marienborn began his resentment);[29]

(3) that the charge of scandalously trampling upon religion and virtue could not be sustained;

(4) that the charge of 'closeness and darkness and guile' did not apply to Christian David, Michael Linner, and others;

(5) that Molther had been withdrawn.

He pays this high tribute, one which he was to repeat in a letter to Benjamin Ingham:[30]

[28] II.496.

[29] Wauer, *The Beginnings of the Brethren's Church in England*, p. 66; Benham, op. cit., p. 40; Tyerman, *Life and Times of the Rev. John Wesley*, I.199; Hutton, *History of the Moravian Church*, p. 295.

[30] *Letters*, II.80.

I cannot speak of them otherwise than I think. And I still think (i) that God has some thousands in our Church who have the faith and love which is among them without those errors either of judgement or practice; (ii) that, next to them, the body of the Moravian Church, however mistaken some of them are, are, in the main, of all whom I have seen, the best Christians in the world.

This is John Wesley at his best, and is so far removed from some of his later writings, notably his letter to Stonehouse, as to demand some explanation.[31]

The solution is to be found, in part at any rate, in two circumstances. Contemporary opinion, official and popular, regarded Moravians and Methodists as of the same stock. Both were apparently separatist, both adopted evangelical methods which were foreign to accepted Church practices, both were 'enthusiasts', though their 'enthusiasm' took different forms, both were, quite unjustly, suspected of disloyalty to the reigning House. The critics of one were generally critics of the other. As early as 1740 a pamphlet attacking 'a certain modern sect of enthusiasts, called Methodists' had been addressed by William Bowman, Vicar of Dewsbury, to his parishioners. As yet the Wesleys had not been in Yorkshire, and he was probably thinking of the work of Ingham and Delamotte, who had already had startling results. Of these, Delamotte was in close touch with the Moravians, and Ingham was within a year or two to hand over his Societies to the Brethren. A pamphlet of the Rev. Josiah Tucker, published in 1742, attempted to show that the Methodists, after having been first the disciples of William Law, *then of the Moravians*, were now 'a medley of Calvinism, Arminianism, Quakerism, Quietism and Montanism, all thrown together', and Wesley stoutly defends his teaching against this attack in *The Principles of a Methodist*. Further controversy was precipitated by a pamphlet published anonymously, but known to be written by Dr Gibson, Bishop of London. In this pamphlet, which was entitled *Observations upon the Conduct and Behaviour of a certain Sect usually designated by the name of Methodists*, some reference was made to the Moravians as 'a new sect'. This so hurt the Count's pride (or loyalty) that he not only wrote a letter to the Bishop, in which he spoke of 'the trackless wilds of Methodism', but published in the *Daily Advertiser* of 2nd August 1745, a Declaration in which he stated that the

[31] *Letters*, III.52, and p. 139, *infra*.

Moravians had now no connexion with the Wesleys. In a later letter to the Bishop, he wrote:

> The author of the aforesaid writing is plainly mistaken, confounding Moravians with Methodists; the Methodists themselves being far from allowing it, and it being very difficult to decide whether the Moravians have a greater dislike to the Methodists' plan of salvation, or the Methodists to that of the Moravians. Methodism, as we comprehend it, being a pure means of reintroducing through another door, though more refined, the old *opus operatum*, and sadduceeism become phariseeism, and now transmuted into enlarged esseneism.[32]

Zinzendorf was quite justified, of course, in disowning all connexion with the Methodists, but unfortunately he went further than this, and threw out a hint that Methodists were willing servants of sin, and that they would 'soon run their heads against the wall'. On this, Wesley has a philosophic comment:

> Many of our friends were grieved at the advertisement which James Hutton had just published, by order of Count Zinzendorf, declaring that he and his people had no connexion with Mr John and Charles Wesley. But I believed that Declaration would do us no more harm than the prophecy which the Count subjoined to it—that we should soon run our heads against the wall. We will not, if we can help it.[33] You declare . . . if a controversy should arise from this declaration, you will not meddle with it in any way. That is, you strike a man on the head as hard as you can, and then declare you will not fight.

Wesley's reply is addressed to 'That part of the People called Methodists who are commonly styled the Moravian Brethren', and includes the following caustic comment:

> You are safe! No controversy will arise on my part from any declaration of this kind. Your unusual conduct does not hinder me from still embracing you with candour and love.[34]

There is a noticeable change of tone and temper in these effusions, a new note of asperity and a subordination of doctrinal difference to personal antipathy, in spite of the lavish professions, in both declaration and reply, of 'candour and love'. It is not surprising to find the controversy becoming increasingly bitter. During the same year (1745), Wesley published two other tracts, *A Dialogue between an Antinomian and his friend* and *A Second Dialogue between an Antinomian and his friend.* These are not

[32] Benham, op. cit., p. 165. [33] *Journal*, III.206. [34] *Letters*, II.40.

avowedly an attack on the Moravians. 'Antinomian' is a term of very vague connotation, and Wesley cannot be exonerated from the charge of using it too freely and indefinitely. These pamphlets were written in reply to a Dialogue published by William Cudworth, an Independent minister, of whom Wesley spoke with a disparagement approaching bitterness,[35] but the opening words are so similar to the Gray's Inn conversation with Zinzendorf that it seems probable that an attack on the Moravians was intended.

The Moravians denied and indeed resented the charge of Antinomianism, and at several of their Synods at this time they laid stress on the need for a gradual growth in inherent righteousness of character. It took them a long while to live down the impression given by Molther, who had decried the necessity of the commonest Christian duties, and at one time by Zinzendorf, who had expressly denied any gradual growth in inherent righteousness.[36]

The second explanation of Wesley's change of tone is to be found in the internal history of the Moravian community, which was at that time passing through deep waters. It was the 'Sifting Time', a period of seven years when the Brethren at Herrnhaag, at the instigation of the Count himself, sentimentalized their relations with one another, adopted gross physical analogies for their relationship with Christ, indulged in high and even riotous living, spoke with complete lack of restraint about sexual matters, and over-emphasized the 'blood and wounds' of Jesus in their hymns. Though these practices were quite unworthy of Christians who had so vigorously protested against the 'convulsions' of the early Methodists, and though Zinzendorf cannot be excused, however high his evangelistic zeal, for his indiscretions, it must be remembered that the worst features of the 'Sifting Time' did not last long, and that no one condemned its excesses more than the Brethren themselves, and especially the English Brethren. After all, one does not judge Wordsworth by 'The Idiot Boy' or Beethoven by 'The Battle of Vittoria', and there are chapters in the history of every Church which are best forgotten.

But though this distressing period did not last long, it left its mark on contemporary judgements, and laid the Moravian Church as a whole open to criticisms which only a small part of it had

[35] *Journal*, IV.302-3, VI.511.

[36] See pp. 89 and 114, *supra*.

deserved. It had already been attacked (in 1743) by Gilbert Tennent, an American, whose book, *Some Account of the Principles of the Moravians*, was published in an English edition, and did immense harm to the Brethren. It went far beyond any criticism that John Wesley had made: it accused the Moravian leaders of exercising a tyrannical control over the lives of their followers; it charged them with despising learning and reason; and it insinuated that they were Papists in disguise, a dangerous accusation in an age which within forty years was to see the Gordon Riots. In very self-defence the Moravians had to establish themselves, and the petition presented in the House of Commons, which owed much to the support of Oglethorpe, was a masterpiece of wise and effective advocacy. On 12th May 1749 an Act was passed which recognized the Episcopal nature of the Moravian Church, granted its members the privilege of affirming in place of taking the oath in all cases of law, at home as well as in the Colonies, and, by implication, exonerated them from the charge of disloyalty. But it did more than that: it marked the end of Zinzendorf's dream of a Tropus, of an *ecclesiola in ecclesia*, and recognized the independence of the Moravian Church in England of the Church of England. Perhaps it was its very success which caused the outburst of attack which followed; perhaps the Brethren themselves precipitated the conflict of words, now feeling strong enough to meet and refute the criticisms of Wesley and the rest; for they seem to have fanned the smouldering embers by sending a communication to the *London Daily Post*, in which they drew attention to a supplement of the *Büdingische Sammlung* which gave Wesley's conversation with Zinzendorf in Gray's Inn Walks, as well as his dedication of Part IV of his *Journal* and his sharp criticism of Luther's *Commentary on the Epistle to the Galatians*. The Brethren seem to have been particularly disturbed by Wesley's dedication to Part IV of his *Journal*, which on the face of it is mild enough and even complimentary.[37] *The Short View* and the two *Dialogues* are certainly severe, especially the last-named, but, unlike Gilbert Tennent's book, they do not specify the Moravians by name, and, at their worst, they cannot compare in severity with other writings of the time, and especially with the later writings of Oldknow, Roche, Whitefield, Rimius, Frey, and Lavington.

Here is the letter to the *London Daily Post*:

[37] II.309-11.

SIR,

Whosoever reckons that those persons in England who are usually called Moravians and those who are called Methodist are the same, he is mistaken. That they are not the same is manifest enough, out of the declaration of Louis, late Bishop and Trustee of the Brethren's Church, dated at London, March, 1745, which I here send you . . .;[38]

and here is Wesley's comment:

The Methodists, so-called, heartily thank brother Louis for his Declaration; as they count it no honour to be in any connexion either with him or his Brethren.

But why is he ashamed of his name? The Count's name is Ludwig, not Louis; no more than mine is Jean or Giovanni.[39]

Wesley's rather trivial complaint about the Count's name is paralleled by a similar entry on 15th September 1750:

I read over a short *Narrative of Count Zinzendorf's Life*, written by himself. Was there ever such a Proteus under the sun as this Lord Freydeck, Domine de Thurstain, &c., &c.? For he has almost as many names as he has faces or shapes. Oh when will he learn (with all his learning) 'simplicity and godly sincerity'? When will he be an upright follower of the Lamb, so that no guile may be found in his mouth?[40]

Zinzendorf's titles were used when he travelled incognito, but Wesley's gibe can hardly be called worthy controversy.

There was obviously some personal dislike here, but there is good evidence for believing that the English Moravians in general cherished no animosity against the Wesleys and their followers. There is an illuminating document in the Moravian Archives at Herrnhut, which reveals the attitude of representative English Brethren during this period of controversy. It is headed: *Minutes of the Committee for finding out the first Aim and Intention of our Saviour by the Awakening in England going under the name of Methodism, how and in what respects this Aim and Intention has been deviated from and in what manner it might best be restored again.*[41] It relates how the movement began with the Holy Club in 1729, though it does not use this title, and how 'Br. Ingham

[38] Original at Moravian Headquarters, Muswell Hill, London.

[39] *Journal*, III.435.

[40] ibid., p. 495.

[41] Copy in Rylands Library, *Eng. MSS*, 1057.

was the first that began what was called a Society, at Osset in Yorkshire'. It then makes this candid admission:

Br. Molther was certainly to blame afterwards in being too positive and rough toward the Methodists and Jno Wesley in particular. This disgusted Jno Wesley, who had already taken some offence in Germany, and from hence he took an occasion first to find fault with Molther's doctrine, and then to make the first separation of the Fetter Lane Society. [There is a marginal note by Zinzendorf here: 'Very surely—but the errors of Br. John!']

Had Molther let J. Wesley be the head [the account goes on], and had he done all things under him, as his servant, he might have done with him what he pleased. Jno Wesley was the beginner of the Fetter Lane Society. . . .

That a misunderstanding and variance began so soon between some of the Methodists and the Brethren was a great pity. It would have been better if the Brethren could have borne with the mistakes and defects of the Methodists [Another marginal note by Zinzendorf: '*Ob in die Welt-hinaus*, I do not know.'] . . . and have wrought upon that which was good in them. Could not the Methodists have been looked upon as a kind of parish which our Saviour designed to put under the care of the Brethren? Have they not been too much overlooked and despised? . . . It is remarkable that the Brethren have got very few but what were Methodist before and they might have got a great many more. . . . Whether it may not be our Saviour's will to remove these objections as far as may be? It appears by all accounts that this is not too far gone to be redressed.

Perhaps this is a time when the Brethren might come under some sort of Tropus, and explain themselves so that the world and all serious people and men of sense might be undeceived in regard to them, they having been charged by Mr Jno Wesley, and looked upon everywhere as a close, secret, and designing people. And this is the most dangerous prejudice now reigning against them in England. . . .

We should now do all in our power to keep in connexion with the Church of England, and some way to shelter under her; this would bring over the most souls to us and free us from the charge of being Dissenters and making a separation. But if this cannot be attained we can always tell the Church of England that they force us from them, and we can go under the denomination of Brethren, as we are most commonly called by most people in Yorkshire and elsewhere.

This important document, which is dated 18th May 1747, is signed 'Ingham, J. Gambold, J. Cennick, F. Okely, Scriba', and is followed by a note in Zinzendorf's writing:

I desire out of a very simple and evident reason that every Brother would be pleased to subscribe to this very plan, and that done I shall lay it for [? before] the Synod. Your poor Br. Lewis.

It makes it clear:

(1) that there was still some hope of a reconciliation with the Methodists;

(2) that there was still some suspicion of the ambition and hostility of John Wesley;

(3) that the Brethren owed their numbers in large part to the Methodists;

(4) that the suspicion of the Brethren's 'closeness and secretiveness' was commonly held, and was not merely an opinion held by the Wesleys, though they may have begun it and increased its currency;

(5) that the Brethren were prepared, as the Methodists were, to leave the Church of England if they could not find scope for their evangelical zeal within it. In view of the criticism expressed by La Trobe and Loretz at the time of the abortive negotiations of 1785-6, on the ground that John Wesley intended to separate from the National Church, this suggestion as early as 1747 is of particular interest.

The inclusion of Ingham's name at the head of the signatures is also noteworthy in view of the statement made by modern Moravians that he was never a member of the Moravian Church.[42]

Did Ingham try to 'run with the hare and hunt with the hounds?' It is noteworthy that though, on 11th June 1740, he 'bore a noble testimony for the ordinances of God and the reality of weak faith',[43] within a month he had associated himself with the Moravians, to whom, a year later, he handed over his Yorkshire Societies; and that he was present, not only at the General Synod of the Brethren at Herrnhaag in 1747, but, as an observer, at the Methodist Conference of 1755.

It seems plain that he was deeply disturbed at the friction between the Methodists and the Moravians, and that, though he

[42] Hutton, op. cit., p. 304. James Hutton, writing to Zinzendorf in March 1740, says: 'Ingham and Delamotte are united to the Brethren' (*Memoirs*, p. 47), but L. G. Hassé, in a pencilled note at Fairfield College, says that Ingham was never admitted ecclesiastically to membership.

[43] *Journal*, II.352.

handed over his Societies to the Brethren, and was therefore in the main the pioneer of their work in Yorkshire, he was not completely satisfied with their attitudes. He raised new Societies—there are still 'Inghamite' churches in Lancashire—and seems to have sought some association with Methodism; for at the Methodist Conference of 1752, Methodists were warned to be very much on their guard against the Moravians, and were advised that although friendship with 'Benjamin Ingham and his Societies' was desirable, there could be no real reunion with him until he returned to 'the old Methodist doctrine'.[44]

It is probable that Ingham was too much of an individualist to commit himself entirely to either Communion. His extravagant claim on behalf of the Brethren in his conversation with John Nelson may be explained in part by his lack of sympathy with Nelson and his methods, and was probably deliberately provocative.[45] Moreover, his close association with the Wesleys in the Holy Club and in Georgia might make him reluctant to break off all connexion with them.

Two days later a Second Committee of the English Brethren met, eleven being present, with Francis Okely again as Scribe, and the substance of its deliberations was as follows: 'Our Saviour's design by the Methodists was without doubt to put a life into the Church of England.' After correcting the previous statement that John Wesley had founded the Fetter Lane Society, the Minutes go on:

> Had the Methodists went [*sic*] on as they began under cover and in the way of the Church of England, in all probability the numbers of awakened people would have been greater and we might have had truth and discipline enough to have saved our souls; but it is quite certain that we could never have been so well and happy and so thankful in that way as we now are by being settled in congregations.

This may help to explain the reluctance of the Moravians to enter into closer negotiations for union.

The Minutes pay a tribute to the Methodists (and to previous influences):

> In one sense we were, all to a man, awakened by the Brethren, but in the common sense of that word most of us seem to have been first awakened either by the Methodists or before that time.

[44] *Minutes of Conference* (1802 ed.), pp. 707-8. [45] See 124, *supra*.

There is another intimation of a possible reconciliation in this:

As our accommodation with and reconciliation to those Methodists who still have something in their hearts toward our Saviour is a very desirable thing, and would be one good step toward recovering our Saviour's first plan with the Methodists in general, especially if this could be done by the advice and mediation of the Brethren, would it not be proper to propose a sort of Synod to the teachers and directors of the Methodists something like that in Pennsylvania?

John Wesley gives frequent hints and intimations that he would be glad of an accommodation and friendship with us, if brought about with honour.

Wesley had already given some evidence of his desire for friendship, if not for reconciliation. On 8th December 1745, after Cennick's departure for Germany, he and his brother had written a letter 'To the Synod of the Moravian Brethren at Marienborn':

MY BRETHREN,

Is it not the will of our Great Shepherd to gather together in one all His sheep that are scattered abroad? Our earnest desire is that this His will may be done. And we are ready to do anything in our power that may in any degree contribute thereto.

If you are willing any of your brethren should confer with us, we are ready, and should rejoice therein.

Might we not, in a free and brotherly conference,

1. See in what points we do already agree together;

2. Consider what points (wherein we do not yet agree) we might suffer to sleep on either side; and

3. Settle how far we might unite, what kind or degree of fellowship we might preserve with each other, even if there should be some points wherein we cannot avoid speaking contrary to each other?

We desire your answer to this proposal, which is made in simplicity of heart by

Your affectionate brethren,
JOHN WESLEY,
CHARLES WESLEY.[46]

There is no record of any reply to this invitation, which is not mentioned by Benham, or, indeed, by any Moravian historian. On 8th September 1746 Wesley wrote his long letter to Benjamin Ingham,[47] in answer to one in which Ingham had defended the Brethren against some of Wesley's accusations. He had, averred Ingham, misunderstood what the Moravians meant by stillness;

[46] *Letters*, II.54. [47] ibid., II.80.

they had not undervalued the ordinances; he had blamed the whole Moravian Church for the imprudences of a few members of the Fetter Lane Society; he had rebuffed those who had 'confessed their faults' and asked his pardon; he had reported unfairly. After answering these points in detail, Wesley paid the warm tribute to the Moravians previously mentioned, and then expressed his earnest desire for union with them. In two letters to William Holland, the first Congregational Elder of the Moravian Church in England,[48] John Wesley declared his continued goodwill. In the first, on 6th February 1748, he wrote:

I was at first a little surprised that the Brethren should so obstinately persist in accounting me their enemy;[49]

and again, on 20th April of the same year:

I have had some trials myself lately from those who are in union with them. I seek for peace; but when I speak unto them thereof, they make themselves ready for battle. . . . They seem determined to believe not one word I say. So much the more may I confirm my love toward them.[50]

The Moravians too frequently declared their desire for peace, and went out of their way to avoid a clash—and also, it is to be feared, to avoid co-operation. At the English Provincial Synod of 1747, held at Fetter Lane, the business 'gave occasion to remind the Conference of our plan with Mr Wesley and the Methodists, consisting in this, that we don't want to be in their way, or to oppose them, but go out of their way as much as possible lest they run against us'.[51] This seems to have been prompted by the fact that both Communions had Societies at Kingswood and Bristol. Again, at the Synod of 1771, some years after Zinzendorf's death,

it was the general opinion of all the Brethren that it would be in vain to attempt a coalition with the Methodists; anything of this kind might prove destructive of our call and destiny; but on the other hand we ought to treat them and their preachers in a friendly manner, particularly whenever they themselves make an overture, and we should be very careful never to speak to their disadvantage, particularly to strangers.[52]

[48] See pp. 64–6, *supra*. [49] *Letters*, II.116. [50] ibid., p. 145.
[51] Rylands *Eng. MSS*, 1054. [52] ibid., 1054, 1056.

The Moravian suspicion of John Wesley's enmity persisted, though there is no adverse reference to the Brethren in Wesley's *Journal* or *Letters* or publications at this time. Indeed, the only mention in the *Journal* is a defence of the Moravians against the animadversions of Lord Lyttelton.[53] Nevertheless, years later, when the 'Battle of the Books' had ended, and some sort of *rapprochement* between the Wesleys and James Hutton had taken place, the Synod of 1771 declared:

John Wesley seems yet too full of enmity; however we will take no notice of it; it is to be hoped he may one day know himself and the ground of his enmity; after all, souls will be saved who are not of our fold.[54]

But much was to happen before the Synod of 1771.

Unhappily, nothing more was heard of the admirable suggestion made by the English Committee at Herrnhaag. Benham, who had obviously seen the account of these deliberations, makes no reference to it, and there is no indication on Wesley's part that it ever reached him. The unfortunate 'Battle of the Books' therefore continued. In order to set at rest rumours that the Act of Parliament of 1749 had been obtained by subterfuge, Zinzendorf published a comprehensive folio volume, entitled *Acta Fratrum Unitatis in Anglia*, which not only gave the necessary documentary evidence which had been produced before the Parliamentary Committee, but supplied a detailed account of Moravian doctrine and practice. It ended with an invitation to the reader to ask for further information. In reply, there appeared a pamphlet summarizing and attacking Zinzendorf's book, entitled *The Contents of a Folio History of the Moravians or United Brethren, printed in 1749, and privately sold under the title of* '*Acta Fratrum Unitatis in Anglia*', by 'A Lover of the Light'. The authorship of John Wesley has been generally accepted, by writers as diverse as G. A. Wauer, Tyerman, Hutton, and R. A. Knox; while in the British Museum Catalogue it appears with the initials J.W. in brackets after it. Yet, in spite of this formidable consensus of opinion, Wesley's authorship is by no means established. The pamphlet begins thus:

The religious Societies under the care of the Reverend Mr J. and C. Wesley, Mr Whitefield and the Moravians, have frequently been

[53] V.383; and see pp. 156, *infra*. [54] Rylands *Eng. MSS*, 1056.

blended under the denomination of Methodists. Messrs Wesleys and Whitefield, I am sensible, have been unwearied in their labours to promote Primitive Christianity.

There is no obvious reason for Wesley, if he was the author, to write approvingly of himself or to refer to himself in the third person. Moreover, though the style of the writing has some resemblance to John Wesley's own literary style, this could be said of many other writers in that age when conventional diction was common; and the structure of the pamphlet, which is hastily and carelessly put together, is very different from Wesley's methodical practice. Moreover, it is dated October 1750, London, at which time Wesley, who was particularly careful about dating his papers, was in Bristol. On the other hand, Lavington, Bishop of Exeter, thought Wesley to be the author, and Wesley, for his part, did not deny responsibility. It is possible that even if he did not write the whole pamphlet he had some share in it.

The matter is of some importance, for the bitterness of the controversy was increased by the publication of this pamphlet. Whoever was the author, he wrote with rancour, accusing the Brethren of having obtained their privileges by false pretences, criticizing Zinzendorf for his autocratic government, charging the Brethren with hypocrisy and with class distinctions. Some of these charges repeat Wesley's acknowledged criticisms, but some are quite new. One section derided the Moravian emphasis on the Wounds of Christ, and at the beginning of the pamphlet some of the 'Blood and Wounds' hymns from the *Moravian Hymnbook* were quoted and criticized. Wesley speaks disparagingly of these hymns in his *Journal*:

Having procured a sight of that amazing compound of nonsense and blasphemy, the last hymn-book published by Count Zinzendorf's Brethren, I believed it was my bounden duty to transcribe a few of these wonderful hymns, and publish them to all the world, as a standing proof that there is no folly too gross for those who are wise above that is written;[55]

and seems to have fulfilled this undertaking in 1749.[56] The Brethren themselves were apparently uneasy about some of these hymns, for in the *Conclusions of the Four Synods of the Brethren's*

[55] III.389. [56] R. Green, *Wesley Bibliography* (1896), p. 65.

Unity of the Years 1764, 1769, 1775 and 1782, the following appears:

The large *English Hymn-book* [which already had omitted some of the worst of these hymns] containing sundry verses and hymns, against which there is an objection, as well in regard to their contents, as also the expressions occurring in them, ought to be used in our English congregations with much circumspection, and only so long, till a new edition of our English hymn-book, which is so heartily recommended, be completed.[57]

The letter to Stonehouse is severe enough, so bitter that it is difficult to reconcile it with Wesley's frequent expressions of good will. George James Stonehouse had been Vicar of Islington, but had sold his living to become a Moravian. He seems to have been somewhat unstable, and indeed did not remain with the Moravians. Wesley speaks of him with some amusement, particularly of his inventive genius—'I really believe he could invent the best mouse-trap that ever was in the world'[58]—and of his original views on pre-existence and the non-eternity of hell;[59] and says of him, in August, 1781:

He is all-original still, like no man in the world, either in sentiments or anything about him. But perhaps if I had his immense fortune I might be as great an oddity as he.[60]

It is surprising that Wesley, if he actually found Stonehouse so amusing, should have troubled to write so long and fierce a letter; but it was probably Stonehouse's warmly expressed admiration for the Brethren which called forth Wesley's acrimonious criticism. He begins by avowing his love for the Moravians, but says that he cannot admire them.[61] He denies them the right to call themselves 'The Brethren' or 'The Moravian Church'; he criticizes their doctrine; he objects to their conduct and especially their 'close, dark, reserved behaviour', he accuses them of heaping up riches for themselves and their own Society; he censures their contemptuous and dishonest attitude toward their opponents; and he regards their teaching as destroying faith and love of God and man, encouraging arrogance, hostile to simplicity, justice, mercy, and truth. Southey acutely comments on this: 'He

[57] Rylands *Eng. MSS*, 910. [58] *Journal*, V.443. [59] ibid., 522-3.
[60] ibid., VI.331. [61] *Letters*, III.51.

should have asked himself whether Methodism did not sometimes produce the same effects.'[62]

Wesley seems to have been in a bad temper when he wrote this letter. His argument about the names used by the Moravians is a mere quibble, his criticism of their doctrine was several years out of date, and the letter as a whole is written with too much passion to be judicial. His suggestion that the Moravians were too fond of money is repeated later. In his *Journal* for 17th April 1780, he speaks of his visit to the Moravian settlement at Fulneck, and says: 'I see not what but the mighty power of God can hinder them from acquiring millions.'[63] Charles Wesley writes of this, somewhat sardonically, in a letter to James Hutton on 23rd November 1786:

> We are all agreed in disapproving the rashness of our *old* friend. When we are as near too, we may be as weak as him. . . . I only wish you could force him to make good his words, and produce the millions you have hoarded up—then, after paying your own, you could generously pay ours, and lastly the National Debt.[64]

Possibly Wesley's strictures in his letter to Stonehouse are due to his reluctance to lose a convert. Something similar is seen in his letter to Francis Okely on 4th October 1758.[65] Okely was a Moravian who had been in charge of the Brethren's children at Bedford. He seems to have kept up his friendship with John Wesley, and actually went with him to Ireland, and to the Bristol Conference in 1758. Wesley was, however, doubtful of his stability. In his *Journal* for 16th March 1758, he wrote:

> I rode through heavy rain to Manchester. I was scarce set down when Mr Francis Okeley came from Bedford. If he comes sincerely (as I believe), God will bless him; but if not, *ego in portu navigo*. He can find out nothing with regard to me: I have no secrets.[66]

Though there was no doubt about Okely's sincerity, he changed his mind about joining Wesley, who in his letter shows clearly the reasons for Okely's reluctance—that the Methodists had not 'real faith', that they seemed 'at best to have the letter of the new covenant and the spirit of the old', and that he had not found what he had expected and therefore could not see his way to join them. In a letter which is neither worthy of himself nor fair to

62 1876 edn. (Bell), p. 222.
63 VI.273.
64 *Moravian Messenger* (1875), p. 423.
65 *Letters*, IV.34.
66 IV.256.

Okely, Wesley suggests that Okely's reasons for not joining the Methodists are five—his wife, his mother, his children, his cowardice, and his love of ease. And then he speaks with increasing bitterness:

'However, *the Brethren* are good men, and I dare not oppose them.' If they are not the *only people* of God (which they cannot be if the Scriptures are true), they are not good men; they are very wicked men. They are as a body deceiving and being deceived; they are liars, proud, boasters, despisers of those that are good, slaves to an ungodly man, and continually labouring to enslave others to him. . . . I dare not but oppose them; for in many places they have well-nigh destroyed the work of God.[67]

There is nothing in the history of the Brethren or of the Methodists at this time to explain the bitterness of this letter. It may be that Wesley was disappointed at the success of the Brethren in Ireland, where he stayed for most of the time between the entry in his *Journal* and the date of his letter. More probably it is a last-minute attempt to influence a possible convert who would have been a valuable helper. Wesley had already had reason to fear defections to the Moravians. His brother Charles had at one time leaned toward Quietism,[68] and his friend William Grimshaw of Haworth, disturbed at what he regarded as Wesley's worldliness in urging the Halifax Methodists to go to law against some rioters at Sowerby Bridge, had in 1749 almost forsaken Methodism for Moravianism. John Bennet visited him at Ewood in May of that year and recorded in his diary:

Mr Grimshaw was under some temptation to join the Germans, and brake off connexion with Mr Wesley. He said he had trusted too much in man.[69]

If, as has been alleged, John Wesley began 'The Battle of the Books', other writers were not slow to follow. The Rev. George Baddeley, Curate of Melbourne, Derbyshire, in a friendly remonstrance, charged the Moravians with doctrinal errors, and with alluring people from their loyalty to the Parish Church; Gregory Oldknow, in an unmeasured and ill-informed pamphlet, attacked Moravians and Methodists alike; John Roche, a Dublin Churchman, in *The Moravian Heresy*, denounced the Moravians as

[67] *Letters*, IV.34. [68] See p. 109, *supra*.

[69] John Bennet, *Journal*; Grimshaw, *Experiences*.

Antinomians, and regarded them as more powerful and more dangerous than the Methodists. But much worse was to come, and for this the Moravians themselves were clearly responsible. The bone of contention this time was not doctrinal but financial. The English Brethren, with amazing folly, embarked upon reckless spending—at Lindsey House, Fulneck, Bedford, and elsewhere—and in foolish speculation. At one time John Wesley visited Fulneck, and admired its fine front.

> The Germans [he wrote] suppose it will cost, by that time it is finished, about three thousand pounds: it is well if it be not nearer ten. But that is no concern to the English Brethren; for they are told (and potently believe) that all the money will come from over sea.[70]

Certainly, much of the money *did* come from over sea, for Zinzendorf, hearing that the Moravian Church in England was in debt to the amount of £30,000, gave his own security for £10,000, and did his best to restore order to the distracted finances. The trouble had, however, gone too far to be cured in that way, and before long the debt had risen to £100,000, and many of the English Brethren were in danger of being imprisoned for debt. Again Zinzendorf, with remarkable generosity, made himself responsible for payment, a grotesquely heavy burden even for a wealthy land-owner.

According to Benham[71] the Methodists seized the opportunity to embarrass the Brethren still further, but the facts do not bear this out. Miss Stonehouse, sister of the Rev. George Stonehouse, who claimed £2,000 which was owing for some land near Nazareth in America, was hardly a representative Methodist, and Whitefield had moved far from the Wesleyan position. The basis of his pamphlet[72] was not primarily financial, but was concerned in the main with Moravian ritualistic and liturgical practices, which had been carried to extravagant lengths; but he went so far as to charge Zinzendorf with robbery and fraud, Zinzendorf who had done so much at great personal sacrifice to save the English Brethren from disaster.

The next attacks, probably the most deadly, came from two Germans, Rimius and Frey. Henry Rimius, a former Councillor to the King of Prussia and now living in London, made a scurrilous

[70] *Journal*, III.292. [71] op. cit., pp. 275, 277.

[72] *An Expostulatory Letter to Count Zinzendorf* (1753).

attack upon the Brethren in *A Candid Narrative of the Rise and Progress of the Herrnhuters* (1753), which he followed by three similar attacks during the next three years. He attacked their government, their teaching, and especially their practices. It is plain that his description was in the main that of Herrnhaag, but he wrote for his public, greedy for sensation, and gave a wrong impression by tearing passages from their context. There is no evidence of similar excesses in England, but the English Brethren suffered in the public mind by their association with their fellows abroad.

Andrew Frey, who had lived for four years amongst the Brethren in Germany, gave a vivid and disturbing picture of their life and ways, all the more disturbing because it was substantially true. Lavington, Bishop of Exeter, who had already denounced the Methodists in his *Enthusiasm of Methodists and Papists Compared* now entered the arena with *The Moravians Compared and Detected*, which is apparently a cento from the writings of Rimius and Frey.

At first Wesley's attitude was negative. On 22nd May 1753 he wrote in his *Journal*:

This week I read over Mr Rimius's *Candid Narrative*. It informed me of nothing new. I still think several of the inconsiderable members of that community are upright; but I fear their governors 'wax worse and worse, having their conscience seared as with a hot iron'.[73]

This was mild enough, but in general there is a marked deterioration in Wesley's attitude. On 11th June, for example, he wrote:

I found the town much alarmed with Mr Rimius's *Narrative* and Mr Whitefield's *Letter to Count Zinzendorf*. It seems that God is hastening to bring to light those hidden works of darkness. And undoubtedly none who reads those tracts with any degree of impartiality will ever more (unless he be himself under a strong delusion) go near the tents of those wicked men.[74]

There is another disparaging entry for 8th October 1753, in which Wesley gives an account of the reports he had received at Bedford, probably from William Parker, afterwards Mayor of Bedford, who had been a Moravian but who had left, or been expelled from, the Society. According to him, the Moravians would not allow their members to remain on the local Corporation;

[73] IV.68. [74] IV.72-3.

they were 'the worst paymasters in the town'; and they exploited their own workers. This informant said:

Mr Rimius has said nothing to what might have been said concerning their marriage economy. I know a hundred times more than he has written; but the particulars are too shocking to relate. I believe no such things were ever practised before; no, not among the most barbarous heathens.[75]

Wesley goes on to say:

In the evening I met the little society, just escaped with the skin of their teeth. From the account which each of these likewise gave, it appeared clear to a demonstration (i) that their Elders usurped a more absolute authority over the conscience than the Bishop of Rome himself does; (ii) that to gain and secure this they use a continued train of guile, fraud, and falsehood of every kind; (iii) that they scrape their votaries to the bone as to their worldly substance, leaving little to any, to some nothing, or less than nothing; (iv) that still they are so infatuated as to believe that theirs is the only true Church upon earth.

In accepting without question such reports Wesley showed less than his accustomed fairness or judgement. Those who leave a community from any sort of discontent are not always ready to speak well of that community: sometimes they criticize it, if only to justify, to their fellows or even to themselves, their action in leaving it. The incident of Richard Viney illustrates this. Viney, a London tailor, had been interpreter to Peter Böhler, and was an original member of the Fetter Lane Society, and went to Germany with John Wesley in 1738. At first an enthusiastic Moravian—in May 1739 he had written a 'letter from an English brother of the Moravian persuasion in Holland to the Methodists in England, lamenting the irregularity of their present proceedings'—he had been appointed Superintendent of the Brethren's school at Broad Oaks, Essex, and later Warden of the Yorkshire Societies, but had become very restive about Moravian Church government, and especially about 'the imperious spirit in which the head authorities ruled the Church'. He visited John Wesley on 19th February 1744, and told him of his discontent. Wesley on this occasion answered wisely:

If you go back, you are welcome to go; if you stay with us, you are welcome to stay. Only, whatever you do, do it with a clear conscience; and I shall be satisfied either way.[76]

[75] IV. p. 86.

[76] *Journal*, III.121.

Viney returned to the Brethren in Yorkshire, where his influence was so disruptive that the Moravians, including his own sister, resolved 'not to meddle at all with him, as long as he does not acknowledge his sins'. Viney now began to associate with Wesley, and may have supplied him with a jaundiced version of his dismissal. This may, indeed, have been the immediate cause of the publication of Part IV of the *Journal*, with its dedication to the Brethren's Church. Wesley records a further visit from Viney on 16th May,[77] at which the latter attacked the aristocracy of Zinzendorf, and the arbitrary use of the Lot by the Moravian leaders. Viney was an unsatisfactory ally. Charles Wesley records:

I met the Birstal Society, whom Mr Viney had almost quite perverted; so that they laughed at all fasting, and self-denial, and family prayer, and such like works of the law. They were so alienated by that cunning supplanter, that they took no notice of John Nelson, when he came back; for Viney taught them that all that was animal love.[78]

Viney underwent another change of heart (or mind) later, and gave some signs of wishing to rejoin the Brethren, but little more was heard of him. He was hardly the kind of informant on whom to depend.

Not only did Wesley listen too readily to unreliable reports, but on more than one occasion he quoted extreme and unrepresentative examples as typical of the Moravians as a whole. He seemed at times very credulous, at any rate in believing scandalous stories, and he forgot, or appeared to forget, that similar stories had been told about the Methodists. Indeed, more than one pamphlet of the day coupled Moravian and Methodist as objects of attack—and rightly so, for the evangelical fervour which made the Methodists unpopular with orthodox Churchmen was the prime cause of the hostility to the Brethren. Lavington, Bishop of Exeter, for instance, who had attacked the Moravians in *The Moravians Compared and Detected*, made three separate attacks on the Methodists, and on John Wesley in particular. Lavington was no more credible when he attacked the Moravians than when he criticized the Methodists. In his spirited reply to Lavington on 1st February 1750, Wesley makes a partial defence of the Brethren:

I was not 'offended' [he writes] 'with the Moravians' for warning men 'against mixing nature with grace', but for their doing it in such a

[77] op. cit., III.139. [78] Charles Wesley, *Journal*, I.385.

manner as tended to destroy all the work of grace in their souls. I did not blame the thing itself, but their manner of doing it.[79]

He soon forsook his negative attitude. The Brethren had become increasingly restive (understandably so) about the number and bitterness of the attacks upon them, and on 31st December 1754, therefore, James Hutton published an advertisement in the *London Daily Advertiser* and in other papers, 'calling for those Queries, the answers to which were alleged to be indispensably necessary for the vindication of the Moravian Brethren'. A week later, a tract appeared entitled *Queries humbly proposed to the right reverend and right honourable* (*Count Zinzendorf*), with an address to James Hutton as an introduction. It has no author's name, but James Hutton believed it to be the work of John Wesley, and the title appears in the catalogues of books published by the Wesleys. Some of the queries are so similar in content and phraseology to those used by Wesley elsewhere as to make his authorship very probable, e.g. 'Do you not judge your Church to be the only true church under heaven?' 'Are these your own words, "There is but one duty, that of believing?" ' 'Are you not of a close, dark, reserved temper and behaviour?' 'Do not you, in many cases, use cunning, guile, dissimulation?'

The *Queries* are bitter, and contain charges in the form of questions. They cover thirty-two pages, and deal not only with the matters mentioned above, but with the Moravians' alleged contempt for the Bible, their subordination of the Father and the Holy Spirit to Christ (a charge made by Sir John Thorold in 1742), their hymns to angels and the Virgin, their 'moral dishonesty' and their occasional 'gross indecency'. There is little good will in these questions, and the only excuse for Wesley's bitterness, if indeed he wrote them, can have been an irresistible sense of moral obligation. J. E. Hutton gives a wrong impression when he makes it appear that these queries *preceded* James Hutton's offer to answer any reasonable questions: it was in response to Hutton's offer that the *Queries* were published. The questions were not specifically answered, but the Brethren issued a series of pamphlets in which they fully and ably defended their beliefs and practice. These pamphlets were chiefly by Zinzendorf, Hutton, and Neisser, and by some anonymous writers who were obviously very much in sympathy with them.

[79] *Letters*, III.269.

Meanwhile, in various parts of the country, the Wesleys found that many of their followers had been estranged by the Moravians, to whom they now generally refer as 'the Germans'. Charles Wesley's *Journal* for 25th January 1747, for instance, contains the following entry:

I resettled the poor shattered Society [at Davyhulme]. One woman delighted me with her scrupulosity, telling me 'she would be of the Society if I would allow her to go to Church, but the Germans used to forbid them'. Through the blessing of God, I have brought back these wandering sheep to His pale.[80]

He wrote to his wife on 5th May 1750: 'I met a band of still brothers, corrupted by the Germans.' Similarly, though more strongly, John Wesley wrote in his *Journal* for 20th October 1750:

I found it absolutely necessary openly and explicitly to warn all that feared God to beware of the German wolves (falsely called Moravians) and keep close to the great Shepherd of their souls.[81]

It is worthy of note that his severe letter to Stonehouse was written only a month later. It ends: 'Art thou the man?' He is referring to a man whose character had been undermined by Moravian preaching. 'If you are not, go and hear the Germans again next Sunday.'[82] On 16th January 1751, he received a letter from 'a friend', which said:

No doubt God had wise ends in permitting the *Unitas Fratrum* to appear just as the people of God began to unite together. But we cannot fathom His designs. . . . 'The dear Lamb', they say, 'has done *all* for us; we have nothing to do but to *believe*.' And ever since this German spirit hath wrought among us, and caused many to rest in a barren, notional faith, void of that inward power of God unto salvation.[83]

It is interesting to note that traces of stillness survived ten years after the disruption.

Thus in half a dozen years the admiration which Wesley had felt and expressed for the Brethren had turned to dislike and reprobation. In 1746, he had expressed his belief that, after those of his own Church, the body of the Moravian Church were, *in the main*, the best Christians in the world. Now, in 1753, he limits his praise to 'several of the inconsiderable members of that community', and regards the rest as 'German wolves', wicked men

[80] I.440. [81] III.499. [82] *Letters*, III.58. [83] *Journal*, III.510-1.

who are guilty of 'moral dishonesty' and even 'gross indecency'. What caused this change of attitude, one which was probably to put an end to all hope of reunion?

No doubt several factors contributed to it:

(1) the scandals at Herrnhaag, though not shared by the English Brethren, could not be dissociated from them in the minds of those who were predisposed to believe the worst, as Wesley seems often to have been;

(2) the question, 'Who began the fight?' is of little more than academic interest. In any conflict, whether of blows or of words, sooner or later the aggressor becomes the defender. Whether or not John Wesley began the 'Battle of the Books', in the controversy which followed he himself had to endure attack, and, not unnaturally, the tempo and temper of the contest increased. It is not difficult to understand how one who was as convinced of his own integrity as John Wesley should resent the criticisms of those who regarded him as an ambitious self-seeker, as one who could not be trusted, and as one devoid of 'real faith'.[84]

(3) The Moravians probably made tactical errors in some of their publications. It was justifiable to disown all connexion with the Methodists, but it was needlessly provocative to criticize the Methodists as being 'wilful servants of sin'. Moreover, James Hutton's invitation of 'queries' was asking for trouble. At any rate, there was nothing 'dark, close and secretive' about this invitation!

(4) The frequent defections from his band of converts were no doubt a source of annoyance to the Methodist leader, and it is noticeable that his language is strongest when he speaks of the 'corruption' of his followers by 'the Germans'.

Thus, though several causes contributed to the growing asperity of John Wesley's comments, it was probably his anxiety lest his own mission should be threatened by what he regarded as error which made him most bitter. His dislike of Zinzendorf, moreover, did not decrease with the years.

On the whole, however, in spite of this attitude, which was one of coolness rather than of heat, there was little actual friction. The one exception was in Ireland, where John Cennick, who, after a fiery period with Howell Harris in Wales, had thrown in his lot

[84] See pp. 158 and 161, *infra*.

with the Brethren, was achieving remarkable success. In Dublin, Benjamin La Trobe, a Baptist student, had since 1745 been conducting a meeting for singing and prayer; and here, in a Baptist hall in Skinner's Alley, John Cennick began his work a year later. Indeed, it was John Cennick, not John Wesley, who began the Evangelical Revival in Ireland: he had been working in Dublin for more than a year before Wesley arrived on the scene.

Wesley, though at first warmly attracted by Cennick—he had called him 'a young man strong in the faith of our Lord Jesus'[85]—became very hostile to him in later years. He bitterly resented his defection from the Bristol Society, where, he says, 'that weak man, John Cennick, confounded the poor people with strange doctrines',[86] and he felt it 'his bounden duty' to record Cennick's unfilial conduct toward his mother.[87] The difficulty in Dublin arose over the possession of Skinner's Alley. Wesley has been accused of buying it over Cennick's head, but this is hardly a fair or an accurate statement. The story is a confused one, Wesley throughout professing his willingness to let Cennick have the hall, and the Moravians accusing him of placing obstacles in the way.[88] There were probably faults on both sides, Wesley perhaps being too insistent on being indemnified against loss, the Brethren being somewhat dilatory in seizing the opportunity when Wesley was in a generous and kindly mood. The trouble was no doubt one of finance, but suspicion, never absent at this time, was deepened. In a letter to William Holland, Wesley complained that the Dublin Brethren seemed determined not to believe a single word of his (rather like his own attitude to Zinzendorf). It is not a pretty incident, but the problem would have been easily solved but for the underlying suspicion on both sides. If it may be maintained that Wesley was too rigid in insisting upon his legal rights, it may equally well be contended that Cennick's delay—he left Ireland at a critical moment—and the suspicions of some of his flock destroyed the atmosphere within which a happy solution could have been found.

Cennick's behaviour in this incident was hardly true to his reputation. There can be no doubt that he was changeable, for he had been in turn Methodist, Calvinist, and Moravian, but he was

[85] *Letters*, I.282-3. [86] *Journal*, IV.415. [87] ibid., III.500.

[88] *W.H.S. Proceedings*, XVII.36-50; Charles Wesley, *Journal*, I.461-2, II.2; *Letters*, II.130-50.

certainly not the 'weak man' whom John Wesley had alleged him to be. Indeed, Wesley's disparagement of him is very similar to his condemnation of Francis Okely later,[89] and probably from the same cause—disappointment at losing a valuable helper. There is little sign of weakness in Cennick's Irish work, and the warm admiration felt and expressed by the Moravians for his evangelistic zeal seems to have been fully merited.

In spite of this clash, the relations between the Moravians and the Methodists were in general peaceful and sometimes even friendly. The passing of the years gradually mellowed the asperities of the leaders, while the death of Zinzendorf in 1760 and of Cennick in 1755 took from the scene two figures which, whatever their merits, stood in the way of reconciliation. John Wesley mentions neither event in his *Journal*! But of his old friends Gambold, Böhler and Hutton he writes with nostalgic affection. As early as 8th January 1745 the Wesley brothers called at James Hutton's, 'desiring to see once more our old acquaintance, Mr Gambold';[90] and mention has already been made of John's happy visits in 1763.[91] Toward Böhler he felt even more warmly. He wrote to him on 5th February 1775, within two months of Böhler's death, and probably because he had heard of its imminence. In his reply, Böhler says:

> You write, 'As to what is to come, I have no desire or design to speak of them [the Brethren] at all'. This I very much approve; and I heartily wish also it may neither happen without a previous design. You add, 'Unless in their favour'. For my part, I could heartily dispense even with this. You conclude, 'I hope I shall never be constrained to do otherwise'. This is properly the sentence which startles me. For I cannot imagine what could constrain you to pass strictures on us or to speak against us. For, dear brother, you have really lost sight of us for these thirty years past. . . . Yet perhaps there may be some things in your mind which do not occur to me; and if they should be of such a nature as to be removable on our part, I beg you to mention them to me, and I will do all in my power to prevent them. . . . Ever since my last coming to England, this consideration (of the breaches in Zion) has been a heart-breaking subject to me.[92]

Wesley's rejoinder is so revealing that it deserves to be given in full:

[89] See p. 140, *supra*.
[90] *Journal*, III.159-60.
[91] See p. 93, *supra*; *Journal*, V.40-2.
[92] *Letters*, VI.140-1.

MY DEAR BROTHER,

When I say, 'I hope I shall never be constrained to speak otherwise of them' [the Moravians] I do not mean that I have any expectation this will ever happen. Probably it never will. I never did speak but when I believed it was my duty to do so. And if they would calmly consider what I have spoken from March 10, 1736,[93] and were open to conviction, they might be such Christians as are hardly in the world besides. I have not lost sight of you yet. Indeed, I cannot if you are 'a city set upon a hill'.[94]

Perhaps no one living is a greater lover of peace or has laboured more for it than I, particularly among the children of God. I set out near fifty years ago with this principle, 'Whosoever doeth the will of my Father who is in heaven, the same is my brother and my sister and mother'.[95] But there is no one living who has been more abused for his pains even to this day. But it is all well. By the grace of God, I shall go on, following peace with all men, and loving your Brethren beyond any body of men upon earth except the Methodists.

It is good to note that after the storms of controversy which embittered the relations between the two Churches in mid-century, Wesley has returned to his former warm regard for the Brethren; but the naïveté of Böhler, who seems to have known little of those storms, possibly because of his absence abroad, is surprising. Böhler died on 27th April, and one more link in the rapidly-weakening chain which had bound Methodist and Moravian together was shattered.

But it was with James Hutton that the relations of the Wesleys, or at any rate of the younger brother, became closest. Charles renewed the friendship in 1770: on 27th October of that year he wrote:

I am glad to hear from my old, my first of friends.

In a very short time we shall meet where all our differences, of party or opinions, shall be no more. Then you and I shall see all things in the true light. Till then let us have patience with each other and as much love as the Lord shall give us.

Your invariable loving
C.W.

On 9th September of the following year, Hutton wrote to Charles Wesley:

[93] i.e. from the beginning of his Savannah ministry, *Journal*, I.176.

[94] Matt. 5^{14}.

[95] Mark 3^{35}.

I got home . . . well pleased that I had spent an hour with you lovingly. It is a pity that we have been these 32 years so estranged from one another. What should hinder our living the short remains of our life on the same friendly footing as of late? . . .

To this letter, Charles Wesley replied:

'Tis high time when a man has one foot in the grave to shake hands with all the world. How much easier for me to love an old friend for whom I never yet lost my love. . . . You are beloved by my wife almost as well as by your first and oldest friend, C. Wesley.

I have business with F.O. of importance (as it seems to me).

'F.O.' is, of course, Francis Okely,[96] whose comment indicates the nature of this business:

C.W. wants to renew a correspondence with me. It seems a matter of great consequence to him how he and the Methodists may behave so as that they may for the future not hurt nor hinder but enjoy the friendship of the Brethren. He told me there was much amongst us which he wished to see among the Methodists, etc. I proposed a total cessation of all hostilities and then it might be left to our Saviour how far we might be serviceable one to another by friendship and mutual good offices. How far his influence extends and how steady he may prove I am unable to ascertain, but I sincerely wish we may be upon a more amiable footing than hitherto.

No practicable scheme of union emerged at this time, though it is probable that some such scheme was already in Charles Wesley's mind. His reason for this may have been purely pacific, and may have been based on a conviction that the two Communions were very closely allied in mission and method; but, as will become evident, the avowed intention of the Brethren to remain loyal to the National Church probably attracted him, in view of the signs of separatism which were already evident within Methodism. On the other hand, the Moravians seemed on their guard against any organic union, and made it clear that all they desired was friendliness and good will.

A letter from Hutton was more promising. Writing to the younger Wesley, he said:

Every symptom of the renewal of your tendency to friendship in these thirty-one years has been constantly received by me with hopes on my side of its going farther, and that it went not farther was always a great disappointment to my heart which catched eagerly after your heart.

[96] See pp. 140–1, *supra*.

The promise held out by this interchange was not fulfilled. The Brethren plainly viewed the elder Wesley with suspicion, and seemed afraid to re-open negotiations, or to give birth to another controversy. As early as 30th July 1770 (?1771), Hutton wrote to Benjamin La Trobe:

Here is a letter I got this evening from Charles W. Pray read it with Petrus [i.e. Böhler] and let me know to-morrow evening.

Whether it be good for me to write at all to John or whether it be better to write to Charles to speak with his brother about it, as he knows my mind, as well as if I wrote another letter to John.

I know not if it will not be wrong to say anything at all to John any more about it, as perhaps we shall be obliged to say something disagreeable to John if ever Cranz's *History* be published in English, in which case it is better to take now no notice any more, in a friendly way, of anything that he does, or does not do.

The reference to Cranz's *History* is rather obscure, for there is very little in it about the Moravian-Methodist relationship. Perhaps this omission itself might be thought to give offence! In any case, Charles made it clear that he was loyal both to Methodism and to his brother:

Take it for granted that I am *fixed*, *resolved*, determined, sworn to stand by the Methodists and my B(rother) right or wrong, through thick and thin. . . . Notwithstanding my incurable bigotry, can you and will you love me?'

At last John Wesley and Hutton met. Wesley records the meeting in his *Journal*:

I met an old friend, James Hutton, whom I had not seen for five-and-twenty years. I felt this made no difference; my heart was quite open; his seemed to be the same; and we conversed just as we did in 1738, when we met in Fetter Lane.[97]

John wrote to Hutton at about the same time, 26th December 1771:

It really seems the time is come when our Lord will roll away our reproach, and Ephraim shall no more vex Judah, nor Judah vex Ephraim.

Frank Okeley and you, with my brother and me, so many at least, are lovers of peace. After having seen above half a century of years,

[97] 21st December 1771; *Journal*, V.441.

we are sick of strife and contention. If we do not yet think alike, we may at least love alike. . . . Nothing will be wanting that is in the power of, dear James,

Your old friend and brother.[98]

There are definite suggestions here that John Wesley thought some kind of union possible. Hutton, however, in his reply, withdrew into his shell, and, while continuing to express good will, made it clear that he wished the two Communions to keep apart:

Let you and your brother &c and I and my brethren consider ourselves and our several people as two different carriages travelling together on the same road only not on the same track . . . let us not cross one another's track . . . you according to the best of your judgement and with all your power helping forward the salvation of souls and thereby giving Christ the most sensible pleasure, and we in our way aiming at the same thing.[99]

The phrases 'not on the same track' and 'we in our way' are further evidence of the reluctance of the Moravians to consider anything like organic union.

Good will, however, continued. In a letter to Hutton on 31st December 1773, John Wesley wrote: 'I am of the same mind still. I love you well; and I love to talk with you.'[100] On two occasions he wrote appreciatively of Spangenberg, once in October 1771, when he said:

Five and thirty years since, hearing that wise man Mr Spangenberg describe the fruits of faith, I immediately cried out, 'If this be so, I have *no* faith'. He replied, '*Habes fidem, sed exiguam*';[101]

and again, on 8th October 1785 (writing to Mary Cooke):

Many years ago, when one was describing the glorious privilege of a believer, I cried out, 'If this be so, I have no faith'. He replied, '*Habes fidem, sed exiguam*'.[102]

The repetition of this after a lapse of so many years is a striking tribute, not only to the impression made upon Wesley by Spangenberg in their early contacts, but to the persistence of his regard throughout the conflicts of the middle years.

[98] *Letters,* VI.294. [99] English Moravian Archives, Muswell Hill.
[100] *Letters,* VI.62. [101] ibid., V.281. [102] ibid., VII.298.

Several of Charles Wesley's letters at this time refer to meetings with Hutton. In a letter to the saintly John Fletcher he wrote on 22nd February 1772:

My old intimate friend James Hutton, and my very good brother and friend Okeley, the chief of the Moravians, have oftener than once commissioned me to give their love and thanks to you for your seasonable letters.

From Moravians this is a desirable testimony, for they did sadly halt and strongly incline to Antinomianism and drew us into their error [an interesting confession]. . . . Their famous Count fairly turns St James out of the Canon;

and on 5th August of the same year, he wrote to Hutton:

We shall never agree about J.G., C.K., and J.H. [Gambold, Kinchin, and Hutton] leaving us, and 'tis no matter if we never do. . . . I find nothing in my heart against loving you and the Brethren with all the power which the Lord gives me;

and a little later:

Let the matter sleep, till we awake up after His likeness and see Him as He is. Our only business now is to love one another and all mankind, whom we shall leave so soon.

This is a hint here of some underlying friction, and this is borne out in a letter from Charles Wesley to Hutton on 17th October 1773:

He (my brother) remembered nothing of the matter. I believe, from your informant's report, that he did mention the Brethren; that he spoke of P.B. or the Count *with bitterness* I do not believe. You know some of your friends (as well as ours) are so weak and touchy that if he named them at all they would call it railing.

Charles was still afraid that the Methodists might cut themselves off from the Church of England, and on Christmas Day 1773, wrote thus to Hutton:

Rather than they should degenerate into a dead formal sect, I pray God the very name of Moravian and Methodist may die together.

Still anxious for peace, Charles wrote again on 19th July 1774:

Write to my B. and second my advice 'to omit all reflections in the new edition of his *Journal*'.

Reference has already been made to John Wesley's sturdy defence of the Moravians (as well as of the Methodists and Hutchinsonians) against the attacks of Lord Lyttelton. In *Dialogues of the Dead*, Lyttelton had said:

Martin has spawned a strange brood of fellows, called Methodists, Moravians, Hutchinsonians, who are madder than Jack was in his worst days.[103]

Wesley asks:

Is the sentiment just? To say nothing of the Methodists (although some of them, too, are not quite out of their senses), could his Lordship show me in England many more sensible men than Mr Gambold and Mr Okeley? And yet both of these were called Moravians.

A charming incident took place in 1783, when John Wesley visited the Brethren's settlement at Zeist, in Holland, and met his old friend Bishop Seiffart,[104] and asked to hear some Moravian singing. By a happy coincidence it was both Wesley's birthday and the 'Children's Prayer Day', and Wesley was invited to take part in the children's Love-feast. He did so, and the children sang a Birthday Ode in his honour.

Indeed charming, but again there was suspicion. Here is Wesley's account:

We went over to Zeist, the settlement of the German Brethren. . . . Here I met with my old friend Bishop Anton, whom I had not seen for near fifty years. He did not ask me to eat or drink, for it is not their custom, and there is an inn; but they were all very courteous, and we were welcome to *buy* anything that we pleased at their shops! I cannot see how it is possible for this community to avoid growing immensely rich.[105]

There is more than a touch of sarcasm here, and an implication of discourtesy which may not have been merited. Whether it was or not, Wesley was still ready to suspect the worst. He had made a similar suggestion that the Brethren were 'wise in their generation' in his letter to Professor John Liden, of Lund, a Swedish Professor of History:

[103] *Journal*, V.383; Martin was the Anglican in Swift's *Tale of a Tub*; Jack was the Puritan. See p. 137 *supra*.

[104] See p. 42, *supra*; and *Journal*, I.179.

[105] *Journal*, VI.428. J. E. Hutton says that the minister was too busy with his pastoral work to ask Wesley to dinner—op. cit., p. 441; *Moravian Messenger* (1871).

They make a profound secret of everything relating to their community. . . . The Count's house at Chelsea is a palace for a prince.[106]

The negotiations for union in 1785-6 have received surprisingly little attention from the 'official' historians of Moravianism and Methodism, and by most of them they are not mentioned at all. Dr Frank Baker, it is true, speaks of them in his little book, *Charles Wesley as revealed by his Letters*,[107] but rightly points out that to Charles Wesley this was a side-issue. After all, Charles Wesley was much more anxious to keep the Methodists within the Anglican Church than to patch up a quarrel between two Communions which were both in danger of seceding from that Church. Nevertheless, a study of the La Trobe–Loretz correspondence, preserved in the Moravian archives at Herrnhut, reveals how important these negotiations were to both Communions, and how much more important they might have been but for some underlying fears, and the letters give a vivid picture of some of the religious personalities of the day.

Benjamin La Trobe, it will be remembered, had been a Baptist student, probably of Huguenot descent, when he first came under Cennick's influence in Dublin. Johannes Loretz was a Swiss, who had been a close companion of Zinzendorf and held the important post of 'Senior Civilis'.[108] Thomas Coke was John Wesley's henchman in his declining years. A curate (of South Petherton) who had been expelled for his evangelistic zeal, he became a Methodist in 1777, and became a vigorous and enthusiastic leader of the United Societies, relieving John Wesley of many of his burdens, but creating for him some awkward problems. John Wesley took a decisive step by ordaining him as 'superintendent' of the work in America in 1784, and Coke became 'the Missionary Bishop of Methodism'.

The first letter, from La Trobe to Loretz, is dated 25th October 1785, and is of an informative character. Of Charles Wesley, La Trobe says:

He has been attached to him [John] in a manner that has made him unsteady in all his connexions with other persons, being his implicit follower in all things;

[106] *Letters*, V.156.

[107] 1948, p. 131.

[108] He has been thought to be the original of 'Major L.' in *Wilhelm Meister's Apprenticeship*.

and of John:

Though it is very doubtful whether John ever knew himself as a sinner or our Lord as his Saviour, yet it is beyond a doubt that many of his people are sincere followers of our Saviour and have experienced the power of His grace, and love to hear the pure Gospel. He has taken up some of our regulations and established them in his Societies.

This differentiation between the leader of Methodism and the rank and file is strikingly parallel with some of Wesley's qualified tributes to the Brethren.

The letter goes on to relate how Coke had recently obtained an ascendency over John Wesley, and expresses the opinion that Coke would not rest until he had formed a Methodist Episcopal Church in England. It says that Charles is opposed to the plan, and that he hopes that 'the Brethren might be of the use they were originally intended for, to nurse these souls who are truly awakened and who adhere to the Church of England'. It reveals that Charles, who thought that the Brethren had forsaken their original plan—hence his opposition to them—had always felt that they had the true doctrine in essentials and the greatest realism; and that many Methodists, preachers and laity, showed an affection for them.

The second letter, from Loretz to La Trobe, sent from Herrnhut on 27th November, 'wishes blessing to La Trobe's preaching and to that of the Methodists', and adds:

Perhaps the time is not distant when many of the Wesleyans may join in receiving blessings along with the Brethren. The Wesleyan scheme came from the Brethren, from Zinzendorf himself, viz. that we would not take people from the Church of England but build them up within the Church. . . . We remain small in England because of our fault. Now it seems Wesley has made the same fault and has abandoned his first plan and is degenerating into a sect.'

The Moravians at this time seem to have believed that the Methodist would allow themselves to be absorbed in the Brethren's organization, and though Loretz disowns proselytizing he advocates 'private visits' and 'individual conversations'—which do not seem far removed![109]

[109] As early as the English Provincial Synod of 1754, the Count had said: 'If we remain friends with all the children of God, we might at last become heirs of the Societies of those servants of God who do not properly belong to our Church.' Rylands *Eng. MSS*, 1054.

The third letter, from La Trobe to Loretz on 6th January 1786, deplores the Moravian departure from their original plan (i.e. of remaining within the Church of England) and implies that it was Wesley's separation from the National Church which encouraged the Brethren to form an independent congregation. It makes the interesting admission that John Wesley, by adopting the Moravian 'Diaspora' plan of 'place-congregations',[110] had at this time a membership of fifty thousand. To this letter there is a most important postscript, covering eight long pages, and bearing the title *Of the Movements relating to the Methodists*. In it La Trobe speaks of the concern felt by Charles Wesley, sick in body and mind, about the possible secession of the Methodists from the Established Church, and of Charles Wesley's belief that the Brethren 'must be the means of preserving the true seed in the established church and of keeping the living souls among the Methodists together'. This would be difficult, for his brother John wished to be 'Pope', and, led away by 'young Coke', looked with suspicion upon La Trobe's influence amongst the Methodists.

The account goes on to say that La Trobe, to his surprise, had received a letter from Coke, dated 23rd December 1785, asking why the Brethren and the Methodists could not unite, in view of the similarity of their doctrine and discipline, and offering to meet La Trobe. Charles Wesley, who obviously suspected Coke's motives, warned his Moravian friend to be on his guard.

The interview, however, took place on 4th January 1786, and La Trobe agreed that it was a pity the two Communions had separated. Coke pointed out the difficulty of keeping the Methodists within the Church of England, for some were dissenters by birth, and others had been refused ordination in the Established Church. Hence John Wesley had been compelled to form a church constitution for America and to ordain 'Superintendents, Elders, and Deacons'. When Coke asked point-blank if La Trobe believed in the possibility of a union, he was told that 'the preliminaries were not yet settled'—apparently from a desire to gain time. It is amusing to record the interchange of courtesies which took place after the interview, Coke sending La Trobe a sermon on *The Godhead of Christ* and receiving in return a copy

[110] According to this, the Moravian congregations were to serve as centres wherein members of other Churches might find a temporary home. (See p. 169, *infra*.)

of Dr Franklin's *Abstract of the Book of Common Prayer*—a work showing the undesirability of making alterations in that book!

There is a further postscript which is illuminating:

I told him candidly that I could not seek an interview with his brother, as I had never done it, for his brother's method of publishing the conversations he had with anyone, and giving the other parties' words such a turn as suited his purpose, made it dangerous to converse with him.

Charles, however, thought the danger might be risked, since both he and John were of great age and probably near their end.

This suspicion of John Wesley peeps out in La Trobe's next report to the Moravian authorities, on 12th January 1786. He admits that he is afraid of an interview, and would not have one without an understanding that there was to be no publication of the conversation without mutual consent. He proposes to visit the Methodist Book Steward, John Atlay, who was friendly to the Brethren—a procedure as dangerous as John Wesley's fellowship with Richard Viney, for Atlay was to be a thorn in Wesley's side. He was bitterly disappointed at not being included in the 'Legal Hundred' formed by the 'Deed of Declaration' of 1784, and though he remained in the Methodist ministry until 1788, he became increasingly hostile to its leader, and finally became a minister of independent congregations in Dewsbury and South Shields.[111] As early as 18th April 1786, he declared that 'he had been attending La Trobe's services, and that he increasingly admired him every time he heard him'. He was hardly likely to be an effective intermediary at this time. La Trobe goes on to say:

As to a union, we apprehend it cannot be thought of. If by a union is meant something similar with that of Herrnhut and Ebersdorf, the reasons are obvious—

perhaps more obvious then than now! He asks whether Wesley is likely to assist in the Moravian 'Diaspora' plan, but adds:

As John is accustomed to be Pope (as his brother says) the old man will, without a particular work of God on his heart making him humble, hardly submit to it.

[111] *Journal*, VII.523; *Letters*, VIII.77, 84-6, 93.

He ends by expressing the opinion that if he were permitted to preach in Wesley's pulpit, both Wesley and Coke might expect the same hospitality; but he calls attention to the Brethren's orders in this matter. One wonders if Wesley would still be regarded as *homo perturbatus*!

In a letter to La Trobe on 17th February 1786, Loretz speaks of Coke's proposals for union, 'a proposition which has given us more fear than joy'. 'If John Wesley and Coke are sincere', he adds, 'we have many doubts. They are chiefs of a party and move in the interests of a party. We cannot suppose they are concerned merely with a spiritual fellowship, since all the children of God in this world should hold communion with one another whatever their constitution. That is not what J. Wesley is after.'

He then enumerates several conditions—agreement on the Diaspora plan, the maintenance of Moravian principles, customs, and methods, especially in the training of their ministers, and the refusal to supply Methodist chapels with ministers, still less administer the sacraments in them.

> We are not meant [he says] for a great company; only men whom the Lord has chosen are our members, therefore we cannot walk with every party. Our relationship is and must remain individual in character and is based on the gracious call of every individual member of the community.

He suggests that the Methodist desire is for an ecclesiastical union, which would legalize their ordinations and ensure their survival. This is a new point, and may have had some validity.

The conversations between La Trobe and Coke continued, the former being somewhat reluctant, the latter pertinacious. Again the suspicion of John Wesley is evident:

> I showed the difference [wrote La Trobe to the Unity's Elders' Conference at Herrnhut on 22nd April 1786] between the conduct of Count Zinzendorf and John Wesley; the Brethren came to him and not he to them. . . .

He told Coke how, under the Moravian constitution, a Union would be impossible; but Coke thought there might be a coalition, and spoke with admiration of the Brethren's constitution and the use of the Lot.

Coke pressed this suggestion of a coalition on the basis of the Diaspora plan, which, La Trobe contended, has the great object of 'keeping awakened souls in the established national church', and Coke's scheme therefore came to nothing. Charles Wesley at this time seemed to have reason for hope that his brother would not begin a new church-system in England, and expressed the wish that La Trobe might meet John in town. La Trobe agreed, with the proviso that the conversation would not be published. In a further report to Loretz in July 1786 La Trobe said:

> Mr Charles Wesley has owned to me that he was formerly very inimical to the Brethren, and his chief reason was that he apprehended the Brethren were undermining the Established Church by drawing the good souls out of it. . . . He is fully persuaded that our Lord aims to make the Brethren useful in bringing souls to Himself and being a blessing to the remnant of the sincere Methodists and of being a salt in the Church of England.

Coke reported his four conversations with La Trobe to John Wesley, and in a letter sent to Wesley on 6th May 1786 gave the following proposal as a result:

> That a conference be formed of an equal number of both Societies who shall meet at specified times to consult in what degree and by what methods a further union may be brought about. . . . The report of this conference to be laid from time to time, on the one hand before you and our General Conference and on the other hand before the Elders' Conference of the Brethren through Mr La Trobe; and in consequence steps be taken for a further union as to the two Governors of the two Societies respectively may be seen necessary.

He stated La Trobe's desire for a preliminary private conversation, and his anxiety lest this conversation should be published, in whole or in part, in Wesley's *Journal*. He sent a copy of this letter to La Trobe, who, in his reply, seemed reluctant to proceed with the matter. He objected to the use of the word 'Governors', which was not, he said, applicable to their constitution. 'Among us', he said, 'order and subordination is established but implicit faith in any man's words and implicit obedience to any man's order exists perhaps in no well-regulated society less than in the Brethren's Congregations.'

In his reply of 17th May 1786 to Coke, John Wesley expressed his great willingness to have a private conference with La Trobe. 'Undoubtedly', he said, 'nothing is more desirable than a cordial union among the children of God. I am not conscious of having neglected any step which had a tendency to this. And I am as ready now as ever I was to do anything that is in my power to promote it.'[112]

Apparently the conference did not take place, nor did the private conversation—why, it is not known. The following letter, however—the last in the series—makes it clear why the Moravians were hesitant, at any rate as long as John Wesley was the leader of the Methodists. It was sent on 12th July 1786, by Loretz to La Trobe, and contains a most significant statement. After admitting Coke's good will—for Coke recognized the importance to the Brethren of Tropus and Diaspora—and the possibility of collaboration on this basis, he adds:

> But I fear that Mr John Wesley will not be content with that and that he will fear to lose his influence and authority in his party. . . . The Methodists know that theirs is not our scheme and plan; we have said in all sincerity that we cannot help them by surrendering our own constitution. . . . That John Wesley is an arbitrary Pope is proved by the protocol of their Conference of last year communicated to you confidentially; he demands that his colleagues give an account but he himself will not give an account of his expenditure or of what he says or does. He is a Pope, as he said Count Zinzendorf was. But it must be doubted whether after J. Wesley's death, another man will be found to whom the Methodists will give so great power. More probably they will fall into parties. They must either remain connected with the Church or make their own Church—that we must leave to the Will of God; we have no call to help or hinder.

It will be noticed that this letter gives no hope of an actual union. All it envisages is collaboration, with the Methodists or with any other Protestant Church; and that, in any case, the Brethren would insist on retaining their own methods and constitution. In view of subsequent divisions in the Methodist Church, the prophecy that the Methodists would 'fall into parties' displayed considerable insight.

There is one more letter which was written on this matter and at this time.[113] It was sent by Charles Wesley to Benjamin La Trobe on 30th July 1786, and gives some indication of the explosive forces latent in Methodism at the end of the life of its founders. It runs:

[112] This Letter is not included in the Standard Edition of Wesley's *Letters*.

[113] Moravian Archives, London; copy (with omissions) at the Methodist Book Room, London; *Wesley Family Letters*, IV.36.

I wanted time yesterday for a fuller account of our Conference. The old preachers and their partisans came fully resolved on a separation. The only question with them was whether to be Independents or Presbyterians. As many as I talked with before the Conference, came over to the Church. In Conference they solicited my B. to ordain a minister for a solitary place in Yorkshire—and to proceed no further. J. Atlay[114] withstood them, and showed that by preserving 500 in the Church (as they pretend) we should lose 50,000. He proved that ordination was separation; and fairly talked them down, comforted if not convinced. My B. and I and the preachers were unanimous for continuing in the Old Ship.

The friendly intercourse of your Society and ours might be another likely means of preserving our children in their calling. My B. is very well inclined to such a correspondence. So is (would you think it?) the writer of these epistles.

Should I live to meet my B. in London he will desire a conference with you. You will first settle your preliminary article, and then venture (I should think) to converse with him and me.

If our Lord is pleased to use us as peace-makers under Him, we may yet do something towards preventing any separation at all. At least we shall deliver our own souls.

The great evil which I have dreaded for nearly 50 years is a Schism. If I live to see that evil prevented,[115] and also to see the 2 sticks, the Moravian and the English Church, become one in our Saviour's hands, I shall then say: 'Lord, now lettest Thou Thy servant depart in peace.'

This correspondence has been given in considerable detail, not only because it shows how near the Moravians and the Methodists came to some form of union, but also because it clearly shows what were the real obstacles to that union. There is no doubt that the Moravians were reluctant, perhaps afraid, to enter into negotiations for a union, and that John Wesley himself was not enthusiastic. Charles Wesley seems to have sought it primarily as a means of keeping the Methodists within the National Church, and Coke to cement the forces of evangelism and possibly to validate Methodist ordinations. Quietism has disappeared from the arena of discussion; the place of faith and works has fallen into the background—indeed, there are several indications in the later letters that there was no serious doctrinal difference; there is no longer any personal rivalry between two outstanding leaders; the criticisms of Methodist 'convulsions' and Moravian 'guile' are no

[114] See p. 160, *supra*. [115] Charles Wesley died on 29th March 1788.

longer heard; and the issues have been narrowed to the personal power and character of John Wesley and the preservation of the connexion with the National Church. There is more than one suggestion that Wesley would arrogate to himself as much power in a united Church as he had already (perhaps necessarily) done amongst his own followers. The Moravians were not the only ones to fear an autocracy. As has been seen, his own brother called him, though perhaps only jocularly, 'Pope John'; and in his letter of 10th March 1741 he had asked,[116] 'Is there not envy, self-love, emulation, jealousy? Are you not afraid lest they should eclipse your own glory or lessen your own praise?' Apparently, Wesley was frequently accused of liking flattery and resenting criticism. In March 1764 a Mrs Ryan of Leytonstone had written to him:

I have often heard you do not take those persons to be real friends who reprove or tell you what they think wrong; but cleave to those who always give praise and respect, though sometimes only from the teeth outward.[117]

and in a letter to Joseph Benson, classical master at Kingswood, he wrote in December 1769:

I have been told a hundred times: 'You love those that flatter you, and hate all that deal plainly and honestly with you.'[118]

How far an autocracy was necessary is a matter for debate; certainly when John Wesley's strong hand was removed, his followers lost their coherence. Wesley defined his position in a letter to Mrs Crosby, another member of the rather critical Leytonstone circle:

I am called to a peculiar work. And perhaps the very temper and behaviour (i.e. refusal to be disturbed by unpleasant circumstances) which you blame is one great means whereby I am capacitated for carrying on that work. I do not 'lessen my authority' (perhaps there have been six exceptions, perhaps not) over two hundred preachers and twenty thousand men and women by any tenderness of speech or behaviour, whether to preachers or people. God exceedingly confirms my authority thereby; of which *I* have such proofs as *you* cannot have. . . . I love you the more, the more free you are. That is another total mistake, that I dislike any one for plain dealing.[119]

[116] See p. 111, *supra*.
[117] *Letters*, IV.232-3.
[118] ibid., V.164.
[119] ibid., V.27.

Wesley's philosophic comment after hearing that Gambold did not wish to associate further with him gives credence to this claim.[120]

The reluctance of the Moravians to commit themselves to any statement which Wesley might subsequently publish or mis-report in his *Journal* is understandable, though the suggestion made by La Trobe that he would twist the conversation to his own purpose is hardly justified. Indeed, there are very few references in the *Journal* to the Brethren after the long account in Part IV; and the absence of any mention of them in the annual Methodist Conferences is striking. There is one such reference in the *Minutes* of the first Conference (30th June 1744):

Q. Can we unite any farther with the Moravians?
A. It seems not, were it only for this reason, they will not unite with us.[121]

Though the doctrinal gulf narrowed through the century, a good deal of suspicion persisted. Wesley regarded the Brethren as Antinomian, as not concerned about conduct as long as they enjoyed a personal relationship with God; the Moravians in their turn thought Wesley, by his emphasis on good works, untrue to the cardinal doctrine of Justification by Faith. Both were mistaken. As has already been pointed out, the Brethren recognized the importance of the ethical side of Christianity.[122] In 1754 they inserted in their Liturgy a number of petitions referring to the prosaic duties of everyday life, praying, not merely for those in authority, but for all in need. It may be contended that this insertion and emphasis were to some extent the result of the example and criticism of John Wesley, and this has probably some foundation. Modern Moravians have a similar and even more specific emphasis: in the dignified and impressive Liturgy of 1914 there are prayers for 'the temporal life, for sanctification and for those in need', while in the *Second Liturgy* prayers are offered for the poor, the aged, the sick, the young, and for all who are in distress. Wesley seems to have ignored the missionary work in which the Brethren were pioneers.[123]

Similarly, the Brethren did Wesley less than justice. They even doubted the reality of his conversion. James Hutton had written

[120] *Journal*, II.472.
[121] *John Bennet's Copy, Wesley Historical Society Proceedings.*
[122] See p. 129, *supra.* [123] See p. 180, *infra.*

in 1741: 'Shortly after Wesley and Ingham's return from Germany, he and his brother were not grounded';[124] and nearly half a century later La Trobe, in his letter to Loretz, said: 'It is very doubtful whether John ever knew himself as a sinner or our Lord as his Saviour.'[125] Undoubtedly, both sides exaggerated: Wesley's vague and comprehensive description of the Moravians as Antinomian came surprisingly from one who generally demanded exact definition; and it is more than probable that Moravian suspicion of Wesley's doctrine of Christian Perfection arose from a misunderstanding of what Wesley really meant. Perhaps the term 'Christian Perfection' was unfortunate, if it suggested that absolute perfection[126] is ever achieved. Wesley certainly never claimed it for himself,[127] but he was continually urging his converts to reach a higher stage in their spiritual careers, 'to press on toward the goal unto the prize of the high calling of God in Christ Jesus'.[128] Indeed, though Wesley sometimes spoke of it as 'perfection', and sometimes as 'entire sanctification', he most commonly referred to it as 'being renewed in love'. He writes of the people in question:

> After being deeply convinced of inbred sin, particularly of pride, anger, self-will, and unbelief, in a moment they feel all faith and love—no pride, no self-will or anger; and from that moment they have continued fellowship with God.[129]

In fairness it must be said that the Moravians who, like good Lutherans, held that justification was imputed, and loved to describe themselves as 'sinner-like', were not the only people to object to this doctrine. Grimshaw, Venn, Romaine and Whitefield all protested. It was Whitefield who invented the phrase 'sinless perfection', a term never used by Wesley himself. Moreover, whatever interpretation Wesley placed upon the doctrine, some of his followers took it very literally and regarded themselves as a spiritual élite—a danger from which the Brethren themselves were not immune. 'It is better for us', they said, 'to decrease in

[124] *Account of the Beginning of the Lord's Work in England to 1741*; Moravian Archives at Herrnhut.

[125] See p. 158, *supra*.

[126] ' "Absolute or infallible perfection"? I never contended for it.' *Letters*, IV.213.

[127] 'I tell you flat that I have not attained the character I draw.' ibid., V.43.

[128] Phil. 3[14].

[129] *Journal*, IV.480.

M

numbers and increase in piety, than to be a large multitude like a body without a Spirit.'

Perhaps at one time one block in the way of union was the theological indefiniteness of the Moravians, though the publication of Spangenberg's *Idea Fidei Fratrum* in 1778 should have made their position clear, following the third constitutional Synod at Barby (on the Elbe) in 1775. It may be true to say, as J. E. Hutton does, that the Moravians 'have always declined to bind the consciences of their ministers and members by any creed whatever', but he goes too far when he claims that they have never had a creed of their own—unless he means by this a creed differing in word and content from the historic creeds.[130] In *Moravian Liturgy and Hymns* (1914), commonly used by Moravian congregations today, there is a 'Confession of Faith', prescribed for use on the first Sunday in Advent, Easter Day, Trinity Sunday, and other occasions, which closely resembles the Apostles' Creed in content, and in part in actual words. But the want of uniformity in belief in the eighteenth century irritated John Wesley, who had a passion for exact statement, and made him suspect their sincerity. At the English Provincial Synod of 1754 James Hutton said:

> We have a good, a loving set of people who shut their minds to all definition; they have no objection against the matter, if they only be happy.[131]

Apart from the Brethren's suspicion of John Wesley and Wesley's reluctance to take a decisive step, the supreme barrier in the way of union was the difference between the attitudes of the two Communions to their own nature as a Church and therefore to the National Church. The keynotes of Zinzendorf's position were the Tropus and the Diaspora. According to the former, he regarded each Church (in the wider sense as a communion and not an individual congregation) as a Tropus, a religious training-ground, which was to be a part of a much larger, comprehensive Church, which should embrace every Church under heaven.

Within this universal community, so diverse in creeds and liturgies, the Moravians could retain their traditional discipline and forms of worship, as could the Lutheran, the Reformed, and the Anglican Churches. Perhaps this conception of a federated Church is not so absurd or so far removed from present-day needs

[130] op. cit., p. 483.

[131] Rylands *Eng. MSS*, 1056.

and possibilities as it seemed to Zinzendorf's critics to be. The position was made clear at the English Provincial Synods of 1764-82:

We have at this time three Tropuses, the Moravian, the Lutheran, and the Reformed, and it is to be remembered that the children always belong to the Tropus to which their parents belong. But these Tropuses are practicable, because of our universality, without which no person could be received into our Congregation till he had abandoned his former religion, but this is contrary to our fundamental plan. . . .

We avoid in the most careful manner all disputes about religion, and since one of the Protestant religions is as dear to us as the other, therefore it is that we can never make it our business to gain proselytes either for the one or the other, but we direct all souls to Jesus Christ, as the Head and Lord of His Church.[132]

The implication in England was that, apart from their settlements, the Moravians made no attempt to increase their own numbers, and therefore looked with hostility on the possibility of Methodist secession from the Church of England.

The idea behind the Diaspora was similar—that the Moravian Church, without losing its entity as a Church, should be regarded as a house of call for the 'Scattered' in all the Churches, and, instead of proselytizing, the Brethren should serve as a bond of union between evangelical Christians of all denominations. This two-fold aspect is shown in the records of the English Provincial Synod of 1765:

Our Saviour's intention with us is surely not only to gather souls out of the world into congregational places, but we are to be a blessing and a salt in other religious denominations. This is particularly our wish with regard to the Church of England.[133]

To this unselfish ideal, which prevented their growth as a Church, the Brethren remained true. Indeed, by the resolutions of their own Synods, proselytizing on behalf of Moravian congregations was forbidden and it has never been easy to obtain membership. It was customary for eighteenth-century Moravians to advise their converts to attach themselves to the nearest parish church, a procedure which has been followed in some respects more recently in 'Religion and Life' campaigns and other evangelistic enterprises. It was not until 1856 that the English Brethren

[132] Rylands *Eng. MSS*, 910. [133] ibid., 1056.

rejected this principle of 'a Church within a Church', an ideal which, however lofty, was an insuperable bar to their own growth.

John Wesley heartily approved of the Brethren's reluctance to form a separate Church, and always regarded his own congregations as ancillary to those of the Established Church. He would not allow them to meet at the same time as the services of the Church of England, except for special reasons, e.g. to prevent any exodus[134] to Dissenting chapels, or where the minister was 'a notoriously wicked man'.

But, as will have been seen already, events were too strong for him. Not only did he feel compelled, in order to secure the American work, to ordain his own ministers, with the obvious consequence of a clean break with the Established Church, but his own somewhat heterogeneous following forced the issue. Some, as Charles Wesley had said in his letter to La Trobe in July 1786,[135] were more inclined to the Independents or Presbyterians; more cared for no side—as converts, they had no traditional loyalties; others, who were loyal to the Church of England, were disturbed by the hostile reception they were given by certain incumbents and by the attacks of some of the Bishops; while those laymen who had in their own Societies tasted authority were hardly likely to wish to return to a system in which they would have none. Moreover, there were already signs of disruption in Methodism. John Cennick was only one of many who became, for a time at any rate, Calvinists; separate independent Societies, of mixed religious parentage, had been set up as early as 1783—several years before John Wesley's death—and were, by union with the 'Singing Quakers', to form the germ of the Independent Methodist Church of today; as early as the Leeds Conference of 1755, a three-days discussion took place on the relationship with the Church of England; the Deed of Declaration of 1784, though it did much to stabilize Methodism, caused a revolt of some of the ministers who were not nominated to the Legal Hundred;[136] and the demand of the laity for the administration of the Sacrament and for financial control caused a serious breach by the setting up of the 'Methodist New Connexion' within six years of Wesley's death.

This schism, regrettable as it was, did little more than recognize

134 *Minutes of Conference* (1786). 135 See pp. 163–4, *supra*.

136 e.g. Atlay; see p. 160, *supra*.

a division which was inevitable and which indeed had already begun. The reforms of Alexander Kilham, the leader of the rebels, merely gave shape to deep-rooted grievances which had been growing for a long time. Sooner or later, separation was bound to take place. A Conference consisting of 'travelling preachers' alone could not persist for ever in a Church which depended so much upon lay support in its respective Societies, and at a time when the demand for political privilege was so vocal.

There was no similar secession from the Moravian body, but there were allied problems: the heavy responsibility of missionary work; the growing desire to enlarge their own Church; a wish on the part of the English Brethren for a greater share in their own development, apart from the control of Herrnhut; and the need to establish town and country congregations rather than settlements. These reforms were yet to come, and their *gradual* achievement probably saved the Moravians from the cleavages which were so sorely to wound the Methodist Church.

If, then, the chief obstacles to a closer union between these two evangelical groups lay in the person of John Wesley and in the determination of the Moravians to retain their association with the National Church, it might be assumed that with the death of the one and the weakening of the other this union might have been achieved. In fact, this did not happen: what movement there was for union among the English Brethren was not toward the Methodists, in spite of the historic connexion, but with the Church of England; and there seems to have been no suggestion of any kind of amalgamation, federation or coalition with Methodism after the abortive negotiations of 1785-6. The possibility of a closer union between the English Brethren and the Anglican Church was envisaged by Bishop Hutchinson of Barbados in 1878, but it was not until 1906 that an Archbishop's Committee was appointed to examine the Moravian claim to the possession of an episcopal ministry. The Lambeth Conference of 1908 proposed certain conditions under which joint recognition of Anglican and Moravian orders might be achieved. These conditions were not equally acceptable to both parties, and were considerably modified later. There were matters on which both sides were hesitant, the Moravians particularly, who feared that union might involve them in some disturbance of their relations with other Christian communities with which they were already in fellowship. The fundamental issue was whether the Brethren, claiming as they did to be both reformed and Catholic, could be organically united with the Church of England, which makes the same claim, even if such a union necessitated some change in their relation to the 'Free Churches', especially in the matter of the administration and reception of the Sacrament. The Moravians, true to their ideal of fellowship in Christ, could not accept such conditions, and the negotiations came to nothing.

Union with the Methodist Church would present no such issues; but there is such strong objection to Episcopacy in British Methodism (though not in American) that anything more than a loose federation is hardly possible. It is to be doubted, indeed, whether the cause of Christian Reunion would be advanced by the union of the Brethren with any other Christian denomination at present. It would be a tragedy if their great contribution to the cause of evangelical religion were ever forgotten; and their absorption in a large Church, possibly with the loss of their historic name and the rationalizing of their distinctive forms of worship, would involve a serious loss to their own specific witness without proportionately influencing the larger body.

But though union with British Methodism seems only a distant dream, and one not universally accepted as desirable in either Church, Moravianism has already profoundly influenced the birth and growth of the Methodist Church, not merely in its effect upon the spiritual life of its founders but in helping to shape its constitution and practice. The former influence has been traced in the early chapters of this book, and to some extent (if only by contraries) in later ones; the latter will be examined in the chapter which follows.

SUMMARY

(1) Throughout the period, with the exception of a few years of sharp controversy, the two Communions kept apart, generally pursuing parallel paths but adopting similar methods. In the verbal contest, 'the Battle of the Books', John Wesley was generally on the attack, the Moravians on the defensive. The Moravian attitude was, on the whole, consistent—guarded, non-committal, avoiding controversy, anxious to pursue their own way undisturbed. John Wesley's attitude, however, was very varied, ranging from warm appreciation of the Moravians as a whole, with

some exceptions in the case of the Fetter Lane Society, to severe and even bitter criticism, usually provoked by some immediate circumstance, though his dislike of Zinzendorf coloured his feelings throughout.

(2) Doctrinal differences, at first acute, fell into the background after the departure of Molther. Wesley persisted, however, in charging the Brethren with Antinomianism, and the Moravians did not cease to object to Wesley's doctrine of Christian perfection.

(3) On the whole, Anglican writers did not differentiate between Moravian and Methodist, regarding both as schismatic and heretical.

(4) Toward the end of the century, there was something of a *rapprochement* between Wesley and the Moravian leaders. The negotiations of 1785-6, which at one time gave promise, if not of organic union, at any rate of co-operation, were sponsored, probably from different motives, by Charles Wesley and Thomas Coke. There is no evidence that John Wesley was keenly interested in the matter, and it became increasingly plain that the Moravian leaders had no intention of pursuing the matter very far. Their reluctance was due to:

(*a*) suspicion of what they regarded as John Wesley's ambition;

(*b*) fear that the Methodists were about to break away from the Church of England, and would thus, if union came, make impossible the retention of the characteristic Moravian plan of Tropus and Diaspora;

(*c*) satisfaction with their own system of settlements, evangelistic methods and modes of worship, and apprehension lest these might be compelled to suffer modification. Coupled with this was a feeling that the Methodist preachers were not sufficiently or properly trained.

On these rocks the hopes of fellowship and united action foundered, and the two Communions remained apart, neither, perhaps, either cognisant of or grateful for the contribution made to it by the other.

CHAPTER SEVEN

THE MORAVIAN CONTRIBUTION TO METHODISM

A—GENERAL INFLUENCES

IT WILL be admitted that in so far as the Wesleys' experience at Whitsuntide 1738 shaped their subsequent thought, and therefore affected the development of Methodism, the Moravians in general and Peter Böhler in particular had no small share in that reshaping and that development. It is not so widely recognized that in the fashioning of the organization of what was afterwards to become the Methodist Church—its social groups, its methods of worship, and its world-outlook—the Moravians exercised a profound, and in some directions a permanent, influence. It was inevitable, of course, that the impression made by the Moravians on John Wesley, not merely in 1738 but before and afterwards, should have shaken his confidence in his previous theological views, and in the Church organization in which those views found expression, viz. in the Church of England and its ordinances. The immediate debt of John Wesley to the Moravians was varied in character but possessed unity in its variety. In general—to use a phrase beloved by the Brethren—it involved the substitution of the religion of the heart for that of the head, or rather the replacement of the 'eudaemonistic ethicism' which he had learned from William Law and Jeremy Taylor by a personal experience of Jesus Christ as Saviour. At first, it was a different emphasis, but later consideration and more mature experience made 'addition' a more appropriate description. But there were other effects derivative from this general influence, effects which were to shape the lives and behaviour of the Methodists as members of the Established Church and later as a separate Communion.

(1) In the first place, the Moravians had a powerful appeal to Wesley in their regard for the order and spirit of the primitive Church. They took him back to the Apostolic age, and though they thus deepened his loyalty to the Church which to him had always been the true heir of Apostolic tradition, by their own regard for the past they revealed to him that the Church of England had no monopoly of that inheritance. Moreover, as will be

seen, the Moravians reminded Wesley of some elements of primitive worship of which the Church of England had lost sight.

(2) In the second place, the Moravians brought to the Wesleys a deeper sense of fellowship. Fellowship had of course been emphasized in the Religious Societies and particularly in the Holy Club. But here was something different, so different that five of the Oxford group joined the Moravian Brethren, and one of them, John Gambold, became their first English Bishop. When Gambold formally resigned his living at Stanton Harcourt in 1742, in order to join an unpopular sect, he explained his reasons in a farewell address to his parishioners:

> That which has determined the choice which I have made was the earnest desire I found in myself of that improvement in the knowledge of the Gospel and in the experience of the grace of Jesus Christ which I stood in need of. The blessings purchased by the blood of the Shepherd of our souls I longed to enjoy in *fellowship* with a little flock of His sheep, who daily feed on the merits of His passion, and whose great concern is to build up one another in their most holy faith, and to propagate the truth, as it is in Jesus, for the good of others.

Whether this fellowship could have been found within the organization of the Church of England is a matter for debate—Gambold obviously thought not—but the Wesleys, at any rate for a long time, apparently cherished the hope that this new emphasis on fellowship did not necessarily involve separation from the Church of their fathers.

Thought often follows feeling, and formulation succeeds impulse, and it is probable that the *doctrinal* influence of the Moravians upon the Wesleys was not immediate. They had already been familiar with the Lutheran doctrine of Justification by Faith—the eleventh Article of Religion would have been part of their staple diet—and, though to a less extent, with the idea of Assurance, or the Witness of the Spirit. But on these points the Brethren had no doubts. They made these two doctrines alive with their own emphasis on feeling, and their fusion of thought and emotion inspired Wesley to fashion his own characteristic doctrine of the Witness of the Spirit. Wesley stressed this change in his views in a reply given at the Bristol Conference of May 1746:

Q. Wherein does our doctrine now differ from that we preached when at Oxford?
A. Chiefly in these two points: 1, We then knew nothing of that righteousness of faith in justification; nor, 2, of the nature of faith itself, as implying consciousness of pardon.[1]

It is noticeable that there is here no mention of the doctrine of Christian Perfection.

How far John Wesley's acceptance of these two doctrines, Justification by Faith, with the exclusive emphasis from which he was in some measure to retreat, and the Assurance of Salvation, which the Moravians maintained should accompany or follow justification, involved inevitable separation from the Church of England, is a matter on which there is considerable difference of opinion. Some writers[2] maintain that separation could not have been avoided, that the spiritual centre of gravity had moved from baptism to conversion, that John Wesley *ipso facto* had forsaken his High Church principles, had ceased to be a priest in order to become a preacher, and that there was no room for an evangelist within the National Church. These assumptions are by no means self-evident. As has been seen, Wesley's change of emphasis did not necessarily involve a breach with the Established Church; indeed, one of the primary causes of his breach with the Moravians was his insistence on the ordinances of the Church of England; and Wesley claimed to be a 'High Churchman' as late as 1775. When the breach with the Anglican Church came, it came over the difficult question of ordination, a question not directly connected with his doctrinal position. In any case, if his belief in the doctrine of Justification by Faith was bound, by the logic of events, to separate his organization from the Church of England, such separation was considerably delayed. It may be added that priesthood and preaching are not mutually exclusive!

On the other hand, it cannot be denied that the teaching of the Moravians, and especially their emphasis on the *individual*, was an indirect cause of the separation of the Methodists from the Church of England. John Wesley, as his work grew, depended more and more upon the assistance of laymen. It was not to be expected that they would eagerly remain in a Church which

[1] *Minutes of Conference* (1746).

[2] e.g. Julia Wedgwood, *John Wesley and the Evangelical Reaction of the Eighteenth Century*; J. H. Rigg, *The Living Wesley*.

limited their effectiveness and, indeed, denied them status. Wesley had loosened a power which he found himself unable to confine, and the secessions from the parent body of Methodism were to arise in the first place from the claim of laymen to a larger share in the government of the Church. The five thousand members who accompanied Alexander Kilham in 1797 to form the Methodist New Connexion did so in the main as a protest against the refusal of the Conference to grant laymen more power in the Church courts and greater control over finance.

In one direction, the influence of Moravianism delayed this separation. The ideal of *ecclesiola in ecclesia* was dear to Zinzendorf's heart throughout his life, and was shared by many of his followers, though there were signs at the end of the eighteenth century that others had forsaken it. Zinzendorf had adopted the idea from the drawing-room meetings of Spener the Pietist, meetings which came to be known as 'Churches within the Church'. Up to 1729, the Brethren had no separate ministry. They were still members of the Lutheran Church, regarded Rothe as their Pastor, attended the Parish Church on Sundays, and took the Communion once a month. In England, long after they had their own ministers, they adopted the same procedure, encouraging their converts to remain members of the Church of England, and placing serious obstacles in the way of new members of their own Communion. When Gambold became a Moravian in 1742, he regarded himself as still a member of the Church of England, though he claimed some kind of independence in his relationship to it. Zinzendorf's idea of a Tropus was akin to his conception of a Church within a Church; and it was in pursuance of this that the Moravian Synod of 1749 invited Bishop Wilson of Sodor and Man to be a Superintendent of the Brethren. 'In future', said Zinzendorf, 'we are all to be Brethren; and therefore in the Church of the Brethren there will henceforth be, not only Moravians, but also Lutherans and Calvinists, who cannot find peace in their own Churches on account of brutal theologians.'[3]

How far Wesley adopted this ideal is doubtful. It is probable that with that practical common sense which distinguished him he saw the many difficulties in the way. It is certain that throughout his life Wesley clung pathetically to the hope that his Societies might find a place within the National Church; and there are

[3] Hutton, *History of the Moravian Church*, pp. 273-4.

interesting evidences that for some considerable time the Methodists regarded themselves as members of the Church of England, and came in parties to take Communion at the Parish Church; and John Wesley's insistence that the hours of Methodist worship should not in general conflict with those of the neighbouring church seems to confirm this. A tract entitled *Observations upon the Conduct and Behaviour of a Certain Sect usually distinguished by the name of Methodist* censures this practice, and quotes the rubric of the Communion Service forbidding the administration of the Sacrament to people who are not known.

Reference has already been made to the reliance at one time placed by Wesley upon Richard Viney. In the latter's *Letter from an English Brother of the Moravian Persuasion in Holland to the Methodists in England, lamenting the irregularity of their present proceedings* (1739), he rejoices at the general revival of religion in England, but deplores separatist tendencies. 'Is that the will of God', he asks, 'to persuade the people to separate from the Churches they are brought up in, and begin new sects? Are there not enough sects already?'[4] The subsequent history of the relations between the Wesleys and Viney may not encourage the belief that this letter had much effect, but there is no doubt that the general insistence by the Brethren on the danger of separation confirmed the Wesleys' own attitude, and that their obvious reluctance, at the end of the century, to commit themselves to any scheme of union arose in large part from fear of the spread of separatist tendencies among the Methodist people. In his letter to Loretz of 25th October 1785, Benjamin La Trobe suggested that John Wesley's intention to remain within the Church of England was, at any rate in part, due to the influence of the Moravians:[5]

> He has taken up some of our regulations and established them in his Societies. He set out as an avowed partisan of the Church of England and his people have kept to it.

In the same letter, he made it plain that Charles Wesley not only abhorred separation, but sought Moravian help in avoiding it. He wrote:

> He declares he will oppose this new schism [involved in the American ordinations] which will end in a number of new sects; and now he

[4] Pages 14-15.

[5] See p. 158, *supra*.

wishes that the Brethren might be of the use they were originally intended for, to nurse those souls who are truly awakened and who adhere to the Church of England.

It was already becoming clear, however, that the Brethren were deserting Zinzendorf's ideal, and, indeed, that they were influenced by the Methodists in this direction. Loretz's letter to La Trobe on 27th November 1785, while claiming that the Wesleyan scheme (viz. of non-separation) came from Zinzendorf himself, implies that the English Moravians had begun to abandon this policy, and were attempting to build up a Church of their own.[6] There is some indication of this in the report of the proceedings of the English Provincial Synod held at Lindsey House on 12th–14th November 1754. At this meeting, Zinzendorf, who is described as 'The Disciple', seems to make a distinction between the English Brethren and the Moravians, and says:

The English Church according to its old principles is the nearest, next to our Church, to the Church of the Apostles.... The English Church... is become something more excellent than what it was intended by its founders, had it not been spoiled by the Methodists and Deists.... We want... a true and able friend among the English prelates, for the good of the English Church, that the awakened souls might abide within the verge of the English Church.[7]

So, too, La Trobe, in his letter of 6th January 1786, says categorically that the Methodists had copied the Moravians in adopting the system of the Diaspora.[8] Wesley therefore had adopted from Zinzendorf not only the conception of a Methodist 'bloc' within the Anglican Church, but also the wider idea of a 'Tropus' in which members of different Churches might meet. Wesley had defined this aim thus:

Two young men sowed the word of God, not only in the churches but likewise literally 'by the wayside'; and indeed in every place where they saw an open door, where sinners had come to hear. They were members of the Church of England, and had no desire of separating from it. And they advised all that were of it to continue therewith, although they joined the Methodist Society; for this did not imply leaving their former congregation but only leaving their sins. The Churchmen might go to Church still; the Presbyterian, Anabaptist,

[6] See p. 158, *supra*.
[7] Rylands *Eng. MSS*, 110.
[8] *Moravian Archives*, Herrnhut.

Quaker, might still retain their own opinions, and attend their own congregations. The having a real desire to flee from the wrath to come was the only condition required of them.[9]

The similarity of this to Viney's letter quoted above is remarkable.

It is reasonable therefore to assume that though John Wesley would, by his early training and prepossessions, have sought to retain his followers within the Church of England, the Moravians, by their advocacy of an *ecclesiola in ecclesia* and the Tropus not only strengthened his determination but defined his methods, until the pressure of circumstances compelled both Moravian and Methodist to perpetuate their existence in separate organizations.

So far, then, the Moravian contribution to Methodism, apart from its influence on the faith and vision of the Wesleys, has been of a general character—first in working methods which tended to separate it from the parent Church, and second in ecclesiastical conceptions which for a time prevented that separation. In one important direction the Moravian influence was even more general, for it was enjoyed by other Churches—in its missionary spirit and example. There are many claimants for the title of pioneers of modern missions. St Francis Xavier went to Goa as early as 1542, and laboured for ten years in South India, the Eastern Archipelago, and Japan. In the same century the Dutch had successful missions in their Far Eastern colonies and in Brazil. There were English missions to the North American Indians in the middle of the seventeenth century; and the Societies for the Propagation of the Gospel and for Promoting Christian Knowledge were founded at the end of that century. It is generally admitted, however, that though Moravian missions did not begin until 1732, their missions were of such a character and magnitude as to entitle them to be called the first modern missions. The two Anglican Societies which preceded them were of a different order, and ministered primarily to white settlers rather than to natives. From the very start, Moravian missionary enterprise was to those who had never heard of the Gospel. Zinzendorf's imagination had been fired by a conversation in 1731 with a West Indian negro slave from the Danish island of St Thomas, and a band of Single Brethren who had already determined to go overseas gladly seized the opportunity now offered. The voice of the Lot decided them, and in August 1732 Leonard

[9] *Works*, VI.276-9.

Dober and David Nitschmann set out, with only a few shillings in their pockets, for Copenhagen, on their way to St Thomas. The Missionary College in Copenhagen had already sent Hans Egede to Greenland and Ziegenbalg to Tranquebar on the Coromandel coast; but these were state officials, whose missionary work was a part of useful colonial policy. In spite of some opposition, the two missionaries went on their way, and opened a new chapter in the history of modern Christianity. They were the founders of Christian work among the slaves. For fifty years the Moravians laboured in the West Indies without any aid from any other religious denomination. They established churches in St Thomas, St Croix, St John's, Jamaica, Antigua, Barbados, and St Kitts. They had thirteen thousand baptized converts before a missionary from any other Church arrived on the scene.

Other fields were tilled—Greenland, where the Danish missionary, Hans Egede, had failed, and where the Moravians, Matthew Stach and Christian David, had at first met with no success. Here a new method, the story of the Cross, produced spectacular results; a settlement was established on the Herrnhut model, and the roving Eskimos adopted a peaceful and settled life. Other enterprises followed—in Dutch Guinea, in spite of the opposition of the Dutch pastors, in South Africa, where the Cape Town clergy accused George Schmidt of heresy, on the Gold Coast, in Wallachia, in Russia, in Persia, in Egypt, and amongst the Jews in Germany.

The Moravian claim to priority, made by other people for them as well as by themselves, is based on the single-mindedness of their effort. It differed from the enterprise of members of other Protestant Churches in being instituted, authorized, and organized by the Church itself. There were, as has been pointed out, Anglican missions, but these were carried out by two voluntary associations, the S.P.C.K. and the S.P.G.; Lutheran missionaries went out as individuals rather than as accredited representatives of the Lutheran Church; Danish missions, like those of Geneva in the sixteenth century, were sponsored by the State; in the Dutch Colonies they were the result of the enterprise of the Dutch East India Company and individual colonial governors; the Baptist Missionary Society, the London Missionary Society, the Church Missionary Society were not formed until the closing years of the century, and the Wesleyan Missionary Society not until the early years of the nineteenth century. But the missionary work of the Brethren was an integral part of their evangelical effort. Their Litany contained, as it still does, prayers for missions; they sang missionary hymns; they held meetings at which missionaries' letters were read; and in other ways they assumed responsibility for the maintenance and supervision of missionary effort.

If the Moravians were the teachers, the Methodists were apt and willing pupils. The Methodist Church is built on its evangelistic foundation, and the John Wesley who looked upon all the world as his parish[10] probably needed no prompting about his missionary duty. As a child, he had abundant encouragement at home. Samuel Wesley, his father, fostered in his children a missionary spirit, and published a comprehensive scheme of missions for India, China, and Abyssinia, while his mother thrilled them by reading to them the story of the work of Danish missionaries at Tranquebar. When the two Wesley brothers were urged to go out to Georgia as ministers to the colonists and missionaries to the Indians, John at first peremptorily refused, but his mother when consulted quietly declared: 'Had I twenty sons I should rejoice that they were all so employed, though I should never see them more.' John Wesley's experiences in Georgia were hardly such as to encourage him to repeat the experiment, and in any case he found sufficient work at home amongst miners and farm-labourers to keep him occupied for a long time; but missionary work was inherent in Methodism, and Methodist missions would have been established whether or not the Moravians had pointed the way. John Wesley's visit to Ireland in 1747, a year after Cennick had begun his remarkable work there, may have sprung from a spirit of emulation, or it may have been his reaction to a good example: it was none the less missionary work of a high order. Methodist missionary work in the West Indies began in 1760, in Nova Scotia in 1765, and in the American Colonies a year later; and it was the call of the work in America which compelled Wesley to take the momentous step of ordination. Indeed, individual Methodists like Robert Strawbridge and Philip Embury, both from Ireland, had taken Methodist beliefs and practices into the American colonies some years beforehand. The Methodist Missionary Society was not to be formed for some years, not until

[10] 'I look upon all the world as my parish'—letter to James Hervey; *Letters*, I.286.

1813, but its extraordinary development since that time shows that whether it was derived from Moravianism, or encouraged by the birth of other Societies, or a spontaneous growth arising out of the very nature of Methodism it was bound, sooner or later, to appear. It is at least probable, however, that its formation was encouraged and challenged by the success of Moravian missions.

B—PARTICULAR INFLUENCES

In attempting to assess the influence of the Moravian leaders upon the spiritual life of John and Charles Wesley, we were careful to take note of, and to examine, other possible factors—the home-life at Epworth, the Holy Club, the Religious Societies, the books they read, Pietism. A similar caution is necessary in tracing the particular influence of Moravian customs on the creation and development of Methodist Church organization and practice. It will be found again that many strands went to make up the texture of Methodist church life. John Wesley had generously admitted the influence of Peter Böhler, Spangenberg, and other Moravians upon the shaping of his own thought and spirit, and he was equally generous, both before and after the split, in acknowledging his admiration of Moravian customs, though he with equal candour declared his detestation of certain individual interpretations. Both in his *Journal* and in his letters he frequently commends their 'discipline'. After his visit to Herrnhut in 1738, for example, in the letter which he began but did not send, he says:

> I greatly approve of your conferences and bands; of your method of instructing children; and, in general, of your great care of the souls committed to your charge.[11]

Again, in the famous letter which prefaces Part IV of his *Journal*, he writes: 'I love and esteem you for your excellent discipline, scarce inferior to that of the apostolic age.'[12] Later, in the letter to the Rev. Thomas Church, he quotes and approves his letter of September 1738 and adds: 'In part, I esteem them still . . . because their discipline is in most respects so truly excellent.'[13] It would indeed be remarkable if his admiration for their organization did not lead in some ways to imitation, and the similarity of Moravian and Methodist church-order, and even of terminology, is too close to be coincidental.

[11] *Journal*, II.496. [12] ibid., II.309-11. [13] *Letters*, II.181.

(a) The Bands

Fellowship has always been inherent in Methodism. In recent times the 'class-meeting' has fallen into disuse and has been replaced by other forms of group-worship and group-study, but even today the 'Leaders' Meeting' is the unit of government of the local church. It cannot of course be claimed that John Wesley's insistence on fellowship took its root in Moravianism, but it is more than probable that its early expression was built on the Moravian model. He certainly knew of the value of fellowship before he ever met the Moravians, for his father had founded a Religious Society at Epworth as early as 1702. John Wesley apparently intended his Societies to be modelled on such a plan, but subsequent events, and especially his contacts with the Brethren, modified his views. It must not be forgotten that the Society at Aldersgate Street, at which Wesley underwent his heart-warming experience in 1738, was an *Anglican* Religious Society, though it has often erroneously been described as a Moravian Society. There were no Moravian Societies in England at that time. In any case, there was a considerable difference between the Religious Societies and the Holy Club on the one hand, confined as they were to the clergy, and the bands and Societies of the Methodists, which consisted largely of laymen, and admitted members of other denominations. There was a difference of function too, as will be seen.

The connexion of the Methodist Societies with the Moravian system is somewhat confused by the terminologies adopted at different times. Not even do Moravian writers give an altogether clear and distinct picture. The best modern account is that given by J. E. Hutton in *Methodist Bands: their Origin and Nature—a New Discovery*;[14] in which he differentiates between the 'Choirs' and the smaller groups, at first called 'Bands', and later 'Societies'. David Cranz explains the term 'Band' as follows:

> The whole congregation was, according to the diversity of age and sex, divided into certain little companies which were called bands, to tie the band of love still faster and to further the inward growth; in which they spoke with confidence concerning the state of their souls, exhorted, encouraged, comforted, and prayed with each other. But to obviate any disorder, the two sexes kept themselves separate, each of them

[14] *Wesleyan Methodist Magazine* (1911), pp. 197-202.

respectively associating in their private edification with their own sex.[15]

There is apparently some confusion with the Choirs here, for, though in both Bands and Choirs the sexes were kept apart, the basis of classification in the Bands was not 'diversity of age or sex' but community of spiritual development. Zinzendorf's own account, as expressed in an address delivered on 2nd July 1747, is clearer:

This day, twenty years ago, whilst the gospel was being preached at Berthelsdorf, Herrnhut and elsewhere to an incredible number of people, a gracious wind from the Lord was felt, which was the commencement of an uninterrupted work of the Holy Spirit in Herrnhut during the remainder of the year. The visit of Mary to Elizabeth, which is that day commemorated in the Christian Church, gave rise to the idea of bands, or societies; these were established throughout the whole community the following week, and have been productive of such blessed effects that I believe, without such an institution, the church would never have become what it now is. The Societies called bands consist of a few individuals met together in the name of Jesus, amongst whom Jesus is; who converse together in a particularly cordial and childlike manner, on the whole state of their hearts, and conceal nothing from each other, but who have wholly committed themselves to each other's care in the Lord. Cordiality, secrecy and daily intercourse is of great service to such individuals, and ought never to be neglected, but whenever slothfulness creeps in, the individuals ought to feel ashamed of it and amend.[16]

According to Spangenberg, the Count, as Superintendent of the Church, and with the consent of his 'fellow-labourers', divided the Brethren into these little societies 'according to their different states of mind.'

Though Wesley owed something also to the Religious Societies, his debt to the Moravians in this matter is obvious. The similarity of these bands to those established by him is immediately clear, especially in the basis of choice, the inner activities, the nomination of leaders, and the disciplining of unsatisfactory members, who were 'moved on' by the Brethren 'after mature deliberation'. When Wesley was in Georgia, he instituted bands

[15] David Cranz, *The Ancient and Modern History of the Brethren*, trans. B. La Trobe (1780), p. 115.

[16] A. G. Spangenberg, *The Life of Nicholas Lewis Count Zinzendorf*, trans. B. La Trobe (1838), pp. 86-7.

which were much on the Moravian model—fellowship meetings on Sunday afternoons and evenings, at which 'the more serious' took part in reading, singing and conversation. On 26th February 1737, for example, in a letter to the Founders of Parochial Libraries, he wrote:

> Some time after the evening service, as many of my parishioners as desire it meet at my house (as they do also on Wednesday evening), and spend about an hour in prayer, singing, and mutual exhortation. A smaller number (mostly those who design to communicate the next day) meet here on Saturday evening; and a few of these come to me on the other evenings, and pass half an hour in the same employment.[17]

It is probable therefore that the later establishment of bands and the appointment of leaders was based on the system seen and tested by Wesley in Savannah. There were differences: there is no suggestion that the groups were formed on the basis of spiritual progress, or segregated according to sex, but they met frequently (as Wesley's Diary indicates), they consisted in the main of the laity—on 13th February 1737, for example, 'the people came—sung, read, sung, read, prayer'[18]—like the Moravians they sang hymns, they even bore the name of band-meetings. Some hint that these meetings were not open indiscriminately to those of varied spiritual equipment is found in a Diary entry for 16th February 1737, which refers to a 'devotional meeting' at which Mr Campbell, Mrs Gilbert, and 'Miss Sophy' were present:

> It was a fast-day, and there was no dinner, or any other refreshment, except tea at six in the morning and three in the afternoon. The whole day was given to letter-writing and devotional exercises.[19]

As Wesley had already been in contact with the Moravians for a full year, it is very probable that he knew of their use of the bands, though J. E. Hutton says[20] that he did not learn of the system until after his return from Herrnhut, and that Böhler was his mentor, in this as in other ways. Böhler's Diary for February to May 1738 records how he had established a band of three students at Oxford:

> The 9th of March a band was organized among the students mentioned above. I talked with them about the chief principles of the Society, and they resolved to assemble three times a week. . . . In the

[17] *Letters*, I.214. [18] *Journal*, I.318. [19] ibid., p. 319.
[20] *Methodist Bands;* see p. 184, *supra.*

afternoon [14th March] I was with the associated student brethren. It was our day of band meeting. First we talked somewhat about the death of the Saviour; then each one related something of his circumstances, concerning which there then was further conversation. . . . In the evening the students assembled. The older Wesley was also present. . . . I read to them the last half of the 3rd Chapter of John.[21]

Wenzel Neisser also records: 'On 31st March I went with Böhler to Oxford, and there we established a Band for women.'

It is possible that the 'little society' which was formed by Wesley and Böhler at James Hutton's house on 1st May 1738,[22] was actually a Band, and not a Religious Society. Böhler's own account gives colour to this assumption:

At nine in the evening I met the elder Wesley at Hutton's. . . . We now settled the names of the brethren who were of one mind, who wished for fellowship with each other, and who were willing to form a Band—Hutton, Bray, Edmund, Wolf, Clark, Otlee (? Okely), Procker, Harphrey [corrected to Harvey], Sweetland, Shaw, and the elder Wesley. . . . Some of them are full believers, others are still in search of saving faith. It is probable that others will soon join us . . . and then they will break into groups, and the youths and men will have separate meetings.[23]

William Holland also refers to this society as a Band,[24] and though Wesley speaks of it as a 'little society' he seems to have used the term elsewhere in referring to a smaller group. Moreover, in speaking of this Society, he uses the same language as that which he afterwards used to describe the Bands at Herrnhut —to confess their faults one to another, and pray for one another, that they may be healed'.[25]

On the other hand, it must be pointed out:

(1) that this 'little society' was much larger than the usual Band;

(2) that its members were not of homogeneous spiritual development;

(3) that it soon broke up into smaller groups.

On June 9th, the following rules were added:

[21] *Moravian Archives*, Herrnhut.

[22] *Journal*, I.458.

[23] *Moravian Archives*, Herrnhut.

[24] Rylands *Eng. MSS*, 1076.

[25] *Journal*, II.50.

'(*a*) that the persons desirous to meet together for that purpose be divided into several bands or little societies;

'(*b*) that none of these consist of fewer than five, or more than ten persons;

'(*c*) that some person in each Band be desired to interrogate the rest in order, who may be called the Leader of the Band'.

There is some difference of opinion, as has been stated earlier, about the respective shares of Böhler and Wesley in the rules of this fellowship.[26] In all probability, the original rules were few—perhaps only two[27]—and the others were added at later dates, and not completed until the end of September. It is of interest to know that Benham, giving no doubt the views of Hutton, a member of this fellowship, does not mention John Wesley's part in drawing up these regulations, implying that they were the work of Böhler, and that a letter sent to Zinzendorf on 2nd May, on the very day following the formation of the Society, is signed by fourteen English names, eleven of which had been mentioned in Böhler's account.[28] The name of John Wesley does not appear—a striking omission. This omission bears out the suggestion made in Mrs Hutton's letter to Samuel Wesley on 6th June that Hutton and his friends were already becoming restive, either about Wesley's 'wild enthusiasm' or about his ambition.[29]

It seems plain, however, that the Rules as a whole reflect Wesley's views. The reference to his favourite apostle, St James, which is found in the title would certainly not have gained the enthusiastic support of Zinzendorf. Rule 21, enjoining entire openness and the avoidance of any kind of reserve, is closely allied to the undispatched letter of September 1738, probably written at about the same time, and to several similar suggestions later; and the emphasis on method—fasting, punctuality, separation from worldly associations, and discipline—are entirely in accord with Wesley's regard for order and obedience. In particular Rule 11 ('that all Bands have a Conference at eight every Wednesday') and Rule 31 (enjoining regular payments) seem to be innovations of Wesley's. At Herrnhut, only the Leaders met in Conference, and no such payments were made. Regular contributions became a distinctive feature of Wesley's Methodist Societies, and in many individual churches still are—'class moneys'.

[26] Pages 62-3, *supra*.
[27] *Journal*, I.458n.
[28] op. cit., p. 29.
[29] See p. 116, *supra*.

Wesley undoubtedly learned a good deal about the Band system during his visit to Herrnhut. In his *Journal* for 8th August 1738, he wrote, 'Several evenings this week I was with one or other of the private bands';[30] and in his account of the Herrnhut constitution he recorded:

The people of Herrnhut are divided . . . into about ninety bands, each of which meets twice at least, but most of them three times a week, to 'confess their faults one to another, and pray for one another, that they may be healed'. . . . The Church is so divided that first the husbands, then the wives, then the widows, then the maids, then the young men, then the boys, then the girls, and lastly the little children, are in so many distinct classes; each of which is daily visited, the married men by a married man, the wives by a wife, and so of the rest. These larger are also (now) divided into near ninety smaller classes or bands, over each of which one presides who is of the greatest experience. All these leaders meet the Senior every week, and lay open to him and to the Lord whatsoever hinders or furthers the work of God in the souls committed to their charge.[31]

Wesley adopted a similar, though less complete, segregation in his own Societies; in his *Plain Account of the Methodists* (1748) he wrote:

In compliance with their desire, I divided them into smaller companies, putting married or single men, and married and single women together.

Very shortly after his return from Herrnhut, he introduced the Band system into his Society at Bristol. He did so at the instance of Whitefield, whose preaching had resulted in a considerable increase in the number of members, and who seemed to think that a closer form of organization was desirable. Accordingly, on 4th April 1739, Wesley began to form his bands, on the Fetter Lane model, the men and women meeting separately under leaders chosen by lot, new members being received into fellowship by the vote of the Band:

In the evening three women agreed to meet together weekly, with the same intention as those in London—viz. 'to confess their faults one to another, and pray one for another, that they may be healed'. At eight four young men agreed to meet, in pursuance of the same design. How

[30] II.22. [31] ibid., II.50, 53.

dare any man deny this to be (as to the substance of it) a means of grace, ordained by God?[32]

This seems to indicate that already some of the company were expressing such a denial—several months before Molther's arrival. There is a reference in Wesley's Diary for 6th June 1739—'6.30 at home, the leaders'—which seems to indicate that he met the leaders of the bands, at any rate occasionally.[33]

He continued the same system at the Foundery, after the breach with the Fetter Lane Congregation in 1740. Many lists of Bands in Wesley's handwriting are preserved in the Colman Collection, with days and times of meeting, names of leaders, and so on. According to these, the Bands had generally four or five members, though a few had as many as six, and one (reproduced in the Standard Edition of Wesley's *Journal*)[34] had seven. It is interesting to note (*a*) that the sexes are grouped separately; (*b*) that (if the pages given are typical) women were much in the majority; and (*c*) that there were frequent expulsions or deaths. There are contemporary references to the Methodist adoption of the Band-system. The pamphlet mentioned earlier,[35] *Observations upon the Conduct and Behaviour of a Certain Sect usually distinguished by the name of Methodists*, makes it clear that the Methodists were multiplying Bands and Societies 'in the Moravian way'; and William Holland also records that the Methodists connected with Howell Harris had their 'private Societies, Choir Meetings, and Bands'.[36]

It is important to note that the Bands were not only smaller in size than the Societies, but were more advanced in their spiritual growth, both in Moravianism and in Methodism. John Wesley had expressed approval of the Brethren's 'exact division of the people under their charge, so that all may be fed with food convenient for them'; and he seems to have followed their example in the division of his own Societies. At the first Methodist Conference, held at the Foundery in June 1744, Wesley's followers were allotted to four groups:

The United Societies (which are the largest of all) consist of awakened persons. Part of these, who are supposed to have remission of sins, are

[32] ibid., II.174.
[33] ibid., II.215.
[34] ibid., II.480.
[35] See p. 178, *supra*.
[36] *Moravian and Methodist;* a sidelight on their early relations; *William Holland's Journey through South Wales in 1746*, by E. R. Griffiths, p. 9.

more closely united in the Bands. Those in the Bands, who seem to walk in the light of God, compose the Select Societies. Those of them who have made shipwreck of the faith meet apart as penitents.[37]

Gilbert Tennent, in *Some Account of the Principles of the Moravians*, says:

The Moravian Leaders, I am persuaded, dare not deny that though persons may be admitted upon pretty easy terms into what they call their Bands, in order to instruction and preparation for more close fellowship, yet they receive none into their intimate church communion but such as profess sinless Perfection—

a statement which is only partly true.

It is clear, not only from Wesley's own tribute to Böhler's help and advice, but from the similarity of the Fetter Lane Rules to the Herrnhut constitution, that Wesley owed much of his conception of a Methodist 'Society' to the Moravians; and it will also appear that the Rules of his own United Societies, published in February 1743, have striking likenesses to these Rules. It is interesting, however, to compare the Rules for the Fetter Lane Society with typical sets of Rules of the earlier Religious Societies in order to arrive at a just estimate of the debt which Wesley owed to either source.

The two sets of Rules are similar in their provision of weekly meetings, in enjoining religious conversation and in imposing conditions of membership and expulsion; but they differ in several ways:

(1) The Fetter Lane Society, though Anglican in its beginnings, admitted members of other Communions;

(2) it enjoined no general fast, though it prescribed for a continual fast by separating three of its members for this purpose;

(3) it made no definite provision for the celebration of Holy Communion, but only for regular Love-feasts. This however is not a real difference, for the Love-feast implied Holy Communion, which always preceded or followed it;

[37] *Minutes of Conference* (1744). The roll of members in the Bradford Circuit, 1781, is divided into three categories very similar to the first three of these—'seekers of salvation', 'justified persons' and 'the perfect in love'—*The Bradford Antiquary* (1902). Methodist churches still have 'Select Classes' and 'Band Rooms'.

(4) the Fetter Lane Rules insisted on spiritual catechism;

(5) the Fetter Lane Society had no prescribed administrative officers, Stewards, and Treasurers;

(6) the Religious Societies had nothing comparable with the small Bands.

It is easy of course to exaggerate debts and influences. The whole of Wesley's spiritual progress had convinced him of the value of fellowship, and he would no doubt have been assured of the impossibility of 'a solitary Christian' in answer to the promptings of his own heart even if he had never met the Religious Societies or the Moravian Bands; but the differences between the Rules of the Religious Societies and those of Fetter Lane or his own Societies are so marked as to suggest that he owed them no more than a general debt. It is more likely that his immediate debt was to the Brethren. A French account of the Fetter Lane Church, written in 1758, speaks of the United Bristol Society thus:

The United Society, it will be observed, is classified after the most approved Moravian fashion, as is the roll of the Moravian Congregation of the Lamb . . . settled in London, 30th October 1748—married men, unmarried men, and the like.

It is important to note that the Rules of the Band Societies, adopted at Bristol in 1741, and subjoined to the Rules of the United Societies, are the same as those of Fetter Lane, and that the Rules of the United Societies, though fuller and more didactic than the Band Rules, are based on the same general principles.

Wesley did not, however, copy the Moravian system slavishly, and in some ways he outstripped his teachers. The Rules for the United Societies are not only more elaborate than those of Fetter Lane, but they contain an emphasis on 'good works' which may have sprung from a reaction against Molther's Quietism. The implied threat of expulsion in Section 7, 'I will bear with him for a season. But if then he repent not he hath no more place among us', parallels Rule 32 of the Fetter Lane Society: 'If any person or persons do not, after being thrice admonished, conform to the Society, they be not esteemed any longer as members.'

These rules were actually applied at Bristol in the dismissal of Cennick and his supporters on 24th February 1741. Here is John Wesley's own account:

The bands meeting at Bristol, I read over the names of the United Society, being determined that no disorderly walker should remain therein;

and, four days later,

I met the Kingswood bands again, and read the following paper: 'I, John Wesley, by the consent and approbation of the band-society in Kingswood, do declare the persons above-mentioned to be no longer members thereof. Neither will they be so accounted, until they shall openly confess their fault, and thereby do what in them lies to remove the scandal they have given.'[38]

This is the earliest recorded instance of disciplinary action in the Methodist Societies, and was apparently so effective that Wesley followed it by a similar procedure at the Foundery in April of the same year, though there is no record of actual expulsions at that time. It is important to recognize that the Bands were not identical with the Societies, and that they were consulted by Wesley about matters which concerned the Society as a whole. In his letter to the Rev. Thos. Church on 17th June 1746 Wesley wrote: 'The Bands are not called the United Society', and added:

The good consequences of their meeting together in Bands I know; but 'the very bad consequences' [he is quoting a charge by Church] I know not.[39]

In thus expelling a member, Wesley seems to have gone somewhat beyond Moravian precedent. The Moravian procedure, according to Spangenberg, was as follows:

Each brother or sister in the congregation who observes anything wrong or offensive in another, be it who it will, is bound, according to the rule which our Lord had given, to mention it to the persons themselves and to exhort and reprove them. If this doth not avail, their duty then requires that they neither conceal it, nor make it imprudently known in an improper place, but they are to acquaint their elders of it that it may be examined into. If the person who has committed the offence can, by hearty conversation and exhortation, be brought to a real sense of his fault, and to repentance, the elders try to make an end of it in stillness. But such a person abstains as is fitting from the holy communion for a longer or shorter time, according to the nature of the case and circumstances; and if he does not abstain of himself it

[38] *Journal*, II.429-30. [39] *Letters*, II.238.

is then declared unto him in the name of the congregation that he cannot be admitted unto it. Finally, he may be expelled from and 'dwell no longer in the congregation place'.[40]

This procedure, which is in accordance with Scripture (Matt. 18^{15-17}), is recorded by Wesley in his account of the Herrnhut constitution:

If any man among us, having been often admonished, and long forborne, persists in walking unworthy of his holy calling, he is no longer admitted to the Lord's Supper. If he still continues in his fault, hating to be reformed, the last step is, publicly, and often in the midst of many prayers and tears, to cast him out of our congregation.[41]

No doubt, Wesley would have known of this procedure quite apart from Moravian example. A similar practice is specified in the Savoy Declaration of 1658, a statement of the Faith and Order of the Congregational Churches of England, in which (Article XIX) 'individuals are told that they must admonish in private if they are the only ones who know about the sin, but in public if it be a public sin. If there is no amendment of a private offence, then it may be told to the Church, and if the sinner does not repent, the Elders must admonish in the name of the Church. If this fails, Excommunication, the act of the whole Church, follows.' That Wesley was familiar with this general procedure is shown by his sermon on 'The Cure of Evil Speaking', based on Matthew 18^{15-17}, in which, following our Lord's injunction and the Moravian practice, he advocates, first, personal reproof by an individual, then a remonstrance by a group, and, lastly, a report to the elders of the Church. He does not seem to have adopted this procedure in full in dealing with Cennick; but it is interesting to note that it is in general followed in the Methodist Church today, whenever a 'charge' is to be made, and that matters are still discussed 'in band', although the court of discipline and appeal has become the Leaders' Meeting.

With the growth of the Societies, the bands lost much of their early importance, and after being under the control of Wesley—in the expulsion of Cennick, they were virtually ordered to accept his judgement—they passed into that of the itinerant ministry.

[40] *A Concise Historical Account of the Present Constitution of the Unitas Fratrum* (1773), pp. 68-9.

[41] *Journal*, II.56.

But they, and the wider Societies of which they were a part, are the heirs of Moravian practice. Long before the separation of 1740, 'testimonies' formed a considerable part of the Band-meetings; and Samuel Wesley, the conservative elder brother, wrote with some anxiety:

> Will any man of common sense, or spirit, suffer any domestic to be in a band, engaged to relate to five or ten people everything, without reserve, that concerns the person's conscience, howmuchsoever it may concern the family?[42]

(*b*) *Hymns*

It would be an exaggeration to say that John Wesley learned the importance of hymn-singing from the Moravians. Hymn-singing, in one form or another, was the precious heritage of the Universal Church, and had been a familiar feature of English worship for generations. The psalms sung in Jewish synagogues were hymns; the disciples sang a hymn just before the Crucifixion; the writer of the Epistle to the Colossians enjoined his congregations to 'sing psalms and hymns and spiritual songs, with thankfulness' in their hearts to God; the Crusaders sang hymns on their way to battle as they carried forward 'the royal banners'; the medieval monks chanted their plain-song melodies; the Lutherans worshipped God in their chorales, the Calvinists in their metrical psalms. But it is probably true to say that John Wesley's knowledge of hymns and hymn-singing was at first limited to the metrical paraphrases of the psalms which held sway in the seventeenth century, to the verses of Sternhold and Hopkins, of Tate and Brady, and to the foursquare tunes of Ravenscroft, Playford, Wilkins, and Chetham. It was the sublime achievement of the Moravians that they introduced him, and through him thousands of his followers, to the beauty, the dignity, the reverence, the fitness of the German chorale,[43] and to the personal and intimate song of the great Pietists. Isaac Watts, it is true, had invaded the field with his *Hymns of Private Composure*, a revolution in their way, but his literary aims were limited: his lines were 'end-stopped' in order to meet the current practice of 'lining-out', and the shape of his verses was governed by conventional psalm-tunes; and there were many private hymnals published toward the end

[42] Tyerman, op. cit., I.287.

[43] A good hymn-tune has been defined as '*dignus, pius, suavis, decorus*'.

of the seventeenth century, though these were intended less for singing than for meditation. The Moravians revealed a new purpose in hymn-singing—not merely the worship of God, but the preaching of the Gospel.

Though John Wesley was to learn of the treasures of German hymnody from his Moravian friends, and therefore to spread a love of hymn-singing amongst his converts, it is important to recognize that he had appreciated the value of the hymn in worship long before his voyage to Georgia. Hymns were a staple diet in his Epworth home. His father produced volumes of verse, and one hymn of his has deservedly survived;

Behold the Saviour of mankind[44]—

with its fine third verse:

'Tis done! the precious ransom's paid;
Receive my soul! He cries:
See where He bows His sacred head!
He bows His head, and dies!—

recalled in the lines of Philip Doddridge:

'Tis done, the great transaction's done!
I am my Lord's, and He is mine.[45]

Samuel Wesley, the elder brother, also wrote several hymns, none of which are in common use today, though five appeared in *Wesley's Hymns* (1876), and two, *The Lord of Sabbath, let us praise* and *The Morning flowers display their sweets*, were included in the *Methodist Hymn-book* of 1904. John Wesley had long been familiar with *Reformed Devotions*,[46] by Dr Hickes, a prominent Non-juror who was removed from the Deanery of Worcester because of his refusal to take the oaths to William and Mary, and who wrote a preface to a 'reformed' edition of the original book by John Austin, a Roman Catholic. Hickes had resisted the tyranny of the psalm-versions of Sternhold and Hopkins, and was an early advocate of the singing of hymns in the Church of England. Wesley took the same view, and used some of the hymns in his meetings in Georgia, as many entries in his Diary show.

[44] *Methodist Hymn-book* (1933), No. 193. [45] ibid., No. 744.
[46] *Journal*, I.122, 267-9, 230, 307.

Among the list of 'Grievances presented by the Grand Jury for Savannah' in August 1737 appears the following:

. . . the said Revd. person (as we humbly conceive) deviates from the principles and regulations of the Established Church, in many particulars inconsistent with the happiness and prosperity of this Colony, as

Prima, by inverting the order and method of the Liturgy;

2. by changing or altering such passages as he thinks proper in the version of Psalms publicly authorized to be sung in the Church;
3. by introducing into the Church and service at the Altar compositions of Psalms and hymns not inspected or authorized by any proper judicature.

He was to deviate a good deal more!

What were the innovations which he introduced? An examination of the *Collection of Psalms and Hymns* published at Charlestown in 1737 gives some indication. Of the seventy-eight hymns, one-third are by Isaac Watts, a remarkable number in view of Wesley's High Church predilections, for Watts was a Dissenter, seven by John Austin (culled from Hickes's *Reformed Devotions*), six based on George Herbert, three by the two Samuel Wesleys, three from Joseph Addison, and five translations from the German. Amongst those of Isaac Watts, in this book and in the revised edition of 1738, were:

Come, ye that love the Lord (*Come, we* in the original);

O God, our help in ages past (originally *Our God*);

Awake, our souls! Away, our fears!

I'll praise my Maker while I've breath (originally *with my breath*);

while the best-known hymn of Herbert was

Teach me, my God and King.

In view of the claim generally made of Wesley's debt to Moravian hymnody, the number of his translations from the German in this book is small. Indeed, it would be only fair to assume that his debt to Watts was much greater. Probably his knowledge of the Dissenter's hymns dates from the days of the Holy Club. It is gratifying to know that John Wesley's admiration for Isaac Watts was returned by Watts's keen appreciation of the work of Charles Wesley. In the obituary notice of his brother, presented to the Conference of 1788,[47] John Wesley said: 'Dr Watts did not scruple to say that that single poem, *Wrestling Jacob*,[48] was worth all the verses he himself had written.' The frequent references to 'Herbert' in the Diary suggest that Wesley spent some time in selecting and adapting poems from *The Temple*. On 5th July 1736, for instance, he spent a full hour in 'Transcribing and "singing George Herbert"';[49] and in John and Charles Wesley's *Hymns and Sacred Poems* (1739), the number of Herbert's hymns increased to forty-two. As the century progressed, the increasing output of Charles Wesley left less room—and perhaps less taste—for Herbert's hymns. Not all the advocacy of Wesley could suffice to make George Herbert an acceptable voice in modern church psalmody. In the latest *Methodist Hymn-book* (1933), while Watts is represented by forty-three hymns, Herbert has only four, of a total of nearly a thousand. Both are easily and understandably outstripped by Charles Wesley, of whose hymns there are two hundred and forty.

It is somewhat surprising, therefore, to find that in this Charlestown Collection, and in the *Collection of Psalms and Hymns* which appeared a year later, and which Tyerman suggests was compiled for the use of the Moravian bands in London,[50] Charles Wesley is not represented. Indeed, the earliest hymns of Methodism are translations from the German, and are the work of the elder Wesley; it was John Wesley, not Charles, who was the pioneer of that change of form and spirit which was to revolutionize English hymnody. It was from German sources that John Wesley received his first impulse to become a hymn-writer.

The Moravians were well qualified to be his tutors. It was as early as 1501 that Luke of Prague issued the first Brethren's hymn-book, said to be the first church-hymnal in history. According to Julian,[51] Zinzendorf himself edited five hymn-books between 1725 and 1735, from *Sammlung geistlicher und lieblicher Lieder*, a

[47] *Minutes of Conference.* [48] *Methodist Hymn-book* (1933), No. 339.

[49] *Journal*, I.242.

[50] This is incorrect: there were no specifically Moravian bands in London till 1740.

[51] *Dictionary of Hymnology* (1907), pp. 767-8.

book of nearly nine hundred hymns, of which twenty-eight were by the Count himself, to a collection of one hundred and twenty-eight poems, all by Zinzendorf. These, however, were not *Moravian* hymn-books, though most of the hymns in the Moravian hymn-book of 1735 were taken from them. This last-named, *Das Gesangbuch der Gemeine in Herrnhuth*, is of particular interest, for it is certain that John Wesley was acquainted with it. In his Diary[52] he includes four of his own translations from the German, three of them prefixed by the numbers 24, 215, and 306, which, as Dr Bett has shown,[53] correspond with the numbers of the pages on which the originals appear in the Moravian book. They are

O Jesu, Source of calm repose,
(*Wer ist wohl wie Du*—Freylinghausen);
My soul before Thee prostrate lies
(*Hier legt mein Sinn sich vor dir nieder*—Richter);
Jesu, to Thee my heart I bow
(*Reiner Bräut'gam meiner Seelen*—Zinzendorf);
To Thee with heart and mouth I sing
(*Ich singe dir mit Herz und Mund*—Gerhardt).

As has been mentioned, there is a reference to the first of these hymns in a letter sent (in Latin) to Zinzendorf some months before the entry in the Diary.[54] It seems a pity that this fine hymn, like many others of historic interest, does not find a place in the most recent *Methodist Hymn-book.*

The first standard Wesleyan hymn-book appeared in 1741, and was followed by the first Moravian hymn-book a year later. These two books, the first Church Hymnals in the English language, derive much of their quality and material from the Herrnhut hymn-book of 1735; and the close fellowship of Moravian and Methodist until the breach in 1740 is shown by the fact that Wesley's own books of 1738 and 1739 were commonly used at Fetter Lane.[55]

Benjamin La Trobe pays a tribute to the Wesleys for their translations from the German in his preface to Spangenberg's *Life of Zinzendorf*:[56]

[52] *Journal*, I.299.

[53] *The Hymns of Methodism*, p. 13.

[54] See pp. 38-9, *supra*.

[55] Bishop L. G. Hassé in *Moravian Messenger* (1891).

[56] Trans. P. La Trobe (1838).

This debt the Moravian Brethren are forward to acknowledge, nor is their sense of gratitude at all affected by the consideration that it was at the brilliant flame of German psalmody that these distinguished hymnologists appear to have kindled their own poetic touch. Whatever benefit the Wesleys derived from this source, it must be confessed they amply repaid to the religious community which had been the channel of imparting it.

Later in the same preface, Benjamin La Trobe questions whether Wesley or Gambold translated Spangenberg's fine hymn, *High on His everlasting throne*,[57] presented to Zinzendorf on his birthday, 1734. This translation appears in Wesley's *Hymns and Sacred Poems* (1742), and is ascribed by Julian[58] to John Wesley.

Zinzendorf wrote so many good hymns that it is to be regretted that he sullied his fame by the 'Blood and Wounds' hymns of later years. It might be said of him as Ben Jonson said of Shakespeare, of whom an admirer had said that 'he never blotted a single line', 'Would he had blotted a thousand'. Methodism still treasures some of his best hymns, notably

Jesu, Thy blood and righteousness
(Christi Blut und Gerechtigkeit);
O Thou to whose all-searching sight
(Seelen-Bräutigam, O Du Gotteslam); and
Jesu, still lead on (Jesu, geh' voran);

the first two of which were translated by John Wesley.[59]

It was on the voyage to Georgia that Wesley was most deeply impressed by the Moravian hymns. During the storm in which the Brethren had displayed such fortitude, they were singing a psalm ('mentioning the power of God') when

> the sea broke over, split the mainsail in pieces, covered the ship, and poured in between the decks, as if the great deep had already swallowed us up. A terrible screaming began among the English. The Germans calmly sang on.[60]

John Wesley had already begun to learn German, and seems to have translated German hymns as early as May 1736. On the

[57] Some verses of this are included in the *Methodist Hymn-book* (1933), No. 784.

[58] Page 1,070.

[59] *Methodist Hymn-book*, Nos. 370, 505, 624.

[60] *Journal*, I.142-4.

5th of that month, he tells us in his Diary,[61] he 'transcribed', or translated, a German psalm. Two days later, he not only translated hymns from the German, but sang or recited the verses already written.[62] At Frederica, Wesley began to carry out what he had planned to do at Savannah:

Our design was, on Sundays in the afternoon, and every evening, after public service, to spend some time with the most serious of the communicants in singing, reading and conversation.[63]

The singing of hymns, indeed, took a prominent place in the services which Wesley conducted—in the early morning devotions, in the Wednesday, Friday, and Sunday meetings of fellowship, in the daily public prayers, and especially at the weekly celebration of Holy Communion. It would be going too far to assume that these hymns were generally translations from the German. Indeed, the frequent references in Wesley's Diary to Hickes's *Reformed Devotions* imply that he had by no means forsaken his early love; while it must be remembered that most of the entries which concern German hymns speak of transcription and translation rather than of singing. On the other hand, hymns are meant to be sung, and Wesley would hardly have written them without thought of that prime purpose. Moreover, the Diary references to singing follow so closely upon the record of translations from the German as to make it almost certain that these hymns were sung. It is interesting to note that Wesley's translations were from the Pietists, and not from Luther himself—somewhat surprising in view of the Moravian devotion to Lutheran doctrine. Perhaps one reason is that it was Moravian Pietism rather than Moravian doctrine which attracted him in the first instance. Moreover, it was from a Moravian hymn-book, *Das Gesangbuch der Gemeine in Herrnhuth*, that John Wesley made his translations.

It is therefore more than probable that, but for the voyage to Georgia and the contacts with the Moravians on the *Simmonds* and in America, Wesley would not have made his wonderful translations, without which English hymnody would have been incalculably the poorer. Wesley admitted as much when near the end of his life. In his sermon 'On knowing Christ after the flesh',[64] recalling his first meeting with the Brethren, he says:

[61] *Journal*, I.211.
[62] ibid., p. 212.
[63] 10th June, 1736; *Journal*, I.226-30.
[64] cxvii.

I translated many of their hymns, for the use of our own congregations. Indeed, as I durst not implicitly follow any man, I did not take all that lay before me, but selected those which I judged to be most scriptural, and most suitable to sound experience.

Wesley adopted this policy of careful selection by including only five in his Charlestown collection, three of the four already mentioned[65] and two others, one of which is perhaps the best of them all, *Thou hidden love of God, whose height*,[66] his great version of Tersteegen's *Verborgne Gottesliebe du*, a translation which Emerson declared to be the greatest hymn in the English language. It is to this hymn that Wesley refers in his *Plain Account of Christian Perfection* (1766):

We embarked for America in the latter end of 1735. It was the next year, while I was at Savannah, that I wrote the following lines:

Is there a thing beneath the sun
That strives with Thee my heart to share?
Ah, tear it thence, and reign alone,
The Lord of every motion there!

One of these hymns was mentioned earlier[67]—*My soul before Thee prostrate lies*—so intimately connected with Wesley's Aldersgate experience. The fifth was a hymn also by Richter, *Thou Lamb of God, Thou Prince of Peace* (*Stilles Lamm und Friedenfürst*). But these were not the only translations made by Wesley from the German. In all he translated thirty-six: seven by Zinzendorf, four by Gerhardt, two by Tersteegen, two by Freylinghausen, one by each of eleven other writers, and one a cento from four hymns by Zinzendorf and the two Nitschmanns.[68] Five of these appear in the *Collection of Psalms and Hymns* published in 1738, including Zinzendorf's fine hymn, *O Thou to whose all-searching sight*;[69] thirteen more in *Hymns and Sacred Poems* (1739); and six more in the 1740 hymn-book. Spangenberg's *Der König ruht, und schauet doch*, translated by John Wesley as *What shall we offer our good Lord*,[70] appeared in 1742.

Most of these writers were Pietists or Moravians, and one

[65] See p. 199, *supra*; *To Thee with heart and mouth I sing* was apparently never published; Bett, *The Hymns of Methodism;* p. 31; *Journal*, I.299, II.6.

[66] *Methodist Hymn-book*, No. 433.

[67] Page 55, *supra*.

[68] *O Lord, enlarge our scanty thought* (*Methodist Hymn-book*, No. 449).

[69] ibid., No. 505.

[70] ibid., No. 784.

hymn by Johann Andreas Rothe, the Lutheran pastor whom Zinzendorf appointed to the pastorate of Berthelsdorf, can challenge Tersteegen's famous hymn for the fame of being the greatest hymn ever written. *Ich habe nun den Grund gefunden* is a magnificent hymn of faith in adversity which Wesley has made even more magnificent in *Now I have found the ground.*[71] That all these German originals are found in the Herrnhut *Gesangbuch* is incontrovertible evidence of the influence of Moravian thought and practice in this field.

It was not only in the words and content of the hymns that Wesley's own thought and practice were shaped. His frequent references to the music to which they were sung reveal that the German chorale strongly attracted him. He appears to have sung with the Moravians quite early during his voyage to Georgia, and his Diary for 19th March 1736 records[72] how deeply impressed he was both by the hymns and by the tunes. No doubt the tune-book they used was the *Gesangbuch* of Freylinghausen. John Wesley's first tune-book, *A Collection of Tunes, set to Music, as they are commonly sung at the Foundery*, was published in 1742, and contains forty-two tunes. They are badly printed, the melody only being given; some are wrongly barred, and a few are obviously incorrect, but they show the influence of German hymnody. Thirteen of the tunes are definitely of German origin, and two others may possibly be German. The others are, as might have been expected, mainly psalm-tunes, though Wesley showed his catholic spirit by including one air, *Jericho Tune* (819)[73] from Handel's opera *Riccardo Primo.* In view of the deep impression made upon Wesley by the tunes sung by the Moravians a larger proportion of their tunes might have been expected, particularly as there had been published in England in 1722 *Psalmodia Germanica*, edited by John Christian Jacobi, the minister of the German congregation in London. This contains a considerable number of fine German tunes, many of which have more recently been adopted into Methodist hymnody. Of these, only three—*St Leonard* (*Frankfurt*), *Vater Unser* and *Bremen*—and three other tunes from Freylinghausen's *Gesangbuch—Hemdyke*, *Savannah* (*Irene*; 233) and *Second German*—find their way into Wesley's little book, the last-named somewhat surprisingly, for as written

[71] *Methodist Hymn-book*, No. 375. [72] *Journal*, I.185.

[73] The numbers in brackets refer to the *Methodist Hymn-book* of 1933.

it is extremely difficult to sing. Wesley may have used both these German collections, but it is probable that he knew Freylinghausen's the better. In the library of Richmond College there are two copies of it, both initialled 'J.W.'

Why are there only thirteen (or possibly fifteen) German tunes in the *Foundery Collection*? Possibly because Wesley's dispute with the Moravians was still fresh in his mind; more probably because of the inherent conservatism of English congregations, which then, as now, regarded a new tune as an intrusion,[74] and preferred the psalm-tunes to which they were accustomed. Moreover, many of the best German tunes were of a shape unfamiliar to English singers, and not in accordance with the new metres with which Charles Wesley was experimenting.

The Rev. G. W. McLeavy, a Moravian Bishop, writing[75] on Bernard Manning's comment on the variety of metres used by Charles Wesley,[76] suggests that he found his models in Freylinghausen and the Moravians, and points out that in the Moravian hymn-book of 1735 there are a hundred and fifty-six different metres. In particular, he refers to what Manning calls 'the perverse, unnatural, and almost ludicrous metre, two 6's and four 7's', and reminds us that in the *Methodist Hymn-book* of 1933 the tune *Irene* (233) which is of this shape was taken from the Freylinghausen *Gesangbuch* of 1704. (Of the other tunes of that metre, *Fulneck* (440) is by Christian Ignatius La Trobe, a distinguished Moravian musician.) There is probably some truth in this, but Charles Wesley went far beyond his models in his predilection for metres with additional syllables. In the *Standard Hymn-book* of 1780, for example, there are fifty hymns of the unusual metrical scheme 7.6.7.6.7.7.7.6. Moreover, Charles Wesley seemed particularly fond of the stanza-form generally known as 'six-line eights' (8.8.8.8.88)—there are nearly forty of these in the present *Methodist Hymn-book*—a form in which there were very few good German tunes before that time. Indeed, the *Moravian Liturgy and Hymns* of 1912, in which chorales play an honourable part, has hardly any of this metre, and of those that are included ten are by the Wesleys. On the other hand, German chorales are

[74] John Wesley himself, late in the century, enjoined his people to 'sing no new tunes'.

[75] In a letter to the writer of this essay.

[76] *The Hymns of Wesley and Watts* (1942) p. 50.

often of the form 8.7.8.7.88.7 (e.g. *Luther*, *Aus Tiefer Not*, *Dettingen*, *Mit Freuden Zart*), a form which Charles Wesley hardly ever, if ever, used.

In the circumstances, the proportion of one in three in the *Foundery Collection* is high, and is evidence of the regard felt by John Wesley for tunes with which he had been, until his visit to Georgia, unfamiliar.

Later influences were of a slighter character. In all probability, the weaknesses of Moravian hymnody during the 'Sifting Time'[77] acted as a deterrent. John Wesley was particularly chary about any approach to familiarity in addressing Christ. For that reason he gave *Jesu, Lover of my soul* no place in his large hymn-book, though A. E. Bailey[78] declares that the amatory suggestions of the first two verses are 'clearly a hangover from Wesley's associations with the Moravians'. This is very improbable. Neither Charles Wesley's diction nor his brother's dislike of it had much connexion with the Moravians. The hymn was written in 1740, at a time when the relations of both brothers with the Brethren were strained; and John Wesley's objection to it sprang in all probability from his native cast of mind.

By 1780, in any case, the worst features of Moravian hymnody were a thing of the past, and the 'Blood and Wounds' hymns of the middle of the century had disappeared from the Brethren's hymn-books. It is possible that John Wesley's criticisms hastened their disappearance, though it is just as likely that they fell into disuse because of the good sense of the Moravians themselves. In any case, as has been suggested, it would be unfair to judge Moravian hymnody by its worst examples. Some of the hymn-singing of the Methodists toward the end of the eighteenth century became so vulgar and so overweighted with flamboyant ornament that John Wesley fiercely, though fruitlessly, attacked it. The Conference of 1763, for instance, asked: 'What can be done to make the people sing true?', and two years later preachers were exhorted to teach the congregation to sing 'by note', viz. without shakes, passing-notes, or repetitions. The late Mr H. P. La Trobe, of Fulneck, had in his possession a collection of Moravian hymn-tunes which showed that at one period it was customary to sing separate lines and to follow them by a more or less elaborate organ interlude. This practice has an interesting parallel in

[77] See p. 129, *supra*.

[78] *The Gospel in Hymns* (New York, 1950), p. 95.

Methodist hymnody at the end of the eighteenth century in the interpolation of an instrumental phrase between the verses of a hymn. In Gresham's *Psalmody Improved*, for example, there appears a setting of *Old Hundredth* in which a trivial six-bar phrase is inserted between one line and the next. Perhaps both Moravians and Methodists resorted to the extravagant expression which so often is used to hide a decline in spiritual fervour!

The influence of Moravian hymnody over the Wesleys was not primarily concerned, however, with the knowledge of hymn-tunes which the Methodist leader thus acquired, nor even with his monumental translations, but in a new conception of the function and power of sacred song. What had formerly been to the Wesleys a means of worship, an approach to God, on the part of the believer, now became a medium by which the unbeliever might find salvation. 'Preach faith until you have it', Böhler had said; he might well have added: 'Sing about faith until you have it.' For there can be no doubt about the amazing influence of hymn-singing on the evangelistic work of the Wesleys and their followers. Indeed, it might well be contended that Charles Wesley did at least as much by his songs as his brother did by his sermons. It is not an accident that the amazing outflow of Charles Wesley's hymn-writing did not begin until after his conversion in May 1738. Though he probably wrote two or three hymns in the early months of that year, the real beginning of Charles Wesley's work as the poet of Methodism came with the wonderful experience of Whitsuntide 1738. Immediately thereafter, he wrote two hymns which have a new accent. *Where shall my wondering soul begin?* (361) is almost certainly the hymn mentioned in his *Journal* for 24th May: 'Toward ten, my brother was brought in triumph by a troop of our friends, and declared, "I believe".' It has been suggested that *And can it be that I should gain* (371) is more directly connected with Charles Wesley's conversion. Verse 4 runs:

Long my imprisoned spirit lay
Fast bound in sin and nature's night;
Thine eye diffused a quickening ray;
I woke, the dungeon flamed with light.
My chains fell off, my heart was free—
I rose, went forth, and followed Thee;

but Charles Wesley's *Journal* entry cannot easily be divorced from the third verse of No. 361:

Shall I, the hallowed Cross to shun,
Refuse His righteousness to impart,
By hiding it within my heart?

His *Journal* runs: 'I will perform my vows of not hiding His righteousness within my heart.' If this identification is correct, the effect of the conversion on Charles Wesley's sense of mission and on his hymnody was crucial. It is a striking fact that the first act of the two brothers after their Whitsuntide experience was to sing a hymn. The difference may be seen in a comparison between the somewhat monastic hymns of the early months of 1738, written after Charles's recovery from sickness, and this one, also written from a sick-bed, but deeply concerned with 'the world of sinners lost':

Outcasts of men, to you I call,
Harlots, and publicans, and thieves!
He spreads His arms to embrace you all;
Sinners alone His grace receives:
No need of Him the righteous have,
He came the lost to seek and save.

Come, O my guilty brethren, come,
Groaning beneath your load of sin!
His bleeding heart shall make you room,
His open side shall take you in;
He calls you now, invites you home;
Come, O my guilty brethren, come!

There is a new note here, as if the cloistered devotee had seen a vision of a world to save, as if a lisping, stammering tongue had suddenly become eloquent; for from this time Charles Wesley's hymns flowed out in a continuous stream which endured until 1785, three years before his death.

The Tunes Edition of the *Methodist Hymn-book* (1933) has this striking passage:

When at Whitsuntide 1738 the Lord turned again the captivity of John and Charles Wesley so that their chains fell off and their heart was free, their mouth was filled with laughter and their tongue with singing.

For that singing the Methodists have much to thank the Moravians, and it is gratifying therefore to know that the Brethren are still well represented in Methodist song. In the 1933 book there are in all twenty-three hymns: four by Zinzendorf, one by the Count and the two Nitschmanns, one by Spangenberg, three by Cennick (all written, however, before he joined the Moravians), and fourteen by Montgomery; while there are three tunes by Moravians: one each by Christian Ignatius La Trobe, Peter La Trobe, and L. R. West, as well as the fine swinging tune of the Brethren of the sixteenth century, *Mit Freuden Zart* (415), and the more meditative tune, *Atonement* (181).

Hymn-singing has survived and perhaps grown in both Methodism and Moravianism. Methodists certainly sing more hymns (generally five) in a particular service than their founder would have approved—he even threatened to expel a preacher who had more than two![79] One reason for this was that, in the absence of books and (at first) of instrumental music, the hymns were 'lined-out' one or two lines at a time. Another more cogent reason was the inordinate length of some of the hymns. *O for a thousand tongues to sing* (1), for instance, had eighteen verses, while *God of all power, and truth, and grace* (562) had twenty-eight! The fact that the latter was printed by Wesley at the end of his sermon on *Christian Perfection* and by Fletcher at the close of his *Last Check to Antinomianism* seems to indicate that it was probably meant to be read rather than sung. The former, however, demands vocal expression, in spite of its length. It is commonly supposed to have been the direct result of some words spoken to Charles Wesley by Peter Böhler. In May 1738 Charles Wesley spoke to Böhler about confessing Christ, and received the reply: 'Had I a thousand tongues, I would praise Him with them all'. This story is, however, open to question. Mentzer's hymn *O dass ich tausend Zungen hätte* had been published in 1704, and George Whitefield had been heard to exclaim in April 1739—a month before Charles Wesley wrote the hymn—'O that I had a thousand tongues with which to praise my God!' Moreover, this famous verse is not the first, but the seventh, in the original hymn.

[79] See *Letters*, VII.301, 304.

(*c*) *The Love-feast*

But though hymn-singing has persisted, in two other directions the influence of the Moravians upon Methodist practice has waned. The Band-meeting changed its methods and its purview even during Wesley's life and today has almost disappeared, though Class-leaders and Leaders' Meetings are still part of Methodist organization, and though fellowships of different types have taken the place of the earlier groups. The Love-feast, however, which was so conspicuous and characteristic a feature of Methodist and Moravian life in the first twenty-five years of their relationships, has fallen by the wayside. It still forms part of the regular worship of the Brethren, though much less frequently than in the early days of the Renewed Church, but it has almost entirely disappeared from Methodism. An attempt to revive it was made at the Methodist Conference at Preston in July 1952, but it is to be feared that many of the large congregation were attracted more by curiosity than from any urgent wish to resuscitate a moribund tradition. Indeed, 'information as to the correct procedure for a Love-feast had first to be sought through the columns of the *Methodist Recorder* . . . a commentary on the desuetude of the institution'.[80]

The Love-feast of the Moravians was, of course, a revival of the Agape of the Primitive Church, the communal meal which preceded the Eucharist, and at which, even in those early days, abuses took place;[81] and it was probably the fact that it *was* a revival that attracted Wesley in the first place. At first these Love-feasts, as practised by the Brethren, were of a private character. On special occasions, such as weddings, or on Sunday evenings, they were held at Zinzendorf's house, and only a few people attended. The Elders also had their own Love-feasts, and both in these and in similar meetings held in one another's houses the Brethren sought to recapture the fellowship of the Primitive Church, singing, conversing and exchanging experiences. As a rule, the meal consisted merely of rye-bread and water, and the participants, as they ate and drank, wished one another, 'Long live the Lord Jesus in our hearts', and talked freely about the Kingdom of God. It is not clear from contemporary accounts whether the conversations

[80] Frank Baker, *Methodism and the Love-feast* (MS).

[81] 1 Cor. 11$^{17-21}$; Jude 12. Jude actually uses the word ἀγάπαι—R.V. 'love-feasts', A.V. 'feasts of charity'.

took the form afterwards so common in Methodist Love-feasts, personal testimonies, though the rather vague terminology admits of this interpretation. At first, the English Brethren used wine and bread at these services, but in order to prevent any confusion with the Eucharist, they soon used tea and a specially made bread.[82] The need to maintain this distinction was mentioned by Zinzendorf in his account of Moravian polity presented to the House of Commons in 1749:

> In order to remove [from the Eucharist] the least idea of an ordinary repast, we subjoin always Agapes to the Communion; but leaving it to the conveniency of our respective Churches, whether they keep them before or after.

The Moravians took the custom of the Love-feast to America, where John Wesley first met it.[83] In his *Journal* for 8th August 1737, he records:

> After evening prayers, we joined with the Germans in one of their love-feasts. It was begun and ended with thanksgiving and prayer, and celebrated in so decent and solemn a manner as a Christian of the apostolic age would have allowed to be worthy of Christ.[84]

It is noteworthy that in the parallel entry in his Diary he refers to the Love-feast by the name used by the early Church—Agape.

The favourable impression received by Wesley in Savannah was apparently confirmed during his visit to Herrnhut. In the *Journal* for 2nd August 1738 he writes:

> At four in the afternoon was a love-feast of the married men, taking their food with gladness and singleness of heart, and with the voice of praise and thanksgiving;[85]

and in his account of the Herrnhut constitution he says:

> For the further stirring up the gift that is in us, sometimes we have public, sometimes private, love-feasts; at which we take moderate refreshment, with gladness and singleness of heart and the voice of praise and thanksgiving.[86]

[82] *Journal*, II.122 n.

[83] Canon Overton (*John Wesley*, p. 30) maintains that Wesley obtained the idea of the Love-feast from the Primitive Church and not through the mediation of the Moravians, but it is significant that there is no reference to it in letter, Diary or *Journal* before 1737.

[84] *Journal*, I.377. [85] ibid., II.20. [86] ibid., p. 56.

It is not surprising therefore to find that to the Rules of the Fetter Lane Society drawn up on 1st May of that year was added on his return Rule 28, which ran:

> That on Sunday se'ennight following (the day of general intercession) be a general Love-feast, from seven until ten in the evening.

There is no record that this rule was immediately kept, but Wesley's *Journal* speaks of a momentous Love-feast held on 1st January (a *Monday*):

> Mr Hall, Kinchin, Ingham, Whitefield, Hutchins, and my brother Charles were present at our Love-feast in Fetter Lane, with about sixty of our brethren. About three in the morning, as we were continuing instant in prayer, the power of God came mightily upon us, insomuch that many cried out for exceeding joy, and many fell to the ground. As soon as we were recovered a little from that awe and amazement at the presence of His majesty we broke out with one voice: 'We praise Thee, O God; we acknowledge Thee to be the Lord.'[87]

It has been pointed out earlier[88] that these sixty were members of the Church of England, and that there were seven ordained clergymen present. None at this time were Moravians, for there was not yet any organized Moravian community in England; but the enthusiasm displayed and the long continuance of the practice reveal how deep was the impression made by this simple act of fellowship and worship.

From this time onward, Love-feasts were frequently held. If the Diary is a complete record, the earlier ones were for women only, for on several occasions the following entry appears: 'Love-feast for the women, tea, singing, prayers.' On 5th February 1739, however, there was one at Fetter Lane—no sex is specified—which lasted until three o'clock on the following morning.[89] These meetings were generally held on Sundays, and it is probable that they were held more frequently than the Diary indicates. Apparently, according to a careful comparison of the Diary with Charles Wesley's *Journal*, men's and women's Love-feasts alternated, once a fortnight, the omitted references being to occasions when neither of the Wesleys could be present. The Bristol Society carried on the same procedure, the women holding their first Love-feast on 15th April 1739, and the men on 29th

[87] II.121-3. [88] Page 76, *supra*. [89] *Journal*, II.139.

April. Before long, however, the two sexes were to meet at the same time.

This was the time when the 'stillness' controversy was reaching its height, and it is not surprising therefore that the Diary references become less frequent. There is no reason to suppose, however, that Love-feasts were less often held. At a special Love-feast at Kingswood on 13th July 1740, Charles Wesley tells us:

Two hundred were assembled in the Spirit of Jesus. Never have I seen and *felt* such a congregation of faithful souls. I question whether Herrnhuth can now afford the like.[90]

This was written at a time when the feelings of the two brothers were exacerbated by the forthcoming breach, then only a week distant; but, apart from this, there is some evidence that, in their manner of conducting the Love-feast as in other ways, Moravian and Methodist were drawing apart. John Wesley thus describes a Moravian Love-feast held in February 1742:

For above an hour all was silent: no singing, no prayer, nor word of exhortation. Then Mr S . . . said: 'My sisters, I was thinking in my heart how many Scripture-names there are among you.' (Might he not as well have been thinking how many barley-corns would reach from London to Edinburgh?)[91]

That the Methodists had wholeheartedly adopted the Love-feast is shown by the many entries in Wesley's *Journal* and Diary even after the breach with Fetter Lane. There are Diary entries which show that in December 1740 Wesley attended three of these 'feasts of charity', one in London and two in Bristol,[92] while Charles Wesley records Love-feasts as far apart as Newcastle and St Ives. John Wesley's *Plain Account of the People called Methodists*, written to Vincent Perronet in 1748, shows that he still regarded them as an integral and valuable part of Methodist organization:

In order to increase in them a grateful sense of all His mercies, I desired that, one evening in a quarter, all the men in band, on a second all the women, would meet, and on a third both men and women together, that we might together 'eat bread', as the ancient Christians did 'with gladness and singleness of heart'. At these Love-feasts (so we termed them, retaining the name as well as the thing which was in use from the beginning) our food is only a little plain cake and water.

90 Charles Wesley, *Journal*, I.244. 91 *Journal*, II.526. 92 ibid., pp. 408-9.

But we seldom return from them without being fed not only with the 'meat which perisheth' but with 'that which endureth to everlasting life'.

Apparently, from the phrase 'one evening in a quarter', these Love-feasts were already being held less frequently than at first. They were still confined to the bands; in a letter to James Brewster on 22nd February 1750 Wesley wrote: 'I admit none but those to our Love-feasts who have "the love of God" already "shed abroad in their hearts".'[93] They seem to have become more and more meetings of testimony, especially after the extension of the privilege of attending from the bands to the whole Society on 9th December 1759. On 1st March 1761, for instance, Wesley wrote: 'Many of our brethren spoke plainly and artlessly what God had done for their souls';[94] and again, on 29th November of the same year: 'We had a comfortable love feast, at which several declared the blessings they had found lately';[95] and again, on 21st September 1767: 'We had a love feast for all the Society, at which many spoke their experience with all simplicity.'[96] An unusual one took place on 17th June 1770: 'Our love feast took up the next two hours, at which many were filled with solemn joy.'[97] John Nelson took part in this meeting, and relates: 'There was not enough bread to supply the great congregation. William Ripley went out and procured a quantity of gingerbread.'[98]

It seems therefore that by this time the Love-feast had extended its borders even beyond the Societies. On 11th October 1767, for instance, John Wesley wrote: 'I permitted all of Mr Whitefield's Society that pleased to be present at the love feast which followed. I hope we shall "not know war any more", unless with the world, the flesh, and the devil';[99] and, on 29th July 1770 he wrote: 'We closed this day with a Love-feast, during which four mourners found peace with God.'[100] On the other hand, in a letter to Thomas Carlill on 13th May 1777, he wrote:

I commend you for letting none but the members of the Society stay when the Society meets, and more particularly at the love feasts. You cannot give a ticket to any who rob the king by selling or buying uncustomed goods.[101]

[93] *Letters*, III.33. [94] *Journal*, IV.439.
[95] ibid., p. 480. [96] ibid., V.232. [97] ibid., p. 371.
[98] *Methodist Recorder* (3rd December 1908).
[99] *Journal*, V.235. [100] ibid., p. 379. [101] *Letters*, VI.265.

Why smugglers should wish to come to a Love-feast is not very clear, except perhaps as a cloak to their nefarious activities! Apparently there was some need of a tight hand, in view of the charges made against the Methodists about their behaviour in these services. A letter to the *Freeman's Journal* on 9th July 1767,[102] refutes the suggestion that Love-feasts went on till midnight, and another, on 31st March 1780,[103] stoutly denies that Methodist Love-feasts and Watch-nights roused the vigilance of the magistrate and influenced the rage of the rabble. The very name 'Love-feast' aroused suspicion and invited comparison with the abuses which had taken place in the early Church. According to one Joseph Nightingale: 'Breaking the cake with one another was peremptorily forbidden, because people would clatter down the aisle or scramble over the pews, in order to share their bread (or cake) with some particular friend.'[104]

Like the Moravians, though to a less extent, the Methodists sang hymns at their Love-feasts. Indeed, it was customary to break out into song when no spontaneous testimony was forthcoming. There is one hymn, still in use in Methodism, which was specifically written for the Love-feast. It begins:

Come, and let us sweetly join
Christ to praise in hymn divine;
Give we all, with one accord,
Glory to our common Lord,

Hands and hearts and voices raise;
Sing as in the ancient days;
Antedate the joys above,
Celebrate the feast of love.[105]

Another begins:

Let us join—'tis God commands—
Let us join our hearts and hands.[106]

It is possible that the reference to 'hearts and hands' may be connected with the Moravian practice (still preserved) of clasping

[102] *Letters*, V.55. [103] ibid., VII.11.
[104] Frank Baker, *Methodism and the Love-feast* (MS).
[105] *Methodist Hymn-book*, No. 748. [106] ibid., No. 713.

hands at the Eucharist and at the 'the Cup of Covenant'; and it is particularly appropriate that the tune to which this latter part is set is named *Lovefeast*. It appeared in the *Foundery Collection* of 1742, and was based on a tune which Wesley would have heard at Herrnhut.

It is evident, therefore, that Wesley adopted the idea and the early practice of the Love-feast from the Moravians, but that he extended its scope (i) to include the whole Society, (ii) to consist in large part of testimonies, and (iii) to act as an evangelistic agency, a converting ordinance. At some Love-feasts numerous conversions were made—fifty at Birstall on Christmas Day 1793, fifty more at the same place on Easter Day 1794, and similar numbers at Beverley and Hull.

As was said earlier, the Love-feast has virtually disappeared from Methodist usage, though two-handled Love-feast mugs may still be seen in some vestries. Even among the Moravians, with whom it has survived, there is very little in the way of personal testimony. At Fulneck, for example, where there is a Love-feast for members once a month, it precedes the service of Holy Communion, and takes the form of a kind of family party—hymns, food (tea and buns), conversation, an address, but neither testimony nor prayer. The women still wear the traditional black dress, shawl, and cap.[107]

It is customary for Methodists to lament this departure from time-honoured practice. Some Methodist writers deplore the disappearance of the Love-feast as involving a breach with the usages of the Primitive Church, and as evidence of a lowering of the spiritual temperature of the Church. It is more probable that its disappearance, like that of the traditional 'testimony meeting' is connected with a reluctance to speak too freely of religious experience. Many Christians, enjoying a rich spiritual fellowship with God, are unwilling to talk about it, partly because it is too intimate to bandy about in an open meeting, partly because it may look like (as it has sometimes been) a mere display, and partly because the Methodist Church, like other Churches, has become less concerned with cultivating its own spiritual life than with facing the religious, social, and economic problems of a larger world. It has not been all loss.

[107] There are also two or three public Love-feasts at Festival times, but these are not followed by Holy Communion.

(*d*) *The Watch-night Service*

The debt of Methodism to Moravianism in the matter of the Watch-night Service is much less certain, though still probable. Unlike the Love-feast, it has survived, and gives no sign of disappearing. Perhaps its survival has been in part due to its having been adopted by other Churches. Like the Love-feast, the Watch-night had its origin in the practice of the early Church, and again this may have been one reason for its attractiveness to John Wesley, in his early manhood a doughty traditionalist. In a letter to the Rev. John Baily, Rector of Kilcully, Cork, on 8th June 1750, he wrote:

> You charge me . . . with holding 'midnight assemblies'. Sir, did you never see the word 'Vigil' in your Common Prayer Book? Do you know what it means? If not, permit me to tell you that it was customary with the ancient Christians to spend whole nights in Prayer, and that these nights were termed *Vigiliae*, or Vigils. Therefore, for spending a part of some nights in this manner, in public and solemn prayer, we have not only the authority of our national Church, but of the Universal Church in the earliest ages.[108]

The Moravian institution of the Watch-night seems to have grown out of their concern for the people in their settlements. At Herrnhut the night-watchman on his rounds sang a verse of a hymn at each hour of the night. Wesley mentions this custom in his account of the Herrnhut constitution:

> Two men keep watch every night in the street; as do two women in the women's apartment; that they may pour out their souls for those that sleep, and by their hymns raise the hearts of any who are awake to God.[109]

He does not mention the actual Watch-night service, but that is because the Moravians, like Churches today, held it on New Year's Eve, by which time Wesley was back in England. The first Moravian Watch-night service took place in 1733,[110] so that it had probably not established itself so firmly in Georgia as to make any great impression on Wesley's mind.

There was undoubtedly such a service at Fetter Lane on

[108] *Letters*, III.287. [109] *Journal*, II.56.
[110] J. T. Hamilton, *History of the Moravian Church*, p. 43.

the last day of 1738, coincident with the Love-feast previously mentioned.[111] Either there is some confusion here—for Wesley gives the date as 1st January, and does not mention the Watch-night—or they met just before midnight, as is the custom today. Wesley's Diary has the bare mention of 11.45, so that this seems a possible interpretation. This seems to have been the first Watch-night service held in England. If so, as it was probably directly due to the suggestion of the Brethren at Fetter Lane, the influence of the Moravians has gone even farther beyond their own borders.

Wesley gives his own account of the Watch-night in *A Plain Account of the People called Methodists*:

> About this time I was informed that several persons in Kingswood frequently met together at the school, and when they could spare the time spent the greater part of the night in prayer and praise and thanksgiving. Some advised me to put an end to this; but, upon weighing the thing thoroughly and comparing it with the practice of the ancient Christians, I could see no cause to forbid it. Rather I believed it might be made of more general use. So I sent them word I designed to watch with them on the Friday nearest the full moon, that we might have light thither and back again. I gave public notice of this the Sunday before, and withal that I intended to preach; desiring they, and they only would meet me there who could do it without prejudice to their business or families. On Friday abundance of people came. I began preaching between eight and nine; and we continued till a little beyond the noon of night, singing, praying, and praising God.
>
> This we have continued to do once a month ever since in Bristol, London, and Newcastle, as well as Kingswood; and exceeding great are the blessings we have found therein.

There is some doubt about the date of this first Methodist Watch-night service. John Wesley records such a service on Wednesday 21st December 1740,[112] but it is difficult to reconcile this with the reference to *Friday* quoted above. It is more likely that the service mentioned in the *Plain Account* took place early in 1742. In that year two hymns appeared which seem to have originated in the immediate circumstances of a Watch-night service, *Oft have we passed the guilty night* (a reference to the dissolute habits of the Kingswood colliers who, now converted, chose another form of nocturnal engagement), and *Hearken to the solemn voice*, the

[111] See p. 211, *supra; Journal*, II.121-2. [112] *Journal*, II.412.

hymn with which the first Watch-night services concluded. On Friday 12th March 1742 there took place a service which satisfied the conditions, for Wesley records:

Our Lord was gloriously present with us at the Watch-night, so that my voice was lost in the cries of the people. After midnight about a hundred of us walked home together, singing, and rejoicing and praising God.[113]

This would explain the close proximity of the first Watch-night in London, held, according to Wesley's *Journal*, on Friday 9th April 1742:

We had the first Watch-night in London. We commonly choose for this solemn service the Friday night nearest the full moon, either before or after, that those of the congregation who live at a distance may have light to their several homes. The service begins at half an hour past eight, and continues till a little after midnight. We have often found a peculiar blessing at these seasons. There is generally a deep awe upon the congregation, perhaps in some measure owing to the silence of the night, particularly in singing the hymn, with which we commonly conclude:

Hearken to the solemn voice,
The awful midnight cry!
Waiting souls, rejoice, rejoice,
And feel the Bridegroom nigh.[114]

It appears then that John Wesley generally used the term 'Watch-night' to refer to these week-night meetings, and not to the service held on the last day of the year. As has been mentioned, the term is not used in his account of the meeting at Fetter Lane on 31st December 1738, nor is it found in his description of that held in Bristol on 31st December 1740.[115] There are many references to Watch-night services in the *Journal*: most of these were held on Fridays at different times of the year. That the New Year's Eve services do not usually carry the term 'Watch-night' (though they sometimes do) is probably because it was not necessary to designate them thus, and possibly because Wesley regarded them as being of a somewhat different order from the others. Late in his life, if his *Journal* and Diary are in any way a complete record, Watch-night services became fewer and fewer in number, and tended to be limited to the annual service on

[113] *Journal*, II.534. [114] ibid., p. 536. [115] ibid., pp. 121, 412.

New Year's Eve, in accordance with modern Methodist practice and with Moravian custom throughout. In the last nine years of Wesley's life only eight are mentioned, and five of these were held on the last day of the year.

In general, these services seem to have been well-conducted, and the suggestion that they were the occasion of loose conduct is without foundation. The emphasis was on solemnity. On 22nd August 1750, for instance, when the first Cornish Watch-night was held, Wesley recorded: 'Great was the Holy One of Israel in the midst of us';[116] and the word 'solemn' appears in many of his entries. Perhaps it was this limited emphasis which made his services less frequent. Appropriate as it was for such services to be held on the last night of the year, there was less need for them at other times, and there must have been some over-crowding of the Methodist programme with band-meetings, Society meetings, Love-feasts, and the ordinary services which they were encouraged to attend. In this the wisdom of the Moravians is evident, and Wesley's debt to them confirmed.

It is necessary to quote one doubter. Canon J. H. Overton, speaking of John Wesley's Oxford days, writes:

> It is a far cry from Ritualism (so-called) to Methodism (so-called); but it is not fancy, but plain historical fact, that Wesley derived his ideas about the Mixed Chalice, Prayers for the faithful Departed, and the observance of the Stations, from precisely the same source from whence he derived his ideas about the Class-Meeting, the Love-Feast, the Watch-Night, and the tickets of membership; and they date from this period[117] (i.e. before he had met the Moravians).

Unfortunately, Overton gives no evidence for this 'plain historical fact'; and as far as the Class-meeting, the Love-feast, and possibly the Watch-night are concerned, it is far more reasonable to hold that, whether they were inherited from the Primitive Church or not, they came to Wesley through the Moravians rather than through his Oxford High Church associations.

If Overton granted too little to the Brethren, J. E. Hutton seems to claim too much for them. In his article on Methodist bands he spoke of the remarkable system which the Moravians had built up at Herrnhut, and specified their lay-preaching, their open-air services, their Love-feasts, their Watch-night services

[116] *Journal*, III.491. [117] *John Wesley*, p. 30.

and their Covenant Service. If it is implied that the Methodist Covenant Service originated in Moravian precedent the case is by no means proved. Indeed, Wesley himself suggests a different origin in his *Journal* entries for 6th and 11th August 1755:

> I mentioned to the congregation [in London] another means of increasing serious religion, which has been frequently practised by our forefathers and attended with eminent blessing, namely, the joining in a covenant to serve God with all our heart and with all our soul. I explained this for several mornings following, and on *Friday* many of us kept a fast unto the Lord, beseeching him to give us wisdom and strength to promise unto the Lord our God and keep it.
>
> I explained once more the nature of such an engagement, and the manner of doing it acceptably unto God. At six in the evening we met for that purpose at the French church at Spitalfields. After I had recited the tenor of the covenant proposed, in the words of that blessed man, Richard Alleine, all the people stood up, in testimony of assent, to the number of about eighteen hundred persons. Such a night I scarce ever saw before. Surely the fruit of it shall remain for ever.[118]

To Alleine he pays a further tribute in his entry for 3rd April 1757:

> On Good Friday, in the evening, at the meeting of the Society, God was eminently present with us. I read over and enlarged upon Joseph [*sic*] Alleine's *Directions for a Thorough Conversion to God*, and desired all who were able would meet me on Monday that we might 'perform our vows unto the Lord'.[119]

It was from Joseph Alleine (not Richard, whose fame depends upon a different book, *Vindiciae Pietatis*) that Wesley received the impulse to a Covenant Service, though he may have seen this in operation in Georgia. There is no mention of it, however, either in the Georgian narrative or in the account of the Herrnhut constitution, and it is improbable therefore that Methodism owes anything to Moravianism in this respect.

(*e*) *Field-preaching*

All the meetings discussed so far appear to have been held indoors. But the inevitable result of the doctrinal influence of the Moravians upon the Wesleys was seen in a change of method and

[118] *Journal*, IV.126. [119] ibid., IV.200.

emphasis. The Brethren taught John and Charles Wesley the importance of experience, and showed him that salvation and assurance were available to all who believed. The logical implication was that this joyous privilege should be *shared*, and though it was left to the events of Whitsuntide 1738 to supply the dynamic impulse, that impulse would have had little power without the conviction which the Moravians had supplied. Henceforward, the Wesleys were evangelists first and foremost, though it was to be some time before John consented to 'make himself more vile' by field-preaching.

Some of the more orthodox Methodists looked upon this practice with anxiety (thereby anticipating the suspicion of 'camp-meetings' a century later), and on several occasions John Wesley was constrained to defend it. On 28th August 1748 he wrote:

> I wonder at those who still talk so loud of the indecency of field-preaching. The highest indecency is in St Paul's Church [i.e. Cathedral] when a considerable part of the congregation are asleep, or talking or looking about, not minding a word the preacher says. On the other hand, there is the highest decency in a church-yard or field, when the whole congregation behave and look as if they saw the Judge of all, and heard Him speaking from Heaven.[120]

'O what a victory', he cried on 20th May 1759, 'would Satan gain if he could put an end to field-preaching! But that, I trust, he never will; at least, not till my head is laid.'[121] Again, on 23rd September 1759 he wrote:

> A vast majority of the immense congregation in Moorfields were deeply serious. One such hour might convince any impartial man of the expediency of field-preaching. What building, except St Paul's Church, would contain such a congregation? And if it would, what human voice could have reached them there? By repeated observations I find I can command thrice the number in the open-air that I can under a roof. And who can say the time for field-preaching is over, while (i) greater numbers than ever attend; (ii) the converting as well as convincing power of God is eminently present with them?[122]

He wrote on 30th September 1767:

> In field-preaching, more than any other means, 'God is found of them that sought him not'. By this, death, heaven, and hell come to the ears, if not the hearts, of them that 'care for none of these things'.[123]

[120] *Journal*, III.373. [121] ibid., IV.315. [122] ibid., IV.354. [123] ibid., V.234.

'What but field-preaching', he asked on 17th September 1763, 'could reach these poor sinners?'[124] He believed that one hindrance of the work of God was the neglect of field-preaching, though apparently he himself did not enjoy doing it.

He wrote on 6th September 1772:

To this day field-preaching is a cross to me. But I know my commission, and see no other way of 'preaching the gospel to every creature'.[125]

Opposition came from many quarters, and its success made the opposition fiercer. John Nelson was told: 'We allow all you say is true; yet you deserve to be set in the stocks for delivering it in the streets.'

Even the Moravians seemed half-hearted in their approval, though they (and especially Cennick) practised it themselves. James Hutton, for example, damns it with faint praise when he says: 'It was a jumble of extremes of good and evil—and so distracted alike were both preachers and hearers, that it was enough to make one cry to God for His interference.'[126] Hutton admits, however, that 'some well-known examples of good' were effected, and adds: 'A large number of persons was truly awakened to their spiritual condition.'

This may be regarded as high praise; Zinzendorf was more restrained. Spangenberg, in his biography of the Count[127] (a book which, like other books on the Moravian side, scarcely mentions the association of the Methodists and the Moravians and the breach between them), makes the following comment:

The Count did not refrain from stating to them [Whitefield and Wesley] what he found objectionable in both; nor did he wish that the Moravians and the Methodists should be looked upon as one body; and openly expressed his sentiments to that effect. He did not find fault with their preaching in the market-places, streets, and fields, although he differed in opinion from them in that respect; it was to their doctrines that he chiefly objected.

From whom then did John and Charles Wesley learn these methods, or did they spring in panoply from their own minds? John Wesley, it is true, had preached in the open-air long before Whitsuntide 1738. Both on the way to Georgia and in Georgia

124 *Journal*, V.30.

125 ibid., V.484.

126 Benham, *Memoirs of James Hutton*, p. 42.

127 1838, pp. 229-30.

itself he had held religious services, free from the restraints (and deprived of the hallowed associations) of a church building. On 19th October 1735 he wrote: 'We had the morning service on quarter-deck. I now first preached extempore.'[128] Even after his arrival in Georgia, he preached several times on the deck of the *Simmonds*,[129] and it is probable that he witnessed open-air preaching in Herrnhut, though his *Journal* makes no reference to it. He does, however, record that

> after the evening service . . . was ended, all the unmarried men (as is their custom) walked quite round the town, singing praise with instruments of music; and then on a small hill, at a little distance from it, casting themselves into a ring, joined in prayer.[130]

Apparently, his brother Charles too had already begun to preach in the open-air. His *Journal* for 19th July 1738 recounts how, in accordance with his custom, he visited the condemned at Tyburn:

> I got upon the cart . . . the Ordinary endeavoured to follow, but the mob kept him down. . . . I spoke a few suitable words to the crowd; and returned, full of peace and confidence on our friends' happiness. That hour under the gallows was the most blessed hour of my life.[131]

This form of open-air meeting was very different from that on the *Simmonds*, in Georgia, and in Herrnhut, which was in the main if not entirely to professing Christians. This was the fulfilment of Charles's determination as expressed in his 'Conversion Hymn', written only two months before.[132]

On a similar occasion, his brother John was with him, as the latter's *Journal* records:

> My brother and I went . . . to do the last good office to the condemned malefactors. . . . My brother took that occasion of declaring the gospel of peace to a large company of publicans and sinners;[133]

and his Diary for the same day states that he too 'preached to the mob'. It must be remembered, of course, that the Wesleys had visited the prisoners while at Oxford, but their work then appears to have been social rather than evangelical.

Thus Charles was John's immediate tutor in the work which

[128] *Journal*, I.111. [129] ibid., p. 169. [130] ibid., II.21-2.
[131] I.122-3. [132] *Methodist Hymn-book*, No. 361. [133] II.100.

was to transform his ministry; but the evangelical campaign which was to set England on fire did not begin until the following February, when George Whitefield took, at Bristol, a step which profoundly influenced the whole course of the Revival. He had earlier suggested open-air preaching, but had been deterred by his friends, who called it a mad notion. Even he was not the first to adopt these evangelistic methods, for, according to Cennick,[134] a Rev. William Morgan, a year earlier, 'pitying the rude and ignorant condition of the Kingswood colliers, sometimes preached to them in the fields'. Whitefield, finding the pulpits of the diocese closed to him, preached on 17th February 1739 to a congregation of two hundred colliers on Kingswood Hill. His preaching was so remarkable that before long the number had reached five thousand.

Whitefield's success inspired not only John Wesley but Howell Harris, the Welsh Calvinist, with whom he joined hands and laid the foundation of the Calvinistic Methodism of Wales. But Harris himself had been preceded by another Welshman, the Rev. Griffith Jones, Rector of Llanddowror, who, as early as 1711, finding his own parish too small for his own missionary zeal, went to the villages around and, when the churches were not large enough to hold all those who wished to hear him, preached in the churchyards and the fields. Howell Harris himself, though not ordained, began to preach, at first in private houses and then in the fields and streets. This was two years before Wesley and Whitefield preached in the open air in and around Bristol.

It would therefore not seem easy to trace the process by which John Wesley took to the open-air. His early experience in Georgia may have suggested possibilities to him, his brother's ministrations to the prisoners may have changed the direction of his thought, and the evangelistic achievements of Harris and Whitefield may have revealed to him the amazing opportunities which this method presented. Certainly, Whitefield's venture was followed by Wesley after a very short interval, for on 2nd April 1739, only a few weeks afterwards, he wrote:

> At four in the afternoon I submitted to be more vile, and proclaimed in the highways the glad tidings of salvation, speaking from a little eminence in a ground adjoining to the city, to about three thousand people.[135]

[134] *Wesley Historical Society Proceedings* (June, 1908). [135] *Journal*, II.172-3.

There is no reason for surprise at the almost simultaneous adoption of open-air preaching by so many young men. Whether or not Whitefield was following the example of Griffith Jones, his own success was so amazing that it would have been surprising if others had not followed him. In any case, the appearance of so many young men full of evangelistic zeal early in the century affords some criticism of the widely-held view of the age as one of artifice and restraint. The extraordinary outburst of the human spirit, finding its expression in the Romantic Movement, in the reform of the penal system, and in a general humanitarian impulse, had been foreshadowed and indeed made possible by the early spiritual strivings of the first half of the century. Indeed, there are evidences that by the end of the century evangelistic fervour was past its peak.

Certainly, if the Moravians appear to have been somewhat half-hearted about embarking upon open-air preaching, they were not slow to follow. Cennick's success in this field was as remarkable as Wesley's, not only during his association with him, but for the rest of his short and crowded life; and though he objected to the scenes which accompanied some of his preaching, he continued to preach to crowds, both in association with Howell Harris and Whitefield and later in Ireland. Here his success was extraordinary, and not even John Wesley was better supported or more bitterly opposed. The Methodists and the Moravians had their own fields of operations. Wesley and his followers ministered to the colliers and miners round Bristol and in Cornwall, Cennick and his helpers to the humble Protestant farm-workers in the north of Ireland.

This is as far as one can go in the matter of *specific* influence. But, of course, the evangelical impulse which sent the two Wesleys into the highways and hedges, to Gwennap and Kingswood and Moorfields, began at Whitsuntide 1738, and the important part played by the Moravians in that epoch-making experience cannot be exaggerated.

(*f*) *Extemporary Prayer and Preaching*

The use of extemporary prayer has become so general amongst the Methodists that it is appropriate to ask what share the Moravians had in establishing this custom and offering an example. No clear case can be made out. In the first place, prayer of this sort seems to have been common amongst English Dissenters during Wesley's early years, and it is hardly likely that he would have been ignorant of it, though his High Church upbringing may have prejudiced him against it. Indeed, his first recorded reference to it has a touch of disparagement. Describing a visit to the Presbyterian settlement at Darien, some twenty miles from Frederica, in the early days of 1737, he says: 'I was surprised to hear an extempore prayer before a written sermon'.[136] Apparently, though he was deeply impressed by the spiritual quality of these Highlanders, he did not at the time approve of this kind of prayer, for he goes on:

Are not the words we speak to God to be set in order at least as carefully as those we speak to our fellow worms? One consequence of this manner of praying is that they have public service only once a week.

It seems that his criticism arose from the fact that the prayer was used in a formal service, 'before a written sermon', and that even at that date he had no objection to extempore prayers in a small, intimate meeting; for in his Diary for the same day he writes: '$7\frac{3}{4}$, Mrs Mackintosh's supper and singing; I prayed extempore!' Perhaps the note of exclamation is his own comment on his apparent inconsistency.

He appears to have made this distinction on other occasions. On 26th March 1738, for instance, he wrote:

I preached at Whitam [?Wytham] on 'the new creature', and went in the evening to a society in Oxford, where (as my manner then was at all societies), after using a collect or two and the Lord's Prayer, I expounded a chapter in the New Testament, and concluded with three or four more collects and a psalm.[137]

On the next day, however, he went with Kinchin to visit a condemned man at the Castle, where they prayed 'first in several forms of prayer, and then in such words as were given us in that hour'. But a few days later, even in the more formal Society meeting, his heart was so full that he could not confine himself

to the forms of prayer which we were accustomed to use there. Neither [he adds] do I purpose to be confined to them any more, but to pray indifferently, with a form or without, as I may find suitable to particular occasions.

[136] *Journal*, I.309. [137] ibid., I.447-9.

It is worthy of note that in his letter of 10th September 1784 to Coke, Asbury, and others, prescribing the conduct of the American Societies, he says:

I have prepared a Liturgy, little differing from that of the Church of England (I think the best constituted National Church in the world), which I advise all the travelling preachers to use on the Lord's Day in all congregations, reading the Litany only on Wednesdays and Fridays, and praying extempore on all other days.[138]

Thus, even at the end of his life, there was no jettisoning of the Prayer Book; extempore prayer was to be used 'when suitable to particular occasion'.

Wesley was much criticized for going so far, and more than once felt impelled to defend his practice. His elder brother early censured him,[139] but that should cause no surprise, for Samuel was a rigid conservative in such matters. In answer to a Mr Allen, who sought to demonstrate that extemporary prayer was no prayer at all, for no man can think and pray at the same time, he replied that this was just as true about *reading* and praying.[140] In two important letters to the Rev. Samuel Walker, Vicar of Truro, he showed that his use of extempore prayer did not involve any disloyalty to the Church of England. On 24th September 1755 he wrote:

At present I apprehend those, and those only, to separate from the Church who either renounce her fundamental doctrines or refuse to join in her public worship. As yet we have done neither; nor have we taken one step farther than we were convinced was our bounden duty. It is from a full conviction of this that we have (i) preached abroad, (ii) prayed extempore, (iii) formed Societies, and (iv) permitted preachers who were not episcopally ordained. And were we pushed on this side, were there no alternative allowed, we should judge it our bounden duty rather wholly to separate from the Church than to give up any one of these points.[141]

Again, in October 1758, he wrote:

Neither dare I confine myself wholly to forms of prayer, not even in the church. I use indeed all the forms; but I frequently add extemporary prayer, either before or after sermon.[142]

138 *Letters*, VII.238-9.
139 Moore, *Life of Wesley*, I.377.
140 *Journal*, II.404.
141 *Letters*, III.146.
142 *Works*, XIII.206 (*Journal*, IV.286 n.).

Thus, though Wesley is on the defensive, he writes with conviction. How far were the teaching and example of the Moravians responsible for this conviction? There is little evidence that they themselves made considerable use of extemporary prayer, or that in this matter Wesley was influenced in either direction by their practice. It is true that one answer given by Spangenberg to the series of questions posed by Wesley on 31st July 1737 indicates that the Moravians used prayer of this kind. Wesley asked: 'Do you prefer extempore to set forms of prayer in public?' Spangerberg replied: 'Our hymns are forms of prayer. For the rest, every one speaks as he is moved by the Holy Ghost.'[143] This, though it allows extemporary prayer, does not enjoin it, and in all probability Moravian practice, then as now, was to use both forms. The following question and answer bear this out:

How do you interpret that commandment of our Lord, 'Ye, when ye pray, say, Our Father'?

As a command to avoid vain repetitions in prayer.

With regard to Wesley's own attitude in this matter at this time, it is well to note that there is no further reference in either *Journal* or Diary to his own use of extemporary prayer, and that he records *without comment* the Moravian use of it at Berthelsdorf on 6th August 1738: 'The minister in the pulpit used a long extemporary prayer.'[144] The word 'long' might seem to imply some criticism, were it not that Wesley uses the same word in describing a liturgical intercession and general thanksgiving, and, indeed, emphasizes the length of the whole service.

The whole of this service, indeed, appears to have been built on a liturgical basis, and this seems to have been the general Moravian practice. The Bill of 1749, which sought successfully the recognition of the Brethren in England, was supported by their Church Litany, which had been revised by Sherlock, Bishop of London. Today the Moravians make less use of extemporary prayer than the Methodists generally do. Their Hymn-book bears the title *Moravian Liturgy and Hymns*, and liturgical forms make up a considerable part of their regular worship.

In so far as the heart-warming experience of May 1738 changed Wesley from a ritualist to an evangelist, the Moravians can claim some responsibility for his adoption of freer methods of worship,

[143] *Journal*, I.374. [144] ibid., II.21.

but here again their influence was more general than specific.

Extemporary *preaching* owes even less to the Brethren, though Cennick appears to have used it. John Wesley certainly did so on one occasion, for on 28th January 1775, referring to a service in 1735, he wrote: 'This was the first time that, having no notes about me, I preached extempore.'[145] The implication is that much of his later preaching must have been extemporary, and this is borne out by subsequent references. On 7th October 1739, for instance, he wrote: 'I was strengthened to speak as I never did before, and continued speaking near two hours';[146] and again on the 19th of the same month: 'My heart was so enlarged I knew not how to give over, so that we continued three hours.'[147] It is difficult to discover how far his preaching, except his *obiter dicta*, was really extemporaneous: it is probable that on many occasions he used notes as a basis. A letter from his brother Samuel to Charles on 1st December 1738, before the actual beginning of field-preaching, suggests this:

> There is a most monstrous appearance of dishonesty among you; your sermons are generally three-quarters of an hour long in the pulpit, but when printed are short snips: rather notes than sermons.[148]

There is no doubt, of course, that Wesley's sermons, *as written*, though excellent as standards of reference, would hardly have been the marvellous instrument of conversion which his preaching undoubtedly was if given in that form; but it is probable that they formed the scheme of thought which lay behind his most effective preaching, and that they were illuminated by illustrations, direct appeals, and all the fire and charm of his personality. Extempore preaching is seldom completely extemporaneous. It depends much upon memory and schematic preparation; otherwise it may become formless, unbalanced, and repetitive; and John Wesley was too great a literary artist to risk such imperfections.

In any case, there is no reason to suppose that he owed much if anything to Moravian precept or example.

(*g*) *Lay Preaching*

If there is one direction in which Methodism traditionally differs from other Churches, Anglican and 'Free', it is in the extent of its

[145] *Journal*, VI.96. [146] ibid., II.287. [147] ibid., p. 296.
[148] Rigg, *The Living Wesley*, p. 145.

use of lay-preachers, or 'local preachers' as they are termed (in contradistinction to the 'itinerant ministry' or 'travelling preachers'). It is calculated that six of every seven Methodist pulpits are occupied every Sunday by laymen and laywomen, and there is an official department which conducts examinations, prescribes courses of study, and awards certificates. Such importance does the Methodist Church give to this aspect of its work that, with very few exceptions (e.g. ministers received from other communions), no one can enter the Methodist ministry without having been an 'accredited local preacher'.

John Wesley realized, quite early in his ministry, that he would need the assistance of laymen, if not as preachers, yet as 'helpers' in his Societies; not merely because of the extraordinary growth in numbers of his followers, but because so few of the ordained clergy were willing to assist him. At first he seemed reluctant to acknowledge them as 'preachers', and appears to avoid the term in speaking of them. This may, in part, account for the doubt about the priority of Humphreys, Cennick, and Maxfield in this capacity. Later, however, he became their enthusiastic advocate. His letters abound with sturdy defence of a practice which his work made necessary and which his reason fully accepted. Sometimes he is more concerned to attack the poor preaching quality of ordained clergy than to justify the use of lay helpers. On 4th May 1748, for instance, he wrote a remarkable letter 'To a Clergyman', in which, in twenty-eight paragraphs, he compared a successful but untrained apothecary with an unsuccessful qualified practitioner, and showed, by analogy, that the lay preacher was justified by his success. He asked:

> Will you condemn such a preacher, because he has not learning? or has not had an university education? What then? He saves those sinners from their sins whom the man of learning and education cannot save. . . . I think . . . that every Christian, if he is able to do it, has authority to save a dying soul.[149]

Again, in a letter of 31st October 1755, he declares: 'Soul-damning clergymen lay me under more difficulties than soul-saving laymen';[150] and says that Grimshaw and Baddeley, two vicars, had no conversions until they formed irregular societies and took in laymen to assist them. In another letter, written on 18th September

[149] *Letters*, II.148-9. [150] ibid., III.151.

1756, he writes: 'O Sir, what an idle thing it is for you to dispute about lay preachers! Is not a lay-preacher preferable to a drunken preacher, to a cursing, swearing preacher?'[151] 'Archbishop Robinson complained to Charles Wesley about this employment of laymen. Charles replied that the fault lay at the door of the clergy: "You hold your peace, and the stones cry out." "But they are unlearned men", said the Primate. "Some are," was the reply, still using Scripture references, "and so the dumb ass rebukes the prophet." '[152] Now all this is somewhat negative, and John Wesley seems to have recognized that some control was necessary. To an objection by the Rev. G. L. Fleury that 'the most ignorant and illiterate' laymen were permitted to preach, provided they had 'the inward call of the Spirit', John Wesley replied:

> They [the Methodists] do not allow 'the most ignorant' men to preach whatever 'inward call' they pretend to. Among them none are allowed to be stated preachers but such as (i) are truly alive to God, such as experience the 'faith that worketh by love', such as love God and all mankind; (2) such as have a competent knowledge of the Word of God and of the work of God in the souls of men: (3) such as have given proof that they are called of God by converting sinners from the error of their ways. And to show whether they have these qualifications or no, they are a year, sometimes more, upon trial.[153] Now, I pray, what is the common examination either for deacon's or priest's orders to this?[154]

Even so, restrictions were placed upon them. They were not expected to make long prayers: 'I advise them not usually to exceed four or five minutes either before or after sermon;[155] they were not allowed to administer the Sacraments: 'I tolerate' (the word is significant) 'lay-preaching because I conceive there is an absolute necessity for it; inasmuch as, were it not, thousands of souls would perish everlastingly. Yet I do not tolerate lay-administering, because I do not conceive there is any such necessity for it; seeing it does not appear that, if this not at all, one soul will perish for the want of it';[156] and it was for a long time the practice, if not the rule, for lay-preachers to preach from the reading-desks or from the congregation.

[151] *Letters*, III.203. [152] Eayrs, *New History of Methodism*, I.293.

[153] Methodist lay-preachers are still expected to remain a year 'on trial' before being admitted to 'full plan'.

[154] *Letters*, V.249. [155] ibid., IV.122. [156] ibid., III.186.

The system of lay-preaching, like that of open-air preaching, came from somewhat mixed parentage, and it is by no means certain that the Brethren had any considerable share in the Methodist adoption of it. Wesley was not unfamiliar with Church history, and must have known of the use of lay-preachers in the Franciscan Revival. He must have known, too, that in the early days of Christianity laymen took a prominent share in the worship and work of the Church. The *Apostolical Constitutions* enjoin: 'Let him that teaches, although he be one of the laity, yet, if he be skilful in the word and grave in his manner, teach; for they shall all be taught of God.'[157] In Virginia, too, in Wesley's time, owing to the lack of clergy, lay readers were generally employed, and, according to Bishop Wilberforce,[158] it frequently happened that a benefice was left unfilled so that the services of the unordained reader might be kept longer. It is not surprising, therefore, that Wesley used Delamotte, a layman, as his substitute in Georgia. Delamotte had already served in the parish school of Savannah, teaching 'between thirty and forty children to read, write, and cast accounts.'[159] Wesley's statement that both he and Delamotte catechized the scholars seems to suggest that the latter's work went beyond mere formal instruction. When Wesley returned to Savannah, he found his little flock in a better state than he could have expected, 'God having been pleased greatly to bless the endeavours of my fellow-labourer while I was absent from them'. This, of course, is no definite proof that Delamotte preached, but Wesley's admission that most of his followers were 'more steadfast and zealous of good works' than when he had left them testifies to his general Christian influence.

There were, of course, precedents in Wesley's family history. His grandfather, John Wesley, in a conversation with the Bishop of Bristol, though not ordained, claimed the right to preach. 'I was called', he said, 'to the work of the ministry, though not the office';[160] and Wesley's mother, with her Presbyterian upbringing, apparently took a similar view. When, in Wesley's absence in 1739, Thomas Maxfield went beyond the terms of his office as leader of the Society and began to preach, Wesley hastened back to London to check him. Susanna Wesley looked at her son as she said:

[157] Clarke's *Ante-Nicene Library*, XVII.246.
[158] *History of the American Church*, p. 141.
[159] *Journal*, I.322. [160] ibid., V.120-1.

John, you know what my sentiments have been. You cannot suspect me of favouring readily anything of this kind. But take care what you do with respect to that young man, for he is as truly called of God to preach as you are. Examine what have been the fruits of his preaching and hear him also yourself.[161]

Wesley did so, and was convinced. In his *Appeal to Men of Reason and Religion* (1745) he points out that our Lord was a layman: 'Is not this the Carpenter?'

Susanna Wesley's defence of Maxfield is akin to that of the aged Mrs Canning's championing of Thomas Westell, whom Wesley wished to preclude from preaching: 'Stop him at your peril. He preaches the truth, and the Lord owns him as truly as He does you or your brother.'[162] It appears from this that though Wesley defended lay-preaching he was not always as enthusiastic about lay-preachers, though he seems to have encouraged Cennick.

In assessing influences, it is important to remember the example and advice of Howell Harris. Harris, though three times offered ordination, remained a layman, and led the way in the lay open-air preaching of the Revival. He and Wesley had a long and intimate conversation on 19th June 1739, and the goodwill which prevailed was such that there was little disagreement on the advisability and indeed necessity of lay-preaching.[163]

But it seems that it was a Moravian layman, Christian David, who made the greatest impression upon John Wesley as a preacher. In his account of his visit to Herrnhut in August 1738 Wesley gives the stories of the conversion of several Moravians—Christian David, Michael Linner, David Nitschmann, Albinus Feder, Wenzel and Zacharias Neisser, David Schneider, Christopher Demuth, and Arvid Gradin. Of these, in Wesley's estimation, pride of place was held by Christian David, a carpenter. Wesley calls him 'the first planter' of the Herrnhut church, and says:

Four times I enjoyed the blessing of hearing him preach during the few days I spent here; and every time he chose the very subject which I should have desired, had I spoken to him before.[164]

Later, he adds:

[161] Tyerman, op. cit., I.369.
[162] Moore, *Life of Wesley*, II.11.
[163] *Journal*, II.223-5.
[164] ibid., II.25ff.

The fourth sermon which he preached, concerning the ground of faith, made such an impression upon me that when I went home I could not but write down the substance of it.[165]

There was obviously no question in Wesley's mind about the right of laymen in general, and the advisability of *some* laymen, to preach.

Apparently the Moravians had similar reservations, though Zinzendorf preached long before he was ordained.[166] The objection to George Schmidt, a Moravian missionary to the Hottentots, on the ground that he had not been properly ordained, cannot be held to reveal any such reserve, for he had received a 'certificate of ordination', and the objection came from the Dutch ministry and not from the Moravians; but Spangenberg's account of the Moravian constitution,[167] while not ruling out lay-preachers, seems to imply that such preachers should at any rate be well-qualified:

Although in the Brethren's congregations no one can and dare teach publicly, who has not been sufficiently proved, regularly called, presented to the congregation, and regularly inducted to his office; yet all the members of the congregation may and should, in a private manner, according to the command of our gracious Saviour, exhort, warn, encourage, and stir one another up to the faithful following of Jesus.

The difficult question of the identity of the first *Methodist* lay-preacher need not be discussed at length here, though it has some relevance to the general theme. Wesley himself gives more than one point of view. Writing, for example, on 9th September 1790, he speaks of Joseph Humphreys, 'the first lay-preacher that assisted me in England in the year 1738'. This has been questioned on more than one ground—that this was before Wesley went to Bristol, and that therefore Humphreys was not a Methodist preacher, but a Moravian one (he afterwards entered the Moravian ministry), and that at the time of writing Wesley was a very old man, faulty in memory. Moreover, it is possible that Humphreys preached, not as a Methodist, but as a member of a Religious Society, for laymen were sometimes used as substitutes for an

165 *Journal*, II.25ff.

166 At the English Provincial Synod of 1743 Neisser opposed lay-preaching: 'He wishes that every brother might not take it in his head to preach, for it is not every one's matter; to believe, yes, but not to preach' (Rylands *Eng. MSS*, 1054).

167 *Concise Historical Account of the Present Constitution of the Unitas Fratrum* (1775).

absent preacher. But there is no evidence that such laymen were permitted to do anything more than read the prayers, conduct the 'conversation', and, when questions of difficulty arose, to read some such book as Hammond's *Expositor*. Wesley would hardly have referred to Humphreys as his 'first lay-preacher' if this was all he did.

Probably the reluctance to accord to Humphreys this priority arises from Wesley's statement in the *Minutes* of the 1766 Conference, naming Maxfield as the first layman who desired to help him as 'a son in the Gospel'. This may merely mean that Humphrey's preaching was sporadic and irregular, while Maxfield's was regular and systematic. Why Cennick, to whom Charles Wesley referred in the same terms in his letter of 8th March 1741—'You served under him in the gospel as a son . . . you ought first to have fairly told him, "I preach contrary to you" '[168]—does not precede Maxfield in priority of place or time is not clear. Perhaps it was Cennick's special position at Kingswood School which placed him in a different category. Certainly the order in point of time was Humphreys in 1738, Cennick in 1739, and Maxfield in 1740. Of these the first two became Moravians, and the last was one of Wesley's right-hand men until he left Methodism in 1763. The importance assigned to lay-preaching by Wesley is shown by the fact that at the first Conference (1744) there were present six clergymen and four lay-preachers, of whom Maxfield was one.

This brings the question of Moravian influence little nearer. Wesley's description of Joseph Humphreys as his 'first lay-preacher' *in England* may mean that Delamotte preached in Georgia. The fact that these three—Delamotte,[169] Humphreys and Cennick—all became Moravians indicates some similarity of view between Wesley and the Brethren in this matter, for Cennick was allowed to continue for some years as an authorized lay evangelist before being ordained in 1749; and the admiration of Wesley for the preaching of Christian David no doubt encouraged him to sanction this practice in his own Societies. Perhaps it is fair to say that the example of Christian David and Howell Harris, reinforced by his mother's persuasions, removed his doubts, and that the need for competent assistants hastened and confirmed his decision. Beyond that it is unwise to go.

[168] *Journal*, II.434.

[169] Bishop L. G. Hassé denies that Delamotte was ever *ecclesiastically* a Moravian, but at any rate he was closely associated with the Brethren.

(h) The Conference

There is an interesting similarity between the Methodist Church and the Moravian Church in England today. Both are *Connexions*, and both are governed by an annual Conference,[170] in which ministers and laymen share, the former by the Methodist Conference and the latter by the Moravian Synod. There is some risk of confusion here, for in Methodism the term 'Synod' is applied to each of the half-yearly meetings of the forty-odd Districts into which British Methodism is divided. It is improbable that Wesley, when he called his first Conference in 1744, imagined that one day it would become the final legislative body for the whole Church, and that in his life-time it would call his own powers into question. At first, it was merely a 'conversation on the work of God', a term used regularly today to describe discussions which take place in the Quarterly Meetings of the Circuits, the Synods of the Districts, and both sessions, Representative and Ministerial, of the Conference. The subjects discussed dealt with doctrine, the relation of Methodism to the Church of England, the organization of Societies, lay-preachers and field-preaching, the duties of officials, the times for services, books, union with the Moravians and with George Whitefield's followers; and, specifically, 'the work of God—what hath God wrought'.

It is surely more than a coincidence that this first Conference was held at the Foundery on 25th June 1744. Wesley's famous letter *To the Moravian Church*, which prefaces the unhappy story of his separation from the Brethren at Fetter Lane, is dated 24th June of the same year! In that letter, the following paragraph appears:

I love and esteem you for your excellent discipline . . . for your due subordination of officers . . . for your exact division of the people under your charge . . . for your care that all who are employed in the service of the Church should frequently and freely confer together.[171]

Wesley's approval of conferences was probably concerned primarily with the meetings of local groups, of 'bands' and 'choirs', but there can be little doubt that the more central meetings were also in his mind. He had learned of them during his

[170] At present, for reasons of economy, the Synod of the English Province meets once every two years.

[171] *Journal*, II.310-11.

visit to Herrnhut in August 1738, and gives in his *Journal*[172] an account of one of them, at which doctrine was discussed, and in this respect, at any rate, some of the early Methodist Conferences and their *Minutes* closely follow the same pattern. The Methodist Conference of 1748, for instance, discussed doctrinal questions of the same kind. There were marked differences, however, for the Moravian conferences were held weekly, and those of this particular type were open to strangers.

It was the Synodal Conference of the Brethren which most nearly resembled the Methodist Conference. These Provincial Synods were an outstanding feature of Moravian history. There was a general Synod at Lhota as early as 1467. They were revived by Zinzendorf, and annual Synods, some general, some provincial, took place at Ebersdorf, Marienborn, and London. It is probable that John Wesley knew of the proceedings at these, and that, to some extent, he modelled his early Conferences upon them.

An interesting Synod was held at Lindsey House, London, in November 1754. It appears to have been a very small meeting, but it did some important work. It asked Zinzendorf to prepare a Book of Statutes, designed for the use of all English Moravians, and it settled the question of Episcopacy in England by appointing Gambold as first Bishop. Zinzendorf still clung to his Tropus idea, and urged the Moravians to keep close to the English Church. He said:

> The English Church, according to its old principles, is the nearest, next to our Church, to the Church of the Apostles, but it is become something more excellent than what it was intended by its founders, had it not been spoiled by the Methodists and Deists. . . . We want a true and able friend amongst the English Prelates, for the good of the English Church, that the awakened souls might abide within the verge of the English Church.[173]

The Methodist Conference held in Leeds a few months later, on 6th May 1755, took a very different stand, for, refused the Sacrament by many of the parish clergy, a few of the preachers had begun to administer it to small groups within their Societies; and the chief question discussed was that of relationship to the Church of England. Thus, though no agreement was reached on this matter, it was plain that the two Churches had already

172 *Journal*, II.13. 173 Rylands *Eng. MSS*, 110.

diverged considerably, but that their Conferences were concerned with similar problems.

(*i*) *Education*

In assessing influences, there is always a risk of exaggerating some and of neglecting others. That danger has already been faced in tracing not only the various factors which led to the conversion of the Wesleys but the particular impact of individual institutions—the Love-feast, field-preaching, and the like. In no aspect of John Wesley's theory and practice is this more necessary than in estimating the various agencies which contributed to his ideas and methods in education. The Moravians had produced one of the pioneers in the training of children, John Amos Comenius, and it is not likely that Wesley, so well-informed on other matters, would have been ignorant of his writings, *Janua Linguarum Reserata*, *The Great Didactic*, *The School of Infancy*, *etc*. But there is no definite record of his having read these works, and there *are* indications that he was familiar with other writings and open to other influences. He knew Milton's work, and had read, criticized, and commended Locke's *Thoughts* and *Essays*.[174] He had read Rousseau's *Emile*, but found it 'a most silly, empty, injudicious thing'.[175] The effect of the teaching of Pestalozzi and Froebel was yet to come. But books are only humanity at second-hand, and Wesley had first-hand impressions in existing institutions. He knew, for example, of the excellent work done by Dr Bray in popularizing the catechetical schools under the control of the Society for the Promotion of Christian Knowledge, and on 26th February 1737 sent a letter by Ingham to Dr Bray's associates, who had sent a library to Savannah in the previous year, and who expected a report in return, from which it appears that he and an assistant taught children 'to read, write, and cast accounts'.[176]

General Oglethorpe, whom John Wesley knew well, had been in close relationship since 1730 with the various enterprises founded by Dr Bray, and at times presided as Chairman at the meeting of the Associates. It is probable therefore that Wesley knew of the Charity School in Georgia before his arrival there.

Nor must the influence of the schools at Jena be forgotten. These were the schools of the Pietists, with whom the Moravians

[174] *Works*, XIII.455; *Letters*, I.136, VII.228. [175] ibid., XIII. 474.
[176] Delamotte; see p. 232, *supra*.

were not on particularly good terms. Indeed, it has been suggested that Francke, 'who behaved with the utmost humanity',[177] used this visit (21st August 1738) to prejudice Wesley against the Moravians in general and Zinzendorf in particular.[178] Wesley was obviously impressed by their schools, for he gives a long and detailed account of their origin and conduct.[179] The emphasis on catechetical teaching makes it clear that this was a common method in the schools of that time, and was not confined to those governed by Dr Bray's scheme.

In the matter of education as in so many other things the background of the Epworth home was of considerable importance. Indeed, it is probable that John Wesley derived more of his opinions about the education of children from his mother than from any other source. There is neither space nor need in this essay to describe her system at any length, but the essence of it may be seen in the remarkable letter written by her to John on 24th July 1732. It prescribes regular hours and meals, quiet behaviour ('crying softly', enforced when necessary by the rod), the conquest of the will—a matter on which Susanna Wesley insisted—prayers, regular worship, restraint on movement, amnesty to the penitent offender, reward of good actions, and in general 'a discipline strict and persistent, but withal calm and unhurried'.[180]

The inability of Dissenters to enter the universities of Oxford and Cambridge had led to the foundation of Dissenting academies, institutions in which the standard of studies was as high as, and often higher than, that of the universities. They were by no means limited to Dissenters. They were not only cheaper than the universities, but they were remarkably efficient. At least six Anglican Bishops were numbered among their pupils, one of them being Joseph Butler, Bishop of Durham, the author of *The Analogy of Religion.* One of the best of these academies was at Northampton, where Philip Doddridge, preacher, missionary enthusiast, scholar, and hymn-writer, was Principal. For twelve years (from 1739 to 1751) he was in close touch with John Wesley, who had asked his advice about a list of books suitable for his preachers to read. This was in 1748, and a year later Wesley issued the first volume of his *Christian Library*, which was within

[177] *Journal*, II.58. [178] G. A. Wauer, op. cit., p. 69. [179] *Journal*, II.58-61.
[180] J. W. Prince, *Wesley on Religious Education* (1926), pp. 104-14.

the next six years to cover fifty volumes, and to involve Wesley in a loss of two hundred pounds.

Now there was a considerable gulf between Northampton Academy and Kingswood School. The former was a college for students of university age, the latter a school for boys from the age of six, but the work done in the higher forms at Kingswood was comparable with that of the academies, and it is very probable that the advice of Doddridge was sought, and his example followed, when, in 1748, the School was founded. Indeed, the reading of the *Christian Library*, which owed so much to Doddridge's advice, was prescribed in the curriculum of 'those who designed to go through a course of academical learning'.[181]

Wesley followed his mother's advice closely. Like her, he believed in conquering the will of children, and more than once said as much: 'In order to form the minds of children, the first thing to be done is to conquer their will'; 'I insist upon conquering the will of children betimes because this is the only foundation for a religious education'. Elsewhere he says: 'The will of a parent to a little child in the place of the will of God!' He maintained that this subjection of the will is to begin as early as possible, by refusing to give the child what it cries for, but to teach it 'to fear the rod and to cry softly'. Like his mother, too, Wesley believed that discipline, though firm, should be kindly undertaken, 'by mildness, softness, and gentleness', 'by advice, persuasion, and reproof'. Both believed that the purpose of all education of children, whether at home, at school, or in the Methodist Societies, was to make them pious, to lead them to personal religion, and to ensure salvation. Perhaps both failed to realize that the achievement of this aim depended less upon systems of instruction and the organization of daily life than upon the character of the teacher.

It might seem that with these many converging streams of influence—traditional usage, the Epworth home, the Pietists, the Dissenting Academies, the Charity Schools, Comenius and Milton—no room was left for further guidance and example. It would be unwise, however, to ignore Moravian influence. How much Wesley derived from his reading of Comenius and how much from the Moravian adoption of Comenius's teaching at

[181] *A Short Account of the School in Kingswood, near Bristol* (1768); *Works*, XIII.283-89.

Herrnhut is doubtful. Certain it is that in his teaching and practice he kept very close to the principles laid down in *The Great Didactic*. Comenius's basic principle, 'The ultimate end of man is eternal happiness with God', is echoed by Wesley, not merely in his writings, but in its practical working-out at Kingswood School; and, as has been pointed out elsewhere,[182] Wesley's pamphlet, *Instruction for Children*, is closely in accord with Comenius's 'Nine Principles of Method'.

We need not conclude that Wesley's views on the necessity for the complete surrender of the child's will to that of his teacher were directly obtained from his stay at Herrnhut. It is true that in the extract which he gives in his *Journal* from the Herrnhut Constitution the Moravians state:

> We . . . study the amending their wills as well as their understanding; finding by experience that when their will is moved, they often learn more in a few hours than otherwise in many months.[183]

Wesley had already imbibed these opinions from his mother—her letters to him had been written seven years beforehand—and it is probable that they were entirely in accord with current educational theory and practice.

Apart from this, Wesley's references to the educational system at Herrnhut are few and slight: 'In Herrnhut is taught reading, writing, arithmetic, Latin, Greek, Hebrew, French, English, history, and geography'—a remarkable curriculum, which Wesley exceeded by teaching astronomy! In the Orphan House, the range was somewhat smaller, the children being taught (according to their several aptitudes) Latin, French, writing, arithmetic, history.[184]

A. H. Body[185] makes an interesting comparison between the time-tables at Herrnhut and Kingswood, and points out obvious similarities which can hardly be accidental. Perhaps the most interesting is the reference in both to 'walks' and the total absence of any mention of games. John Wesley disapproved of children's play—'he that plays when he is a boy will play when he is a man'—a quotation which he seems to have heard in Germany. It may be difficult to harmonize this restriction with Wesley's love of

[182] e.g. by A. M. Body, *John Wesley and Education* (1936). J. H. Prince, *Wesley on Religious Education*; and T. E. Brigden in *A New History of Methodism* (1910).

[183] II.54. [184] ibid., pp. 50-1. [185] *John Wesley and Education*, p. 51.

children and his characteristic kindliness of nature, but the solution may be found in the deplorable condition of the public schools of Wesley's day, in which play often meant brutality and violence. Wesley seems to have thought that children could not be trusted; nor did the passing years bring any mellowness of judgement, for in 1763 he wrote:

The children ought never to be alone, but always in the presence of a teacher. This is totally neglected [at Kingswood]; in consequence of which they run up and down the wood, and mix and fight with the colliers' children. They ought never to play. But they do, every day. . . . How may these evils be remedied, and the school reduced to its original plan? It must be mended or ended; for no school is better than the present school.[186]

It must be remembered that Wesley himself had had a bitter experience at the Charterhouse. The Kingswood regulations were hard, but so were those of all the public schools—very early rising, regular hours for prayer and worship, rigid fare, semi-monastic rules and usages, and special dress prevailed everywhere alike, in Church of England schools, in Quaker schools, and in Moravian schools.

It seems probable, therefore, that though Wesley was subject to many influences in shaping his educational thought and practice, some of the immediate details of his school organization were directly derived from the Moravians. It will be remembered that in his letter of September 1738, drafted but not sent, he had said: 'I greatly approve . . . of your method of instructing children'.[187]

The education of children, and especially of poor children, was intimately connected with their general care, and Wesley, whose anxiety on behalf of the poor was evidenced by the establishment of a collection for them in his Societies, at one time contemplated the foundation of an Orphanage. He may have obtained the idea of such an orphan home from his visit to Herrnhut, but it is more likely that the possibility had occurred to him before that time. Whitefield took possession of a site for an orphan home in Georgia in January 1740, and in *A Brief Account of the Rise, Progress, and Present Situation of the Orphan Home in Georgia* he acknowledged his indebtedness to Oglethorpe and Charles Wesley. Moreover,

[186] 'Remarks on the State of Kingswood School', *Works*, XIII.283-302.
[187] *Journal*, II.496.

Francke, the Pietist, had already established a successful orphanage at Halle, and John Wesley made a point of seeing this on the occasion of his visit on 26th July 1738.[188]

Wesley's own scheme was never fulfilled. He purchased a plot of land at Newcastle, and laid the first stone in December 1742, but his intention of making it an orphanage was never carried out. His ideals, however, were not forgotten, and the widespread work of the National Children's Home and Orphanage is a tribute to his vision.

(*j*) *The Lot*

Some of the effects of Moravian example and teaching upon Methodism have survived to this day, others had a long life. One, however, though adopted by Wesley, did not last long, the use of the Lot. This was an integral part of Moravian practice, private and public, and was consulted on matters which might have seemed of purely personal concern. It was not regarded as an appeal to chance, but as a means by which the will of God in answer to prayer might be learned; and though it is easy, at this distance, to deride it, the loyalty and self-sacrifice of those who obeyed its decisions are beyond praise. Its real value was that it set the minds of the Brethren at rest, and enabled them to face every eventuality with confidence. Its importance was enormous. The decision of the early Brethren to institute their own order at Lhota in 1467 was taken as a result of the Lot; so too were the momentous renewal of the Moravian Church in 1731 and the equally momentous decision to embark on missionary enterprise. The recognition of our Lord as General Elder in 1741, and the establishment of the London congregation as a separate Moravian society in 1742 were both carried out by means of this system. But the Lot went far beyond matters of public policy. A young man could not marry without the consent of the Elders' Conference, after the question had been submitted to the Lot, elections to local officers, and even to membership were based on the same principle, and for a long time no pupil could be admitted to a school unless his application had been confirmed by the Lot.[189]

Though the Pietists had used this system before its readoption by the Brethren, it was from the latter that Wesley learned it. He

[188] *Journal*, II.17.

[189] An exception was made in the early nineteenth century at Fulneck School.

used it to settle an awkward problem on 4th March 1737, when he had an inconclusive discussion with Delamotte about his proposed marriage to Sophia Hopkey:

At length we agreed to appeal to the Searcher of hearts. I accordingly made three lots. In one was writ 'Marry'; in the second 'Think not of it this year'. After we had prayed to God to 'give a perfect lot', Mr Delamotte drew the third, in which were these words, 'Think of it no more'. Instead of the agony I had reason to expect, I was enabled to say cheerfully, 'Thy will be done'. We cast lots once again to know whether I ought to converse with her any more; and the direction I received from God was 'only in presence of Mr Delamotte'.[190]

Subsequent events confirmed his confidence in the Lot, and he used it again when he returned to England to decide whether or not Whitefield ought to go to Georgia.[191] As it happened, Whitefield had already departed. On another occasion, he used the lot to decide whether or not to preach and print his sermon on 'Free Grace'. The important question of his going from Fetter Lane to establish a Society at Bristol was also settled in this way. His brother Charles objected to their going, their fellow-members could not agree, and at length they all agreed to decide the matter by lot, and accepted the verdict, which was that he should go.[192] In view of the unfortunate sequel to his decision not to marry Sophia Hopkey, and of the friction which took place during his absence from Fetter Lane, it may seem that Wesley was somewhat too ready to believe that the Lot spoke with the voice of God; but at any rate Wesley had no doubts. There were other occasions when it was used—in the choice of the leaders of the Bristol bands in April 1739,[193] and on 14th March 1744, when Charles Wesley was in danger of arrest at Birstall, and hesitated whether to leave or stay. He resorted to the Lot, and faced his trial.

This appears to have been the last recorded example of the use of the Lot by either of the Wesleys, though as late as 17th June 1746, in his letter to the Rev. Thomas Church, John Wesley defends the practice:

At rare times, when I have been in great distress of soul, or in utter uncertainty how to act in an important case which required a speedy determination, after using all other means that occurred, I have cast

190 *Journal*, I.325. 191 ibid., I.421 n. 192 ibid., II.158.
193 *Letters*, I.296, 316.

Lots or opened the Bible. And by this means I have been relieved from that distress or directed in that uncertainty.

Instances of this kind appear in pages 12, 14, 15, 28 and 88 of the Third *Journal*: as also in pages 27, 28 and 80 of the last *Journal*.[194]

He then points out:

(*a*) that he was utterly uncertain how to act in a matter which required 'a speedy determination';

(*b*) that though there is no Scriptural injunction to use lots, there is no prohibition;

(*c*) that this is not a matter of chance or of the sacrifice of reason. He had used reason (and so had his fellows) for eleven days, and then left the settlement 'to the Lord'.

He agrees that he had learned this from the Moravians, but, in spite of this continued subscription, there is no evidence that Wesley was enthusiastic in his use of the Lot. It is plain from his own statement

(*a*) that he turned to the Lot only when other means had failed to convince him; and

(*b*) that, even so, he preferred to find Scriptural guidance. Of the references he gives to his *Journal* all but one relate how he turned to his Bible for help, and found it there.

The Lot does not appear to have ever become a normal procedure with himself or in any Church court, and during the nineteenth century it gradually fell into disuse amongst the Moravians themselves. The exception previously mentioned[195] reveals the existence of some disquiet, and the matter reached a climax in 1836. At a General Synod at Herrnhut, a request came from America that the Lot should no longer be enforced in marriages. Gradually, the radicals won their battle. At first, it was conceded that only in the regular settlements need the Lot be thus used; then the settlements complained and obtained exemption; and finally a free choice was extended to ministers and then to missionaries, and thus the enforced use of the Lot passed out of Moravian history. In the next decade, it virtually disappeared from England and America by the admission of new members without its use.

[194] *Letters*, II.245-6.

[195] See p. 243 n., *supra*.

SUMMARY

From the above, it is clear that the influence of Moravian teaching and practice on Methodist doctrine and organization was considerable, but that it varied very much in quality and extent.

General Influences

The Moravians made little addition to the doctrinal views held by John Wesley. Rather may it be said that they strengthened views already held. Of the three doctrines which are generally regarded as characteristically Methodist—Justification by Faith, Assurance, and Christian Perfection—the first two had been held, in some form, by Wesley before he had met the Brethren. The last was his own creation, and was indeed disliked by the Moravians. The doctrinal influence of the Moravians lay in the fact that by their insistence on (i) a personal knowledge of God in Christ, and (ii) the need and duty of evangelism, they strengthened the tendencies which already threatened separation from the Church of England.

Particular Influences

Of the many aspects of Moravian practice and teaching which had their effect upon Wesley and his followers, some appear to have been deliberately adopted by the Methodists, some to have exercised an unconscious influence, and some merely to have reinforced other influences and deepened convictions already held. Of those which were, in some degree, taken over into the structure of Methodism, the chief were:

(*a*) *The Band System*, which, in one form or another, has lasted till today. This is probably the most important contribution made by the Brethren to Methodist worship and organization. Though it is probable that Wesley's knowledge of the Religious Societies may have modified his practice, his own methods and even terminology were so closely allied to those of the Moravians as to make it certain that the influence of the Brethren predominated.

(*b*) *Hymn-singing*. Not only was John Wesley deeply impressed by the part played by hymn-singing in the life of the Moravians at the time when his regard for them was at its height, but his own translations were directly due to them. Moreover, the amazing output of hymns by his brother Charles, hymns which were to be of such incalculable value to him in his evangelistic campaigns, took its origin in the events of May 1738, and was therefore directly due to the Moravians.

(*c*) *The Love-feast.* Though this has not persisted in Methodism, it played a large part in the building-up and cementing of Methodist fellowship in the eighteenth and early nineteenth centuries. Though it is possible that Wesley adopted it from his regard for the customs of the Primitive Church, the similarity of his methods to those of the Brethren makes it extremely probable that in this matter too he deliberately followed Moravian example.

(*d*) *The Watch-night.* This too might have been an authentic revival by Wesley himself, but his adoption of it at the time of his closest fellowship with the Brethren makes it probable that their example caught his imagination and encouraged his imitation.

(*e*) *The Conference.* Wesley's frequently expressed admiration of Moravian Conferences, and the close similarity between his own Conferences in form—question and answer—and in the content of discussion, strengthened the view that Wesley modelled his own assemblies on those of the Brethren.

In other matters, though it is not so easy to trace a direct connexion, the example and advocacy of the Brethren served to strengthen views already held by John Wesley.

(*a*) *Field-preaching* owes no direct debt to the Moravians, who indeed were not in general enthusiastic about it; but it was an inevitable implication of the 'heart-warming experience' of Whitsuntide 1738, in which the Brethren had played so notable a part.

(*b*) *Lay-preaching* was necessitated by the circumstances of Methodism, and owes little to Moravian example, though John Wesley's acceptance of it probably received some confirmation from his admiration of Christian David.

(*c*) *Education.* In all probability Wesley's educational principles were widely held in his time, and therefore he was merely a joint-heir of the teaching of Comenius. The close parallel, however, between the curricula at Herrnhut and Kingswood seems to indicate some deliberate adoption of Moravian method.

In all these matters, whether the direct influence was great or small, the guiding impulse came from the Whitsuntide experience, and the influence of the Moravians, therefore, upon the life-purpose of the Wesleys and the growth and fashioning of the Methodist Church was monumental.

CHAPTER EIGHT

THE METHODIST CONTRIBUTION TO MORAVIANISM

It is generally agreed that Methodism owes something to the Moravians, though there is considerable difference of opinion about the nature and magnitude of the debt. This essay has endeavoured to prove that the debt is a large one. It is not, however, so widely conceded that Methodism, in its turn, has made some contribution, indeed a considerable one, to English Moravianism. The neglect to recognize this fact is due in part to the nature of the case, for the characteristic features of a Church which numbers thirteen millions of members and at least as many 'adherents' are more easily seen than those of one whose *English* membership numbers only a few thousands. Moreover, the Moravians have generally avoided publicity—John Wesley on many occasions referred to their 'closeness'—and have kept their institutions, as it were, within the family circle. Yet it may be maintained that the growth and continuance of Moravianism in England has been profoundly influenced, and its nature, teaching and practice modified, by its contact with eighteenth-century Methodism. The influences were both positive and negative, the following of an example or the response to a stimulus on the one hand, and the reaction to a criticism on the other.

A—DOCTRINE

The doctrinal issue on which Moravian and Methodist were divided was in their respective interpretation of the Lutheran doctrine of Justification by Faith. The area of agreement was wide, much wider than the antagonists on either side were prepared to admit, for the extreme views urged by the one side produced similar extremes on the other. The gravamen of the charge made by the Brethren against the Methodists was that they placed undue stress upon works, and indeed made them necessary to salvation, or at any rate means of grace. In his letter to Zinzendorf on 14th March 1740 James Hutton wrote:

John Wesley . . . having told many souls that they were justified, who have since discovered themselves to be otherwise; and having mixed the works of the law with the Gospel as means of grace, is at enmity against the Brethren.[1]

It is clear that by 'the works of the law' the Moravians were referring to particular forms of worship, the sacraments, and public prayer; but to John Wesley this attitude involved the neglect of social duties, the care of the poor, and the preaching of the Gospel to those outside the Church. It is understandable, of course, that a disbelief in works as a *substitute* for faith may lead to a neglect of them as an *implication* of faith; and it certainly seems evident that, at first, the ethical work of the Brethren was largely confined to their own people. John Wesley pays a tribute to this in the letter which he uses as a preface to Part IV of his *Journal*:

I love and esteem you . . . for your exact and seasonable knowledge of the state of every member, and your ready distribution either of spiritual or temporal relief, as every man hath need.[2]

Either John Wesley's doubts were justified or they were widely shared, for the Moravians felt it necessary to emphasize their ethical aims, inserting (in 1754) in their Litany a number of petitions referring definitely to the common duties of everyday life . . . and expressing their belief in the necessity of good works of a beneficent nature.[3] It is possible, of course, that the insertion of these petitions was merely a statement of what had long been Moravian practice; but it is difficult to dissociate it from the persistent pressure of Wesley. Indeed, there is some hint of this in the account of the Synod of 1765, at which this was said:[4]

Some people of a certain denomination charge us with antinomian principles, though probably they themselves are convinced of the contrary. . . . If we but declare the death of the Lord with hearts on fire, there is no fear of Antinomianism.

Then follows an exhortation to righteous life.

The doctrine of 'stillness', which was a logical development of an extreme interpretation of the doctrine of Justification by Faith, was of a somewhat different order. Apart from Molther, none of the Moravian leaders seems to have been enthusiastic about

[1] Benham, *Memoirs of James Hutton*, pp. 46-7.
[2] II.311.
[3] See p. 166, *supra*.
[4] Rylands *Eng. MSS*, 1056.

it, though several defended it, perhaps out of loyalty to their colleague. Ingham, for instance, in his letter to Wesley of August or September 1746, whittled it down until it could have been accepted by Wesley and his followers:

First, as to *stillness*: The thing meant hereby is that man cannot attain to salvation by his own wisdom, strength, righteousness, goodness, merits, or works; that therefore, when he applies to God for it, he is to cast away all dependence upon everything of his own, and trusting only to the mercy of God through the merits of Christ, in his poverty of spirit to resign himself up to the will of God, and thus quietly wait for his salvation.[5]

It is worthy of note that in this letter Ingham denies the assertion that the Brethren advocated extreme forms of stillness—'that people who are seeking after salvation are all the while to sit still and do nothing—that they are not to read, hear, or pray'; and that in seeking to rebut this Wesley declares that this interpretation had been made by 'Mr Brown, Mr Bowers, Mr Bell, Mr Bray, and Mr Simpson', hardly a representative group of Moravian leaders! Spangenberg, it is true, 'spoke of looking unto Jesus, and exhorted us to lie still in His hand',[6] an exhortation which was capable of wide interpretation, and Hutton, in his letter to Zinzendorf of 14th March 1740 spoke of converts who at first 'could not be reconciled with stillness';[7] but the absence of any authoritative pronouncement by any recognized leader other than Molther seems to imply either that the Brethren did not regard the doctrine as of primary importance, or that Wesley's opposition had affected their judgement. In any case, the doctrine had disappeared from the Moravian vocabulary by the second half of the century, and recent Moravian historians[8] deprecate it. It is difficult to resist the conclusion that in both these directions Moravian teaching was modified by Wesley's criticism.

B—EVANGELISTIC PRACTICE

The amazing results of the preaching of the Wesleys had their effect on Moravian methods. There was some difference in approach; for though the Brethren realized that the Methodist mode of preaching was bound to continue,[9] they deliberately

[5] *Letters*, II.80.
[6] *Journal*, II.313.
[7] op. cit., p. 47.
[8] e.g. Wauer and Hutton.
[9] Synod of 1752: '*Der Methodismus ist zu continueren, der Heiland will es auch.*'

avoided anything which encouraged 'scenes', and preferred to work by what have come to be known as 'cells'. But in Ireland, especially, their preaching took the same form as that of the Methodists, and had striking success. Indeed, there were several tributes at the Synod of 1748 to the results of Cennick's work:

> The Wesley complication has relieved us of the worst members. Wesley's methods make it necessary for us to have labourers there [Dublin].[10]

It was also stated that Wesley's followers admitted that Cennick had the best supporters, '*die besten, die meisten, und auch die reichsten*'. Ingham, too, had adopted much the same methods, with outstanding success, before handing over his Societies to the Brethren, and thus beginning their work in Yorkshire.

It must be admitted, however, that the Brethren were uneasy about these methods, if not about their results. They strongly disliked anything like 'convulsions', and therefore deprecated the emotional appeals which produced them. But there is no evidence that these manifestations were typical of the conversions under Wesley's preaching, or that Wesley, though he defended them, sought their continuance; and it is probable that the preaching of Moravian and Methodist proceeded, not only on parallel lines but on similar lines, though with a different emphasis, and therefore that the methods were largely those of John Wesley, the pioneer of the Revival. It must not be forgotten that the Society of Fetter Lane, which became the nucleus of the Moravian Church in England, by common consent owed much of its impulse and constitution to John Wesley.

The emphasis in preaching was admittedly different. At the Moravian Synod of 1754 Zinzendorf defined the difference as one of mood, the Methodist being comforted 'by more or fewer glimpses into the wounds and merits of Jesus', while the Moravian, happy in the privilege of a similar glimpse, is 'by more or fewer looks into his natural misery and corruption sufficiently humbled', a distinction between Wesley's quest for perfection and the Moravian insistence on 'poor sinnership'; while Watteville, at the Synod of 1748, had regarded Wesley's teaching as unsound, '*eine andere Lehre*'.

The Moravians had their own manifestations, though they

[10] Rylands *Eng. MSS*, 1054.

were of a different sort. The excesses of Herrnhaag were never typical of English Moravianism, and the attacks of Rimius and Frey were largely beside the point as far as the English Brethren were concerned, but the preoccupation with the physical sufferings of Christ produced a crop of hymns which John Wesley rightly criticized. It is probable that the good sense of the Brethren would in any case have prevented the continuance of this kind of hymnody, but the censure of John Wesley, whether or not he was the writer of *The Contents of a Folio History*,[11] would surely have reinforced their determination.

C—HYMNS

In the field of hymn-writing, John and Charles Wesley made a substantial contribution to Moravian worship, the former by his translations, the latter by his own compositions. In view of the enormous output of Charles Wesley in this field, the number adopted at the time by the Brethren was small, but those included in their Hymn-book of 1754 (compiled by Gambold) are of high quality, viz.

Father of Lights, from whom proceeds[12]
Son of the Carpenter (575)[13]
Being of beings, God of love (383)
Where shall my wondering soul begin (361)

If this last is, as is supposed, the 'Conversion Hymn' sung at Little Britain on 24th May 1738, immediately after John's experience at Aldersgate Street, it would have intimate historic associations for both Methodist and Moravian, and its inclusion in the Moravian book was a gesture of goodwill.

Of John Wesley's translations, the following appear in the same book:

Jesu, Thy boundless love to me (430)—*O Jesu, Christ, mein schönstes Licht*—GERHARDT

Thou hidden Source of calm repose (98)—*Wer ist wohl wir du*—FREYLINGHAUSEN

Thou hidden love of God, whose height (433)—*Verborgne Gottesliebe du*—TERSTEEGEN

[11] See pp. 137-8, *supra*.
[12] 1780 *Collection*, No. 98.
[13] The numbers in brackets refer to the *Methodist Hymn-book* (1933).

Thee will I love, my strength, my tower (445)—*Ich will dich lieben, meine Stärke*—SCHEFFLER

Shall I, for fear of feeble man (783)—*Sollt' ich aus Furcht vor Menschenkindern*—WINCKLER

Jesu, Thy light again I view (573)—*O Jesu, süsses Licht*—LANGE

Holy Lamb, who Thee receive (1780, No. 350)—*Du heiliges Kind*—DOBER

I thirst, Thou wounded Lamb of God (449)—*Ach, mein verwunder Fürste*—ZINZENDORF and J. and A. NITSCHMANN

Now I have found the ground wherein (375)—*Ich habe nun den Grund gefunden*—ROTHE

My soul before Thee prostrate lies[14]—*Hier legt mein Sinn sich vor dir neider*—RICHTER

High on his everlasting throne—*Der König ruht und schauet doch*—SPANGENBERG

Jesu, to Thee my heart I bow—*Reiner Bräut'gam meiner Seelen*—ZINZENDORF

Moravian hymnody would have neglected some of the treasures of sacred song if it had not adopted these writings of the Wesleys. It is noteworthy that in the *Moravian Liturgy and Hymns* of 1912, now generally used in English Moravian churches, ten of the above translations are included, together with six others which do not appear in the 1754 Hymn-book; and that there are also thirty-seven hymns by Charles Wesley, as against forty-six by Zinzendorf, forty by Montgomery, and twenty-two by Isaac Watts. The obligation does not end there, for both Cennick and Montgomery, perhaps the best of the Moravian hymn-writers, were set a fine example by Charles Wesley in his breaking of the tyranny of the seventeenth-century metrical psalm, and in the variety of 'shapes' of his hymns.

D—PERSONS

But the contribution of Methodism to Moravianism is seen at its greatest in the men who were influenced by the Wesleys, and who gave their enthusiasm and ability to the Renewed Church of the Brethren. Dr A. W. Harrison[15] says that five members of the Holy Club joined the Brethren. If he is referring to Ingham, Gambold, Hutchins, Hall, and Kinchin, this statement requires

[14] See p. 55, *supra*.

[15] *The Evangelical Revival and Christian Reunion*, p. 35.

some qualification, for Ingham was never 'ecclesiastically' a Moravian, though he made a remarkable contribution to the Brethren's Church, and Kinchin died too early (in 1742) to take any active part in its work. As, however, he resigned his deanery, fellowship, and parish, with the intention of becoming an itinerant preacher, and as members of his family are named in later Moravian lists, he would no doubt have followed in the footsteps of Gambold had he lived. But it is true to say that three of these four—Ingham, Gambold, and Hutchins (or Hutchings)—made a notable contribution to the development of Moravianism in this country. Now there is no doubt that Charles Wesley was the founder and inspiration of the Holy Club. The little group was formed in November 1729, of the two Wesley brothers, William Morgan, and Robert Kirkham; Gambold joined them in March 1730, Ingham in 1732, and others in the same year. No doubt, it was similarity of aim and outlook that brought them together, but the Wesleys were the moving spirits in the little company, and the growth (and indeed the birth) of English Moravianism owed much therefore to John and Charles Wesley, so far as it was assisted by Ingham, Gambold, and Hutchins.

Of the three, Gambold reached the highest distinction in the Renewed Church of the Brethren. He resigned his living at Stanton Harcourt in 1742 to become a Moravian, and threw himself so heartily into the work that he became the first English Moravian Bishop. He translated *Acta Fratrum in Anglia* in 1749, and compiled the great Hymn-book of 1754; and though he differed sharply from John Wesley at the time of the separation,[16] Wesley always thought and spoke highly of him. In answer to an attack by Lord Lyttelton in a book entitled *Dialogues of the Dead*, Wesley replied: 'Could his lordship show me in England many more sensible men than Mr Gambold and Mr Okeley?'[17] Gambold was the statesman of the Moravian Church in England, and kept it secure and stable during the difficult days of the 'Sifting Time'. Wesley entertained a warm regard for him long after the breach with Fetter Lane, and longed to be reunited with him. There is no doubt, too, in spite of the disruption, that Gambold had been deeply impressed by the Wesleys, and his letter 'To a Friend', written about 1736, testifies to this impression. Speaking of 'the little Society' (the Holy Club) he writes:

[16] See p. 93, *supra*; *Journal*, II.472. [17] *Journal*, V.383.

Mr John Wesley was always the chief manager, for which he was very fit. For he had not only more learning and experience than the rest, but he was blest with such activity as to be always gaining ground, and such steadiness that he lost none. What proposals he made to any were sure to charm them, because he was so much in earnest; nor could they afterwards slight them, because they saw him always the same. What supported this uniform vigour was the care he took to consider well of every affair before he engaged in it, making all his decisions in the fear of God, without passion, humour, or self-confidence; for though he had naturally a very clear apprehension, yet his exact prudence depended more upon humility and singleness of heart.[18]

This tribute, so different from the later accusations of autocracy, is generous, and we can understand Wesley's wistful cry of 16th December 1763: 'O how gladly would I join heart and hand again!'[19]

Elsewhere in the same letter, Gambold speaks of Wesley's 'private piety, his watchfulness, his self-control, his "beating down praise", his love of prayer, his cheerfulness, his refusal to be discomposed by any slanders or affronts. He helped one in things out of religion, that he might be more welcome to help him in that.'

It is clear that Gambold regarded Wesley as his 'father in Christ', and that though he was an apt pupil he had Wesley to thank for much of his spiritual training.

Benjamin Ingham, whether he was actually a Moravian or not, served the Brethren magnificently. He was one of the little company which journeyed with the Wesleys to Georgia, and thought so much of them that he kept a copy of Wesley's *Journal* which has been of immense value to later editors. His description of the storm[20] matches Wesley's, though it does not mention the Moravians. He appears to have been warmly welcomed at Herrnhut, where he was allowed to partake of the Sacrament, a privilege denied to Wesley, and was at one time attracted by the doctrine of 'stillness'.

As an Anglican clergyman at Aberford, near Leeds, he disapproved of John Nelson's 'plainness of speech' and of his 'advising people to go to Church and Sacrament'; but his relations with Wesley remained good, and the controversial letter sent to

[18] *Methodist Magazine* (1798), pp. 117-121, 168-172; *Journal*, VIII.265ff.
[19] *Journal*, V.42. [20] ibid., VIII.302.

him by the Methodist leader on 8th September 1746[21] is affectionately worded.

Ingham was a powerful preacher, and carried out a most successful campaign amongst the working classes of the West Riding of Yorkshire. His methods were those of the Wesleys: open-air preaching, visiting of people in their homes, the formation of Societies, and his success was comparable with theirs. At his request, Töltschig visited him in Yorkshire in November 1739, with the result that at one stroke Ingham's societies were handed over to the care of the Moravian Church. The importance of this can hardly be exaggerated, for Moravianism in Yorkshire, built around the remarkable settlement at Fulneck (on land which was at one time Ingham's property), is probably the Brethren's greatest stronghold in England. If then, as seems likely, the initial impulse to Ingham's evangelistic zeal was given in the Holy Club, here again the Wesleys made a notable contribution to English Moravianism.

John Cennick was *sui generis*, as much a master of his own craft as John Wesley was of his, and no doubt he would have preached to salvation had there been no Wesley, Harris, Whitefield, or Böhler. But it must not be forgotten that part, at any rate, of his apprenticeship was with Wesley, and that his methods continued to be like those of his tutor. It may be that Cennick owed his conversion neither to the Methodists nor to the Moravians. Certainly, he had felt assured of his own salvation long before he had met the Brethren. But it is also true that it was through Wesley, Whitefield, and Harris that he found the way to use his gifts and to share his experience. Kinchin, one of the Holy Club, introduced him to Wesley, Hutton to Whitefield; and it was as a *Methodist* preacher that Cennick began his evangelistic work.

Wesley does not appear to have admired him as much as he did Gambold, Böhler, Spangenberg, and Ingham.

> I visited the classes at Kingswood [he says]. Here only there is no increase; and yet, where was there such a prospect till that weak man, John Cennick, confounded the poor people with strange doctrines? O what mischief may be done by one that means well! We see no end of it to this day.[22]

[21] *Journal*, II.80ff. [22] ibid., IV.415.

In view of Cennick's remarkable success in Ireland, perhaps it was not Cennick's weakness but his strength that caused Wesley concern!

Cennick died in 1755, Gambold in 1771, Ingham a year later; James Hutton outlived them all, and did not die till 1795. In a way, he was not only the longest-lived but the most influential of the English Moravians; for not only did he act as a link between the different generations, but he was the virtual founder of the Moravian Society at Fetter Lane after the disruption. It was he who took out the lease of the Fetter Lane *Chapel* from Lady Day 1740, when a breach was inevitable, and when Wesley had already purchased the Foundery; and it was he who was the first Warden of the first Moravian Society in England. He came to the front during John Wesley's absence in Bristol, and during his rule, if not because of it, the Society became more and more Moravian in character. A year later, Hutton became President of the Society, and his work thoughout the century, particularly as official publisher, was invaluable.

What share had the Wesleys in all this? A great deal, for it was through John Wesley that Hutton gave himself to religious work. It was while he was visiting some of his school-fellows at Oxford that Hutton first met the Wesley brothers. At first no more than attracted by their devoutness of life, he became deeply impressed by John's preaching, and under the influence of one particular sermon on 'the renovation of fallen man', and moved by the character and bearing of the two brothers, he was 'awakened'. This was the beginning of Hutton's spiritual life, and therefore a vital link in the chain of Moravian development—and it began with John and Charles Wesley! Gambold, Ingham, Cennick, Hutton, to whom may be added Simpson and the two Delamottes, and, to a lesser degree, Francis Pugh and James Beaumont—it is an imposing list, and, though there is a risk of exaggeration, it is powerful evidence of the influence, direct and indirect, of the Wesleys on the growth of the Moravian Church in England. If it is claimed that but for Peter Böhler there would have been no Methodist Church, it may also be contended that but for John and Charles Wesley the English Brethren would have had to await another time and to find other men by whom the Holy Spirit could change the hearts of men.

SUMMARY

Thus, by restraint upon Moravian practices, by criticism and comment, by example and by personal influence, the Methodists exercised a profound influence on the birth and development of English Moravianism. They modified its doctrine, they checked its excesses, they offered a model of evangelistic methods, they provided it with hymns without which its worship would have been infinitely poorer. Most of all, they ensured for it a succession of able and enthusiastic leaders to whom it owed its inspiration and indeed its very existence. It ought never to be forgotten, though it has not been sufficiently recognized, that every *English* Moravian leader of note at some time or other in this century came under the direct influences of John and Charles Wesley.

Today the two Churches run again in parallel lines, though on a different scale and by different methods. Differences of size and resources preclude the Moravians from organizing and maintaining large City Missions, and from much of the departmental work which a large Church necessitates. On the Mission Field, the similarity is greater, for in this direction the Brethren have a notable record. Moravian and Methodist are good friends, or, rather, acquaintances. Methodist lay preachers sometimes occupy Moravian pulpits, Moravian ministers feel at home in Methodist churches; and for some years a Methodist minister, the Rev. Charles Taylor, M.A., was 'lent' to the Moravian Church as Headmaster of the historic Fulneck Boys' School. But, as a whole, Methodists and Moravians do not know how closely linked they once were, nor do they recognize the debt which each owes to the other. Perhaps this essay will help to repair the omission and bring them closer together.

BIBLIOGRAPHY

FOR A general background of the events leading up to the Aldersgate Street experience, *A New History of Methodism*, edited by Townsend, Workman and Eayrs (1910), is useful, but should be augmented by the many biographies of John Wesley, e.g. by Coke and Moore (1792), Tyerman (1865—detailed but not judicial), Simon (Vols. I-III, 1921-5), Telford (1886), and Overton (1891), and by critical studies such as Maximin Piette's *John Wesley in the Evolution of Protestantism* (1937), J. E. Rattenbury's *The Conversion of the Wesleys* (1938), Umphrey Lee's *John Wesley and Modern Religion* (1936), and A. W. Harrison's *The Evangelical Revival and Christian Reunion* (1942).

John Wesley's *Journal*[1] (1907) is, of course, essential, as are his *Letters* (1931). Charles Wesley's *Journal* (1849) is much slighter in extent and quality. The latter's letters are not yet available in printed form, but a definitive edition is being prepared by Dr Frank Baker. John Nelson's *Journal* (reproduced in *Early Methodist Preachers*, 1865) has some interesting sidelights on the controversial period.

On the Moravian side, J. E. Hutton's *History of the Moravian Church* (1909) is interesting but undocumented. Early histories, e.g. those by Cranz (1825) and Holmes (1825), make little mention of Methodism. *The Beginnings of the Brethren's Church in England*, by G. A. Wauer (1901), is a scholarly record of the early years and gives a balanced outline of the years of fellowship and controversy. Dr W. G. Addison's *The Renewed Church of the United Brethren, 1722-1930* is an able study from an Anglican angle, and is particularly valuable for its account of the abortive negotiations for union in 1785-6.

For the lives of individual Moravians, Benham's *Memoirs of James Hutton* (1856), though badly arranged, is indispensable.

[1] Indicated as *Journal* in the footnotes.

INDEX